EXPLORING SPORTS AND SOCIETY

Also by Karl Spracklen

CONSTRUCTING LEISURE
THE MEANING AND PURPOSE OF LEISURE
HEAVY METAL FUNDAMENTALISMS (*co-edited with Rosey Hill*)
SPORT AND CHALLENGES TO RACISM (*co-edited with Jonathan Long*)
LEISURE, SPORTS & SOCIETY
WHITENESS AND LEISURE

Exploring Sports and Society

A Critical Introduction for Students

Karl Spracklen

Professor of Leisure Studies,
Leeds Metropolitan University, UK

 macmillan education palgrave

First published 2015 by
PALGRAVE

Palgrave in the UK is an imprint of Macmillan Publishers Limited, registered in England, company number 785998, 4 Crinan Street, London N1 9XW

Palgrave Macmillan in the US is a division of St Martin's Press LLC, 175 Fifth Avenue, New York, NY 10010.

Palgrave is a global imprint of the above companies and is represented throughout the world.

Palgrave® and Macmillan® are registered trademarks in the United States, the United Kingdom, Europe and other countries

ISBN 978-1-137-34159-4   ISBN 978-1-137-34160-0 (eBook)
DOI 10.1007/978-1-137-34160-0

This book is printed on paper suitable for recycling and made from fully managed and sustained forest sources. Logging, pulping and manufacturing processes are expected to conform to the environmental regulations of the country of origin.

A catalogue record for this book is available from the British Library.

A catalog record for this book is available from the Library of Congress.

For my mother, Maggie Spracklen

Contents

Acknowledgements

A small part of the ideas and words in Chapters 1, 3 and 9 appear in a significantly modified and re-structured form in my chapter 'Why PE Should be Made Voluntary' (Spracklen, 2014), part of the collection published by Inter-Disciplinary Press, Oxford, called *Game Changer: The Transformative Potential of Sport* (Dun, Spracklen and Wise, 2014). Inter-Disciplinary Press have given permission for this re-use of their material, and I am grateful to Rob Fisher for this and his faith in the Sport Project.

Thanks to all the students who helped me shape the ideas in this book during long hours of teaching. Also, a special thanks to Roland Ingram and Paul Miller who taught with me on the Understanding Issues in Sport and Exercise Science module, and whose conversations and suggestions are reflected in some of this book.

PUBLISHER'S ACKNOWLEDGEMENTS

Articles 22, 24 and 25 Part 1 from the Universal Declaration of Human Rights are reproduced with permission of the United Nations. Article 8 Parts 1 and 2 of the International Convention against Doping in Sport, 19 October 2005, © UNESCO 2005 are reproduced with permission of the United Nations Educational, Scientific and Cultural Organization.

Introduction

AIMS OF THE BOOK

What is sport? What is its relationship to society? How can we understand sports in relation to physical activities, leisure and physical culture? How can we think about sports in an inter-disciplinary way? If you were asking those questions, or your teacher or lecturer asked you to think about those questions, you have come to the right place. Now you have a copy of this book in your hands, you need to know what you have in front of you.

The aim of this book is to provide a critical textbook on the meaning and purpose of sports that can be used by students and lecturers in the full range of sports-related courses, from sports science and physical education to multi-disciplinary sports studies and leisure studies. This is a textbook for exploring sports participation and society. The book combines information, polemic, exposition and critical analysis, using ideas and research from sports studies alongside ideas and research from sociology, history, philosophy and psychology. The textbook is unique in having as its focus the concept of looking at sport and physical culture through an inter-disciplinary lens. It is impossible to think about critically exploring sports and their place in society without drawing on a wide range of academic disciplines, because sports are human creations with histories and philosophies, designed to stimulate bodies and minds, with impacts on social structures and culture. So, although this is primarily about sports and wider physical culture, it examines both through applying theories from the disciplines of sociology, philosophy, history, psychology and cultural studies.

The distinctive nature of this book is its critical lens. This is not an introduction to sports studies that avoids making critical, political, sociological statements. This book is designed and written to provoke teachers and students to question their assumptions about the value of sports and physical culture. I like sports and I think that they can be a good thing for us, but I maintain the right to question and critique the way sports have arisen and the way they are maintained. Throughout the book I take an essentially radical view of sports, making clear that modern sport is full of problems and contradictions.

The critical lens: using the work of Jurgen Habermas

My critical lens is underpinned by Marxist and post-Marxist theories of modernity and capitalism. Capitalism is the system of the free market, where individuals are free to buy and sell goods, their labour and anything else that can be given a price. Marxist political theories suggest that the age of modernity, the age that started with industrialization and urbanization, is the age in which capitalism becomes dominant in society, to the extent that capitalists become the new elites. Marxism originally predicted that capitalism would force a world revolution once the workers realized that they were being used by the capitalists. However, in the twentieth century, when capitalism became global, it seemed to be succeeding without creating world revolution. A number of radical theorists tried to explain why it had succeeded. Gramsci (1971) says capitalism succeeded by fooling people into thinking they were free, through the elites' complete control (hegemony) of culture. This is a very pessimistic view of society and of humanity. Jurgen Habermas (1984, 1987, 1989, 1990) has taken the Gramscian idea of capitalist control and has argued that this is in the form of instrumental rationalities (reducing everything to profit or to material gain) that constrain our ability to think for ourselves. But he also believes that as humans we have free agency and the ability to think and act in a communicative way, that is, without restraint or control, among others who are free to do the same. In my own research and writing on leisure, I have applied these Habermasian ideas to understanding leisure and sport (Spracklen, 2007, 2009, 2011, 2013a, 2013b). I have argued that leisure is a communicative act – that is, an act that is undertaken freely, often in free interaction, agreement and discussion with others. Leisure then is an essentially human act, which is at risk of being taken over by corporate, instrumental leisure. Sports and other forms of physical activity are a sub-set of leisure, so this book will use the same critical lens to understand them. Sports are an ideal subject for this kind of analysis, because they are hugely popular but also hugely problematic for their relationship to political structures and social inequalities. This is the heart of the theoretical framework and argument that runs through each chapter and which is expanded in the Conclusion.

This book is also distinctive in the way it uses examples from research across the sports and physical activity participation spectrum, and the sports-studies parent disciplines from psychology through sociology to philosophy. All of these examples are related to different issues within the framework of sport and physical culture. I have tried to use a wide, international range of sources and examples to make every chapter relevant to students on courses across the world, although my own British background means discussions about particular policies (especially in the chapter on physical education) – and my own research on rugby league, which is used here and there – rely on British contexts. These issues and my critical account of them drive the book's structure, and are framed in the everyday debates and controversies had by sports fans and participants. This textbook shares a similar structure and argument to my earlier textbook *Leisure, Sports and Society* (Spracklen, 2013a). It is designed to complement (and be a sequel to) that book on leisure sociology and leisure studies courses; but it is important to note that this textbook works as a stand-alone textbook for students who are on sports courses.

The book's chapters frequently include my own reflections on sports and physical activity, along with my own critical assertions. This is designed to make students think. Each chapter can be read separately. Along with boxed research examples, and the sectional structure of each chapter, this provides students with easy access to the relevant topics they need to think about. At the same time, there is one common critical argument running across the textbook: the arrangement of the textbook allows students and other readers to gain a cumulative knowledge of the meaning and purpose of sport, the context of sports in society, and the importance of understanding the tensions in the role of sport and physical culture in our everyday lives. This is an unashamedly polemical argument: that sport, while exciting and inspiring and life-changing in so many ways, is an instrument of inequality and a product of capitalist hegemony. A sophisticated critique of sport will develop through the book and be fully developed in the Conclusion.

But before we get to the content of the rest of the book, I need to define two terms I have already used a number of times in this Introduction: what is this thing called physical culture; and what is this thing called sports participation? Physical culture is a term invented by sociologists of sport and physical education to define the whole range of physical activities, practices, pedagogies, sports and pastimes that surround us in modern society – all the things that involve doing or watching or talking about physical exertions of some kind (Evans, Davies and Wright, 2003; Hargreaves and Vertinsky, 2006; Kirk, 1999). There is a controversy about what physical culture actually entails (for example, it is clear that building a house is physical work, but it is not an activity that is obviously part of physical culture), and some sociologists of sport have strongly attacked the phrase for masking the structural inequalities in modern society and modern sports (Tomlinson, 2002).

At times in this book I will use physical culture to describe activities that are physical, a shorthand term for the sports, the physical activities and the education, as well as the cultural products of sport that have become ideologically charged.

Physical culture is a way of thinking about sports participation in the broadest sense of the term. Before you read the rest of the book, I need to define the ways in which I will be talking about sports participation. There are three ways in which people engage with sports. First of all, we do sports by playing them, by being *active participants*. The second way in which we might engage in sports is that of the *fan*, or spectator: watching sports, liking sports and talking about sports. The final way in which people do sports is through being an active volunteer or paid *worker* in a particular sports role. In this book when I refer to sports participation it will usually mean doing sports, being physically active. But there will be times when sports participation is defined more broadly to encompass the three ways defined here. Where this happens I will draw it to your attention.

OVERVIEW OF THE BOOK

The book is divided into fourteen medium-sized chapters, with a Conclusion of half the length. Each of these main chapters introduces an issue or controversy in sport, relates it to wider debates in sociology or philosophy (or other related disciplines), and focuses in on specific problems and issues in sports, leisure and society. The chapters begin with an introduction to key concepts for students unfamiliar with social sciences – and there is a glossary at the back of the book that summarizes the definitions of these concepts. While this textbook is aimed at students with little or no knowledge of critical sociology, there will be some concepts that need to be understood by following up references in the text. Examples from related and relevant current sports research are separated out of the flow of the text in small 'textboxes': three per chapter. These textbox examples will make student users of this textbook think about issues but will be linked directly to the content of the chapter through an identification of key concepts they need to consider. Each chapter ends with a series of classroom exercises for lecturers and students to use, to enhance their learning and teaching experience and their interaction with the textbook's themes.

The chapters are in turn split into two uneven parts. The first part, Positions, covers the meaning, purpose, value and use of sport. This part is called Positions because each of these chapters provides a way to begin to understand the meaning and purpose of sport in society, either through history, philosophy, psychology or sociology. The second part, Problems, attempts to apply some of this positioning about sport to particular problems and areas of sport. I have called this part Problems because each of the subjects, issues and areas are problems that are in the popular domain. That is, these problems are talked about by people who are sports fans and participants, as well as critics of sport. The choices I have made in this book are, of course, partial. There are 'positions' and 'problems' I could have discussed, but have chosen not to, because the issues in this book are, I would argue, the most important if a sports student is to become a critical sports student.

Part I

Positions

Chapter 1

Who Invented Sports?

SUMMARY OF TOPICS

- *Definitions: sports, history and sports in history*
- *The origins of modern sport in the nineteenth century*
- *The social and cultural values associated with modern sport in its creation and development*
- *The establishment of the sports industry*

To begin thinking about the origins and importance of sports in modern society, contemplate your own sports participation.

Yesterday, I went for a run up my favourite hill. It is a hard push up to the top from my house, two hundred and fifty metres straight up. I wore my fancy running shoes with the synthetic cushioning and my lightweight running shorts (along with a cheap, plain tee-shirt). I looked like a runner even before I had started running. It was easy enough to buy the shoes and the shorts as I am a reasonably well-off, white middle-class academic living in a Western country, and running is a popular 'lifestyle' sport with an entire industry surrounding it selling all manner of things: not just clothes and shoes, but various tracking devices, water carriers, energy drinks, dietary supplements, guidance books, magazines, histories and videos. I went up the road to the point where it stops and becomes a rough track, and I noticed someone running ahead of me. They reached the top of the rough track then gave up and turned back down towards me. Lightweight, I thought to myself, as I ran up and past them, though what I said was: hello! I pushed myself to the very top of the hill, onto the moors and over to the far side, across another small hill, then down through pasture fields to reach the road to Bradley, where I followed the canal back home. This was the fourth time I had done this run – extending my heroic conquer of the peak with extra miles of graft. I thought the other runner, the person who gave up halfway up the hill, was a 'lightweight', an English expression for someone who is unable to compete – it is a pejorative phrase, often linked to hegemonic, heterosexual masculinity (Carless and Douglas, 2013). I would not use the word in public, but in the privacy of my mind, as I push myself up the hill, challenged by gravity, I find myself lapsing into the worldview of the modern sports competitor. I present myself as strong, the conqueror of mountains, and those who cannot do what I can do I secretly mock. These thoughts, these attitudes, are not healthy. I might be following the trend of being active to be physically healthy, I might be part of the physical culture of our modern world, but that physical culture – celebrating sports, celebrating the ethics and ideology of modern sports – seems to put me in a frame of mind that, on reflection, disturbs me.

In thinking about my own sports participation, I cannot help thinking about the problematic nature of modern sport. In my reflection I celebrate the joy and pleasure of doing sports, what we might call the positive nature of sport which we have inherited from the people who created modern sport. But the reflection also shows that there is a negative side to modern sport, the obsession with competition, with winning, and the arrogant dismissal of those who cannot perform sports, which again has come to us from modern sport's founders. Sports are so ingrained in our everyday lives that it is difficult to step away and question how and why they have the roles they have today. This chapter starts out by introducing popular debates about the origin of modern sports, as an attempt to understand the how and why of the meaning and purpose of sports. We will explore academic debates about the foundations of modern sports, and debates about the purpose of sports and physical education over the last couple of centuries. I will suggest that the meaning and purpose of sport in this century can only be understood by realizing that sports had a number of contradictory purposes in the nineteenth and twentieth centuries, when sports and physical education as we know them became part of a shared physical culture of modernity.

DEFINITIONS: SPORTS, HISTORY AND SPORTS IN HISTORY

What are sports? This is what is called an ontological question. Ontology is the part of philosophy that looks at the meaning of concepts. Philosophers of sport have tried to answer that question and found it both very simple, and very complicated (Breivik, 2007; Morgan, 1976, 2005, 2008; Suits, 2005). Sports are physical activities of some kind that demand some kind of physical exertion from the participants. Sports are like games, or pastimes. We can all point to an activity and say: 'that's a sport'. But what is it about some activity that makes it a sport? How do we establish what are the necessary features of an activity that establish it as a sport, and not something else? You might think this is trivial. After all, I am sure we would agree with each other that baseball is a sport, and the different codes of football are sports, and swimming is a sport, and gymnastics is a sport. We could go down the list of all the sports that we know about and have no problem at all. But then we might get to walking. Is that a sport? We might say it depends on the conditions in which the activity takes place: walking is clearly a sport where it is part of a competitive structure, with agreed rules about how you walk correctly, and officials who make sure walkers in competitions don't just get a taxi from the start to the finish. Walking might not be a sport if it is just the physical activity of going to the local pizza restaurant. So perhaps a definition of modern sports is they are games that are physical activities, with fixed rules, ordered competitions and independent judges.

Based on this premise, sports depend on formal structures and organizations that establish the rules of the game and monitor the participants. That definition is itself problematic, because it seems to rule out those physical activities that look like what we are confident are sports, but which we have ruled out by linking sports to formality. Where do we place recreational swimming, for example? We have just agreed that swimming is a sport. But we have also suggested that sports are defined by competition and structure, so swimming for fun (or to keep fit) does not fit our definition – and neither does any kind of physical activity that is recreational or leisure-like in nature. This is why some academics have adopted the notion of physical culture, as we saw in the Introduction. Physical culture seems to be more inclusive in its definitional boundaries. It seems to allow more things in its remit than the term 'sport'. For now, perhaps I might argue that recreational physical activities that we call sports, such as swimming, are less regulated versions of an activity that does meet the strict definitions around competition and struc-ture. Swimmers may not be competing against each other in a recreational session, but they are competing against the environment and their own bod-ies. There may not be an official monitoring the strokes the swimmers use, but the swimmers are following the rules of how to move their bodies through the water, and they are obeying the rules of the organization that controls the swimming pool. What is clear in this attempt to define sports is that they are a phenomenon associated with the modern world, of modernity, the form of society that emerged in the nineteenth century and which might be said to be the society which we live in today. So to understand modern sports, we have to understand the history of sport, and the history of modern society.

If we look at the different periods in history, before the modern age, we can see activities that we might identify as sports. If we do this, of course, we seem to be breaking with the ontological definition of sports as something inherently modern. Many historians of sport have done this, especially when exploring the cultures of what is often called the Classical world of Ancient Greece and Ancient Rome (Guttmann, 1981, 1986; Young, 2005). We will look at the Greek example of the Olympics in more detail in the next chapter. The other example from Ancient Rome might be the gladiatorial games and chariot races. The gladiatorial games are well-known in contemporary popular culture, not because we have all been reading our Latin authors at school, but because of Hollywood films and television programmes that focus on the bloody violence of such games (Dunkle, 2008). It is tempting to see in the gladiatorial combat portrayed on our screens a precursor of modern sports, or a fully defined sport in itself: a fight between well-trained, profes-sional athletes, watched over by thousands of shouting spectators. However, although the gladiatorial games provided a visceral spectacle not completely removed from the violence of a football stadium, it is a step too far to see the equivalence as an exact one. First of all, gladiators killed unarmed prisoners, as well as animals and each other, so the focus of the spectacle was slaughter not competition. Secondly, the games were an important part of Rome's re-ligious calendar, paid for by wealthy citizens to promote Roman values and Roman superiority (Balsdon, 2004). We might think the chariot races are more obviously analogous to modern sports. As I have discussed in another book (Spracklen, 2011), chariot-racing was hugely popular, drawing thou-sands of fans to the circus to watch the professional teams compete. There were fan clubs or guilds for the circus factions (the Blues and the Greens), money was won and lost at gambling, and there were even riots between fans of the rival factions. This was clearly something like a modern sport, but the factions served different roles to modern-day football hooligans. The factions were involved in political and religious controversies, and are best seen as a combination of a mafia gang, a trade guild, and a political party. Chariot-racing was one activity undertaken by the circus factions in a wider set of activities that might be described by us as leisure activities – such as watching dancing, singing, and drama, and using prostitutes. The races probably brought the greatest number of people together but they were only one part of the factional culture (Balsdon, 2004; Spracklen, 2011). The culture of the Roman Republic and the Roman Empire was in many ways proto-modern, similar to our society in the way leisure time and leisure activities were used by the ruling elite to maintain their power over the urban masses. But the Roman world was very different to ours, and it is naïve to talk about the games and chariot-racing as sports in the modern sense of the word.

Oiled bodies and the making of Turkish wrestling

Turkish 'oil wrestling' is an important part of modern Turkish identity, modern Turkish masculinity and the contemporary nationalist history of modern, secular Turkey. Oil wrestling describes a specific style of wrestling in which the contestants are stripped down to their bare chests and doused in olive oil: this makes the contest more about skill than strength, as each contestant finds their rival slipping away from them in the holds. The modern sport has its roots in oil wrestling lodges that existed in the time of the Ottoman Empire, the multicultural (but mainly Muslim) empire that collapsed in the first quarter of the twentieth century. The Ottoman Turks who ruled over the Empire had gradually taken over the older Byzantine and Arab areas in Asia and Europe, and captured Constantinople in 1453. The Ottomans adopted many Byzantine Greek customs, and many Greeks remained in the Ottoman Empire. Oil wrestling was definitely an Ancient Greek pastime. Oil wrestling is almost certainly a surviving Byzantine pastime, though under the Ottomans it became associated with the ruling elites, with Islam and with Turkishness. Krawietz (2012) shows how the sport's historical origins have been the subject of Turkification and nationalism in the twentieth century and into this century. In the struggle by the secular nationalists to establish a modern Turkey on the ashes of the Ottoman Empire, there was no space for minority ethnic groups: there were terrible massacres, uprisings and battles; and many of the Greeks of the Ottoman Empire were exchanged for the Muslim Turks of Greece. In such a traumatic upheaval, the Turks found it necessary to make oil wrestling more anciently Turkish, and to forget or ignore its Greek origins.

QUESTIONS TO CONSIDER

What other modern sports have their origins in Imperial cultural practices like oil wrestling? How can we know the true origins of a sport?

REFERENCE AND FURTHER READING

Krawietz, B. (2012) 'The Sportification and Heritagisation of Traditional Turkish Oil Wrestling', *The International Journal of the History of Sport*, 29, pp. 2145–61.

Some historians of sport (for example, see Brailsford, 1992; Holt, 1989) have argued for the origins of modern sports in the emergence of organized competitions in eighteenth-century Europe in horse-riding, boxing, running and walking, which was often referred to in the primary sources as pedestrianism (Lile, 2000). These competitions were organized between professional athletes by local landowners or other rich citizens, and brought together thousands of spectators and the ancillary activities associated with them: fairs, gambling, drinking and eating. Some of these activities are claimed to be even older: fell-running, for example, a modern sport associated with the highlands of the United Kingdom, is often claimed to have its origins in competitions organized as early as the Middle Ages (Askwith, 2004). There is some truth to the claims that such activities were the forerunners of our modern sports, and these activities did have some of the characteristics of our definition of modern sports: competition, spectacle, professionalism. And to confuse the matter slightly, these activities were given the name sports by those involved in them, a word that was first used to describe the leisurely pastimes of elite English gentlemen (such as hunting and fishing) who had so much money they did not need to work (Holt, 1989). These leisure and recreational activities do share many similarities with their modern versions, but their meaning and purpose in society was different to that of sports today. These activities were loosely organized, with rules being decided on the day, and there were no governing bodies of sports or professional sports clubs organizing and making profit from the activities. So fell-runners, boxers and pedestrian athletes made money through winning cash prizes, but they were not full-time professional athletes like the ones that have emerged in modern sports. These activities shared more in common with medieval leisure activities such as village football, pilgrimages and holy feasts than they shared with modern sports (Spracklen, 2011). They were ways of reaffirming the power of the landed gentry in Western Europe at a time when a new bourgeois class of urban capitalists was struggling to gain political supremacy. They were a product of a struggle over hegemony: who had the power to impose their norms, value and culture on the emerging nation-states of Early Modern (seventeenth and eighteenth-century) Europe.

The new elites from the free cities demanded lessons on how to act in a noble manner, so they could prove their distinction and civility (Bryson, 1998). At the same time, the old aristocracies were becoming more concerned with marking themselves out from the masses according to their tastes and morals (Tribby, 1992). These two trends led to the establishment of a refined, courtly high culture, with rules on gentility, decorum and distinction (Arditi, 1998). Elias, in *The Civilizing Process* (1978, 1982), charts these trends and stresses the growth of inhibition and self-restraint, and the growth of privacy in the lives of individuals. Elias argues that these trends originated in courtly society of the late Middle Ages, but grew with the rise of bourgeois, urban middle classes, in Early Modern states such as Venice, France and England. Elias links this 'civilizing process' to the rise of absolute power in the monarchy. Successive kings move to weaken feudal nobility, and legitimate use of violence becomes a monopoly of the state. The outcomes of these 'civilizing processes' were a decline of violence for enjoyment, the banning of rough sports and leisure activities, and a decline in the public exercise of bodily functions (Arditi, 1998; Borsay, 2005).

THE ORIGINS OF MODERN SPORT

Modern sports appeared in the nineteenth century, mainly in the West, that area of the world that is loosely bounded by Europe, the United States of America, and the colonies of white Europeans that emerged in what we now know as Canada, Australia, New Zealand and (to a lesser extent) South Africa. These European and post-European societies shared a common heritage and a common culture. The common heritage was a combination of Christianity, capitalism and state-building, which had given rise to both the growth of Empire and the growth of technological innovation (Habermas, 1989; Spracklen, 2011, 2013b). This was the age of Western economic and military supremacy. The common culture of the West was bourgeois (urban, middle class): the product of the Enlightenment, when middle-class people (generally white men) gained civil rights and political representation. The wealth of the West was built on the exploitation of slavery and military power. The application of scientific reason to the production of goods saw the rise of steam power, precision engineering and the replacement of cottage industries with urban-based factories and mills. The dissolution of feudal ties allowed provincial or colonial towns to become huge cities filled with economic migrants from the countryside, seeking employment in the factories.

This was the age of modernity, the period of history in which people started to claim their own society was better than that of the Classical world, or the many other ages that had led up to the nineteenth century. For the confident elites in these Western societies, industrialization, capitalism and imperialism were forces for good, creating civilization, modern men and modern nation-states (Spracklen, 2013b).

Modern sports were by definition a consequence of this modern, Western culture. Firstly, these sports were the product of a process of invention. They might have been based on older pastimes, but it was only in this period of modernity that official rulebooks were written and governing bodies formed to organize the various sports. The pressure to create and codify sports came initially from the ruling elites who wished to apply the rationality of modern bureaucracy to their hobbies (Collins, 2013a, 2013b; Hargreaves, 1994; Spracklen, 2011). Modern sports were also created in the form we know them as a consequence of the technological changes that were occurring in this period. Transport and communications speeded up the world and made it necessary to standardize things such as time zones and bye-laws. Modern sports became rationalized inside nation-states and, through international governing bodies, in the rest of the world (Hargreaves, 1994). Technological developments also created a market for modern sports products. Soccer balls, for example, could be made more cheaply to standard factory designs, using the latest scientific discoveries. Finally, the rapid industrialization and urbanization of the West led to an enormous rise in populations, and the huge numbers of poor working-class people in the towns and cities became targets of marketing campaigns and moral campaigns, both undertaken by the elites to modify working-class tastes and habits. As the working classes gained more leisure time and more money to spend in their leisure time, various leisure industries emerged to take their money: sports were one kind of leisure activity among many others, albeit a kind of leisure activity that proved enduringly popular (Borsay, 2005; Spracklen, 2011).

Modern sports, then, are an invention of hegemonic, Western instrumental power (Collins, 2013a). Of course, there are sports-like activities that owe their origins to different cultures and societies, such as Turkish wrestling and the variations on polo still played in the highland zones of Pakistan and Afghanistan (Parlebas, 2003); there are also sports-like games that appear in the historical and archaeological records for Central and South America (see discussion in Spracklen, 2011). Even in the West, there are precursors to modern sports, especially in the period of the Classical Age of Europe, when Greeks and Romans played and watched a number of games that are still part of the modern sporting arena (athletics, gymnastics, wrestling) as well as games that are no longer considered to be sports at all (chariot-racing, gladiatorial combat). But despite those exceptions and caveats, the first sentence of this paragraph still holds mainly true: what we think of as sports, the things we play and the things we watch, are all inventions of white, Western modernity.

As mentioned earlier, the concept of 'sports' first appears in the Early Modern period, when white, European elite men used the word to describe their leisured, gentlemanly pursuits in the outdoors: hunting, shooting, fishing and horse-riding (Borsay, 2005). Rural games such as football were identified as the sports of the poor. These games were later described by gentleman authors such as Strutt, who believed they were the remnants of a residual, feudal culture, with informal rules and governance (Strutt, 1801). In the early nineteenth century, the Western elite classes started to take an interest in sporting activities that were threatened by the rise of urbaniza-tion and industrialization. Educators and Christian activists believed that the old, folk sports were a valuable learning tool for young elite men: they should take part in sports to be physically fit to run the empires of the West, and morally fit to be good Christians. Sports would provide these young men with the bodies and minds they needed to keep Western, hege-monic whiteness in its hegemonic state. As the working classes moved to live in towns and stopped playing sports associated with rural, feudal cul-tures, these same sports were adopted and codified by the elites in the schools and other institutions – whether it was soccer in the British uni-versities or baseball (adapted from rounders) in the United States. These sports were believed to be expressions of white, Western modernity, of a shared elite civilization – even where nationalism was also a factor of the modern sport's growth (again, baseball is a classic example). As well as seeking to use the older games as the building blocks of carefully regulated and governed modern sports, the Muscular Christian movement adopted and adapted games from the Classical Age, replicating the similar neo-classicism emerging in elite culture, architecture and literature.

By the second half of the nineteenth century governing bodies of sports had emerged throughout Europe and North America, organizations with individual or club members, which decided on rule-books, competitions and laws over who was allowed to take part in the particular sport. This was the birth of modern sports – sports could not be modern without fixing their rules, developing governance structures, and becoming part of the regula-tory regime of modernity (Spracklen, 2011). Some of these governing bodies had a domestic remit; others were international organizations that had domestic governing bodies of sport as their members. These governing bodies were initially dominated by the elite classes of their countries, the white Westerners – so, for example, when soccer developed in Argentina it was dominated and controlled by British men (Archetti, 1995). Modern sports' governing bodies became quickly fixated on the fear of professionals, lower-class players being paid to play as opposed to middle and upper-class gentlemen amateurs. Rules on amateurism tore some sports apart, such as rugby (Collins, 1999; Dunning and Sheard, 2005); some elites lost the battle and professionalism emerged as the legitimate (and dominant) practice in some sports (for example, soccer); but in most sports, the power of the elites endured and amateurism survived as the prevailing ethic into the second half of the twentieth century. This ideal of the amateur helped to preserve the whiteness and the maleness of sports participation: amateur sports such as athletics, rowing, American football and rugby union became the sports played by the white, Western elites in their private schools and top universities. I will discuss these issues in more detail in the next chapter.

Professional sports such as soccer and baseball were used to keep the poorer classes (white and black) in their place in the Western, modern system, through offering poor men dreams of becoming famous, a chance to cheer their local side and a chance to bet and drink with their friends (Collins, 2013a; Spracklen, 2011). Modern sports transformed from elite leisure activities into mass entertainment almost as soon as they spread out from the elite classes. Professional, modern sports established themselves as the successors of the older spectator pastimes such as racing, bareknuckle boxing and pedestrianism. Professional clubs in team sports such as soccer built fences around their playing fields, made spectators pay to watch, and built stands in which spectators could shelter from the weather. Watching sport – paying to watch it, supporting a club – became a fashion among all classes in the West, and a marker of white, modern masculinity (Vamplew, 2004). The growth of professional sports was phenomenal at the end of the nineteenth and into the twentieth century, both in terms of the number of professional sports clubs and leagues, and the numbers of people who wanted to declare their loyalty to a particular club or sport. At first, the passion aroused by sports fandom was fuelled by the rise in sports coverage in the newspapers: first match reports, then daily news and speculation (Collins and Vamplew, 2002; Vamplew, 2004). Alongside dedicated sports journalism in local newspapers – stories associated with the fortunes of the local club or the particular professional sport favoured in the area – there soon arose a practice of having professional (and high-profile amateur) sports discussed and analysed in daily sections in the national newspapers. The newspapers competed with each other for the money of the sports fan, each trying to find angles and exclusive content that would make their newspaper more attractive than the others. Modern technologies such as the telegraph and the telephone allowed journalists to report on matches and events taking place throughout entire countries and beyond. As well as newspaper coverage, sports were the subject of specialist magazines aimed at adults (such as *Sporting News* for baseball in the United States, which ran from 1886 to 2012) and children (for example, *Boy's Own* in the United Kingdom, which ran from 1879 to 1967): the former allowing fans to discuss the action with their friends and engage in bets; the latter normalizing the novelty of modern sports in the minds of the young. All these forms of print media constructed a public sphere in which sports and sporting success defined local and national belonging, creating a myth of traditions around the novelty of modern sport, making sport a symbol for civilized, white, male Western culture and power. By the first two decades of the twentieth century, professional sports leagues were established in Europe, North America and Australia, and the print media in every Western or Westernized country promulgated the notion that following sport was fashionable, masculine and modern (Briggs and Burke, 2009).

With the commercialization – and commodification – of radio technology, came competition between broadcasters for listeners and advertising revenue. Radio technology allowed companies to broadcast live and recorded material to anybody who bought a radio set and tuned in to the company's programmes. Sports events were a profitable part of any station's programming, and soon companies were negotiating with professional leagues, clubs and governing bodies of sports for contracts and permissions to cover their sports events. News reporting of scores and analysis of the day's sports action were complemented with live commentary on events, which proved profitable and popular. Radio defined a nation or a region, or both, and its novelty made it a mass-market leisure phenomenon in the 1930s (Briggs and Burke, 2009). People listened to the radio at work and at home, discussing the topics broadcast with friends and family. In the United Kingdom, the British Broadcasting Corporation normalized an elite, white version of Englishness through its use of Received Pronunciation, the national anthem and its formal subservience to the Monarchy, the Church of England, the Marylebone Cricket Club, and the British Empire. In the United States, radio established baseball as the national game, allowing live reports and news programmes on the national scene to be syndicated across hundreds of local radio stations, ensuring national identities were linked to the white, small-town, all-American men who played the sport (Silvia, 2007). In Australia, radio created rivalries between cities where different football codes were dominant, but used those different footballs to create a common Australia of working-class white men battling the system, the British and the Aborigines (Moore, 2000).

How the British made soccer global

The modern sport of soccer is seemingly universal, played across the globe and the number-one sport to watch and play in dozens of countries. Soccer's spread across the world started with its export from England to Europe, and its quick establishment on the continent as a professional, mass-spectator sport. The sport also spread rapidly to countries where the British had strong connections through trade, imperialism or cultural hegemony: Russia, Brazil and Argentina, for example. Matthew Taylor (2010) shows how British soccer knowledge in the first half of the twentieth century was distributed to other countries where soccer was played through the migration of individual experts: players, coaches and managers. Taylor suggests that these experts were the equivalent of the British engineers of the nineteenth century, who helped the transfer of technology (and British cultural practices and cultural hegemony) to the wider world. This made the global game of soccer more culturally British, although Taylor suggests the cultural transfer was not always one way. The governing body of soccer in England, the Football Association, was slow to take advantage of the growth of soccer as a global sport, and for many years the Football Association was reluctant to sanction tours and other international competitions: famously, the first three World Cup competitions did not involve England.

QUESTIONS TO CONSIDER

How did other modern sports spread around the globe? Why did soccer struggle to gain popularity in some countries?

REFERENCE AND FURTHER READING

Taylor, M. (2010) 'Football's Engineers? British Football Coaches, Migration and Intercultural Transfer, c.1910–c.1950s', *Sport in History*, 30, pp. 138–63.

The development of modern sport goes hand-in-hand with sports spectatorship. Playing sport was related to spectatorship, which was related to the fashion for sports. There were two routes to modern sports participation, both of which excluded marginalized groups such as women and minority ethnic groups to a greater or lesser extent. For the white, elite men, amateur sports were something they did to become proper men, physically and mentally equipped to rule and give orders, fighting in imperial struggles and capitalist marketplaces. Amateur sports could be obscure, such as real tennis or the Eton Fives game, or they could be sports that were well-known and played by a wider range of classes including the bourgeoisie (such as golf). Especially popular were team sports such as soccer and basketball: these sports promoted the importance of victory, individual endeavour and physical prowess, alongside the importance of working as part of a team to bring glory to one's club. Sports such as these became fundamental in schools, colleges and universities, where the new white elites and the growing white middle classes of the West were trained. As the twentieth century progressed the importance of sports in the elite education curriculum was established, normalized and allowed to spread to women's educational establishments, and throughout the world where modern, Western values were adopted. The second route to sports participation was the evangelization of the working classes by sports advocates, men (and occasionally women) trained in the elite system determined to make the poor better in body and soul through sports. This led to widespread adoption of formal physical education curricula and the rise of state intervention in creating sports facilities, as well as the increase in professional sports activity when young, working-class men realized they could make money from playing sport. This second route to sports participation did allow some non-white participation in sport in Western countries, but the participation was controlled and shaped by the condescending attitudes of the sports advocates. Sports were still viewed as something done at an amateur level by rich white men – sports for poor people were ways of making them healthy, pliant, and less aggressive; a way of giving them something to forget their troubles.

Most modern school systems owe their content and design to Western educational systems devised in the rush to mass education in the late nineteenth century. The Western models of education that have been globalized and modernized today (the primary, secondary and tertiary model of schools and universities) in turn owe their form to the prejudices and assumptions of their founders: the elite, white Western educationalists trained in elite private schools that inherited an assumption about the value of sport learned in the Muscular Christianity revival of the mid-nineteenth century (a revival based partly on the reconstruction of Classical norms of athletic training and modern, scientific fears of moral degeneration). Wright (1996) discusses how this construction of modern sport was played out in the education system, reproducing gender and class inequalities. Mangan (1981, 1986) highlights the centrality of sport in the curriculum of imperialist Great Britain, but sport was not only a hegemonic practice in the British Empire, it was central to the nationalism and struggle for cultural hegemony in all nation-states emerging out of the nineteenth century. Sport, a product of modernity, was the marker of each nation-state's myth-making. For the United States, for example, the local invention of basketball and the home version of football were bound to the nationalism of difference and individualization. In Germany outdoor pursuits gave the new bourgeoisie the opportunity to prove their good taste and distinction while organized and regulated physical activity was encouraged in workplaces, trade unions and schools. Into the twentieth century this model was exported across the rest of the world with Westernization, modernization and globalization, the long-term geopolitical trends that shaped the rise and fall of British imperialism, and the rise of American cultural and political hegemony in the West and the rest of the world. Sports, then, were always connected to two contradictory trends: the power and control of what might be called instrumental rationality (Habermas, 1984, 1987), and the desire to pick and choose one's leisure habits freely. People watch sports and play sports because they like them and find meaning and belonging and identity in sports. But modern sport is the product of hegemonic power. While it might be argued that American power has declined in the century in which we live, there is no doubt that Americanization was – and still is – an important factor in the spread of Western culture and Western ideologies such as capitalism and instrumentality. Sports were and are one part of that wider history.

Danish gymnastics and the Nazis

In much of Europe in the early twentieth century, organized and regimented physical activities – drills undertaken in large, disciplined groups – were seen as ways of instilling healthiness and moral correctness into the participants. Young people in particular were encouraged to take part in such physical activities to ensure they avoided the perils of sexuality, sedition and other activities deemed to be reckless. For Christian nationalists, these regimented physical activities saved the nation and souls. For far-right nationalists such as the Fascists of Italy and the Nazis of Germany, controlled physical exercise was part of a way of demonstrating the racial purity of the nation and the supremacy of its bodies. Hans Bonde's (2009) research on the 1930s Danish male gymnastics innovator Niels Bukh demonstrates the racist, fascist and nationalist ideologies at work behind this form of physical exercise. Bukh wanted his young men to be morally and physically pure, ideal types of the Danish people. The Nazis saw in this display of gymnastics the expression of a Northern European or Aryan racial body and racial culture. This body and culture had no basis in reality – but Bukh's gymnasts and gymnastics seemed to the Nazis to be 'evidence' of their racial superiority. Bonde shows how the Nazis in 1930s Germany invited Bukh to the country to put on displays of his gymnastics. Bonde also demonstrates how Bukh's style of gymnastics was introduced into German physical education. Bukh's gymnasts were ideal Aryan types, and his techniques were adopted in German training to try to make Germans conform to the moral and physical ideals of Nazi racial ideology.

QUESTIONS TO CONSIDER

How were physical drills used in other countries in this period? How did these practices influence the development of physical culture today?

REFERENCE AND FURTHER READING

Bonde, H. (2009) 'The Struggle for Danish Youth: Fascism, Sport, Democracy', *The International Journal of the History of Sport*, 26, pp. 1436–57.

CONCLUSION

Through this examination of the origins of modern sports, we can begin to answer the question posed at the beginning of this chapter: what is the meaning and purpose of modern sports? Modern sports seem to be defined by what Jurgen Habermas identifies as the tension in modernity between different ways of thinking, different rationalities: the communicative reason associated with free interaction, free choices and open discourse; and the instrumentality that reduces debates about value to economics or some other simplified rationality (Habermas, 1984, 1987; Spracklen, 2009). Sports, as we have seen, had a number of contradictory purposes in the nineteenth and twentieth centuries, when sports and physical education as we know them became part of a shared physical culture of modernity. They were activities that allowed individuals to come together to make meaning in their lives, in that free, communicative sense – giving enjoyment and sense of belonging to their participants and to spectators. But sports and physical education were tools of instrumentality right from their invention in the nineteenth century – that is, as we have seen in this chapter, they were partially designed with the purpose of celebrating elite cultures and keeping others in their place – and this use of sports as tools of instrumental power has continued to this day. We will look at the historical use of modern sport as a tool of power in more detail in the next chapter.

EXERCISES

1 Discuss the role of physicality in defining sport and explain whether darts, computer games, fishing and chess are sports.
2 Compare and contrast chariot-racing with modern-day Formula One. What are the similarities and differences?
3 Italians claim modern soccer has its roots in the older pastime of *calcio*. What reasons might you have for agreeing or disagreeing with this claim, and can you find evidence to back up your argument?

Chapter 2

The Development of Sport: Politics, Power and Myths

SUMMARY OF TOPICS

- *Definitions: Whig history and myths*
- *The gentleman amateur and the rise of professional sports*
- *The rise of the modern Olympics*
- *National myths, elitism and modern sports*

We have seen in the last chapter how the purpose of modern sports in their foundational years was to serve the interests of the ruling elites, but in becoming popular, modern sports have become more contested between those who see them as vehicles of control, and those who want the freedom to enjoy them. This chapter will introduce and explore the tension between history and myth by looking at the foundation myths of particular sports, and exploring the development of the modern Olympics. We will explore the construction of history, the invention of tradition, the construction of imagined communities and the mythology of the 'gentleman amateur'. I will argue that sport and wider physical culture is always the product of a tension between those individuals who are able to express their passion for physical activity and those who would use such culture as a means to control others.

DEFINITIONS: WHIG HISTORY AND MYTHS

Histories of sport – sporting histories written by official governing bodies of sport, or sports journalists – are Whig histories. Whig history is a term first coined by Herbert Butterfield (1968). He defined it as the tendency of historians to see the past as the story of conflict between progressives and reactionaries, in which the progressives win and bring about the modern world. He suggested that this was to overestimate the likenesses between present and past and to assure that we always intend the consequences of our actions. Whig history, then, supports a progressivist view of history, as if the entire past was a build-up to the present, a supporting act to the events of our time. Whig history becomes equated with the modernist paradigm, and all historical discourses that use the past to prove a point in the present. Whig history is the propagandist history of ideologies; it is the use of history to justify the actions and interests of the Whig historian. Sports histories are often Whig histories because they describe how sport has become successively better and better, more popular, more successful. Sports histories are discourses that are present-centred (Ashplant and Wilson, 1988; Wilson and Ashplant, 1988), describing the history of sport with the prejudices and biases of the present. This, however, is a problem all histories face. How do I write a history of modern sport if all our interpretive skills and our language are also centred on the present (Skinner, 1969)?

The way around the problem of present-centredness is to look at the actual processes by which historical narratives are constructed (Bentley, 2006; Lorenz, 1994). Who has written the history? Why? What were the sources? Does this agree or disagree with other discourses on the same subject (Ashplant and Wilson, 1988; Wilson and Ashplant, 1988)? In response to the question of what the past of sport really is, or whether we can ever get true access to what sport meant to people in the past, one can only make a leap of logical faith. If, as we have seen, accounts of history that are Whiggish (or biased towards particular nations or cultures) are bad history, then the removal of all these habits from our historical discourses will make them better, that is, more faithful to the events of the past. If we then accept that we are interested in specific parts of history (sports in the last hundred and fifty years), that we have a purpose which is overtly acknowledged, and that to 'know true history' is impossible and a misguided goal, our discourse will be far more credible. I cannot help but write my historical discourse with my interests in mind – why else would we choose to write history? But I can be aware of that and the danger of excessive truth-claims. Hence I am watching out for the pitfalls that make good history bad (Bentley, 2006). Baudrillard (1988) makes the added claim that the past can only be seen as a symbol (or symbols), with a myriad of different interpretations, and we cannot know which historical discourse is the right one. The task then becomes to explore and define these localized historical discourses. Instead of the truth, we look at what people claim to be 'true' history, and ask why they have defined the past in such a way.

In one sense, myths are simply stories that have no foundation in truth. In everyday language, for instance, we talk about the myths of the Vikings – the gods such as Odin and Freya, the stories of Ragnarok and the world-tree Yggdrasil – in fairly certain knowledge that none of these things exist. Myths can also be stories that people believe to be true, but which are not true; or stories that might have had an element of truth in them, but which have been changed through transmission and interpretation. In modern sports, there is the founding myth of the heroic iconoclast, writing down the rules as if they were commandments, or creating the new sport through some brave action: William Webb Ellis is celebrated as the creator of the modern sport of rugby even though the only claim that he created it comes from a time when the governing body of rugby in England was trying desperately to keep its class-based authority against some new clubs from the working-class north of the country (Collins, 1999). These sporting myths are very common, and it is easy for more critical historians of sport to challenge them through the work of exploring primary sources in an academic way (indeed, there is even a book devoted to such myth-busting in the history of sport: see Wagg, 2011). But myths are not merely false stories, or mis-representations of some other true story that needs to be found and published. Myths are rich representations of human culture, stories in which norms, structures and values are (re)established, legitimized and normalized (Baudrillard, 1998; Sahlins, 2009). They operate at a deep psychological level, drawing on archetypes and literary tropes – heroes, gods, demons, quests – to tell similar stories about how to lead a good life and how to conform to the culture in which we live (Barthes, 1972; Eliade, 1963). Myths, then, are the stories that people tell to each other to shape social and cultural belonging and exclusion.

Benedict Anderson (1983) has shown how nation-states create stories about the past, myths of belonging and community, which bind complex and disparate people together into one cultural and political community. Anderson calls these things 'imagined communities'. Imagined communities use history to justify and legitimize their existence. But they do not deal with the past: rather they work with myths and stories that are historicized. They are dealing with 'invented traditions' (Hobsbawm and Ranger, 1983). In other words, people in the present make use of the past as a place where they can place genesis stories, genealogies of structure (Foucault, 1972), in order to legitimate claims and structures they may use in the present. This is not a conscious, manipulative design. Invented traditions serve a real need in the present, as they are the founding stories of the people who use them. It is clear that these invented traditions are more important in the research than a quest for 'what really happened', as they relate to the discourses that surround the invention and evolution of something like modern sports.

American football: exceptionalism or 'global trend' following?

The origin myths of the American version of football are found in every popular history book about the sport, and all over the sports pages on-line and in the print media. Even academic historians of sport and America have argued that American football is an example of America breaking free from Europe's cultural setting and creating a new world of its own. The birth of the sport is accredited to the founding father Walter Camp, who set out his involvement in creating the rules of American football in a now famous 1886 magazine article. Collins (2013b) shows that this interpretation of the origins of American football is false, and the story of Camp's heroic fathering of the sport a half-truth transformed into a myth following its re-telling over the years. As Collins (2013b) suggests, the American obsession with sports in the second half of the nineteenth century followed the trend in England and Europe. Like the European elites, the American elites saw sports like rugby as character-forming forms of physical culture good for body and soul. Migration of people led to migration of ideas, cultural trends and sports. American football's rules were shaped by a wider global trend in football to simplify and adapt the rules of the various codes to solve the problems of play breaking down. Rather than a break with the old world, the birth of American football demonstrated America's strong links with England.

QUESTIONS TO CONSIDER

How does American football reflect American identity today? How did other football codes emerge?

REFERENCE AND FURTHER READING

Collins, T. (2013b) 'Unexceptional Exceptionalism: The Origins of American Football in a Transnational Context', *Journal of Global History*, 8, pp. 209–30.

THE GENTLEMAN AMATEUR

One of the most divisive myths to take hold of modern sport was the notion of the amateur athlete. In the nineteenth century, when sports were being taken up by elite gentlemen and codified across the West, there was an implicit assumption that gentlemen did not need to be paid for their sports participation. They played sports because they enjoyed the physical activity, and this activity was something they did alongside their work as officers, priests, teachers, estate managers and so on. As modern sports became more popular, they became more competitive. In some sports, working-class men were able to take part in their free time, and this made the elite organizers of those sports unhappy as they feared the working-class men would grow to dominate their sports. Some sportsmen (of all social backgrounds) were paid to take part in tournaments, some won prizes for winning, and some started to insist on being paid expenses to attend certain competitions and events (Vamplew, 2004). As more people started to attend sports competitions as paying spectators, there was a pressure on sports clubs, teams and governing bodies to get the best athletes to entertain the paying public. Some sports allowed professionals to appear, athletes who earned money to play their sport, and very quickly some sports became dominated by professional athletes, professional clubs and professional leagues. Other sports created strict, exclusive categories of amateur and professional athletes, who played in different tournaments. Some sports allowed amateurs and professionals to mix under rules that codified class status and gave amateurs more privileges and power over professionals.

In the mythology of the gentleman amateur, the proponents of amateurism and their historians have identified a pure form of sports participation. Professionalism is viewed as a kind of Biblical Fall from a perfect state of participating in sports for the sake of one's health and soul – instead of playing sports to become better humans, professionals play sports merely to earn the filthy lucre of the winning bonus. For the founders of amateurism, the rule was supposedly something close to a 'proper' morality for the athlete, something taken from the Classical world-view: sports were a form of prayer and preparation for young men taking up the leadership of the nation. Elite participants in modern sports were expected to be morally correct, spiritually pure and physically fit – so amateurism was a way of transforming their relationship to sport, removing them from the supposed depravity of playing to win (Collins, 2013a). Professionals – where they were sanctioned in the new governing bodies – were associated with tradesmen, servants, other ranks, and treated accordingly. They might have been a necessary evil of the modern world of sport, but they held low status. Where professionals were not allowed in the rules, the sin of accepting money ran so deep that clubs and individuals accused of being 'professionals' (often on highly political, tangential charges) continued to receive lifetime bans from amateur sports all the way into the 1990s (Thomas, 1997). Of course most amateur sports were in fact 'shamateur' from the invention of modern sports right through the twentieth century: elite amateurs received all manner of payments and all kinds of 'professional' support from coaches. But the breaches of the code were overlooked because the athletes were from social elites who shared the same background as the people who ran the sports (Llewellyn, 2011). Rules about amateurs and professionals were social constructions that maintained the power of the elites and restricted the power and involvement of others in modern sport. This is clearly seen in the modern Olympics.

Sport as nation-making technology

Dyreson (2003) draws on the work of the German philosopher Heidegger to argue that modern sports are a technology – a combination of language, systems and ideas – that, in the twentieth century, drives two paradoxical forces: the globalization of modernity and the development of modern nation-states and nationalism. This identification of sports as a product of the modern, technological turn is not solely Dyreson's, but his use of Heidegger's concept of technology is unique. In the middle of the twentieth century, says Dyreson (2003), the American philosopher Lewis Mumford argued that the growth of sports was a reaction against modernity, a turn to a Romantic diversion keeping the masses stupefied with trivial obsessions about winning and losing. This view of sports as a reaction or rejection of modernity, though a popular one at the time, is mistaken, according to Dyreson (2003). He shows that in fact sports are Heideggerian technologies. They are used as devices to propagate the very ideology of modernity: instrumentality and rationality. In the twentieth century, modern sports were the first markets of national identity in new nation-states embracing modernity. These new nation-states joined the international governing bodies of sport and embraced this globalizing trend of modernity, but sports competitions were also technologies of nationalism, allowing nation-states to create imagined community and symbolic boundaries of belonging and exclusion. Medals and World Cups became the new ways in which nation-states proved their national worth.

QUESTIONS TO CONSIDER

What other parts of culture might be modernizing technologies in Heidegger's sense of the word? What was the role of the media in disseminating modern concepts of nationalism?

REFERENCE AND FURTHER READING

Dyreson, M. (2003) 'Globalizing the Nation-Making Process: Modern Sport in World History', *The International Journal of the History of Sport*, 20, pp. 91–106.

THE RISE OF THE MODERN OLYMPICS

As the nineteenth century drew to a close in the West, the masses and foreigners became associated more with ideas of impurity and degeneracy. Concerns about the effects of unchecked capitalism and the unchecked growth of humanity (Gould, 1997) combined with biological arguments around design and evolution. Although Darwin was cautious about applying the theory of evolution to modern society, this caution was dropped by his successors. Galton and others read *On the Origin of Species* as a moral tale about the declining birth rates of the middle classes and the growth of the working class. Social Darwinism became a movement that promoted the survival of decent middle-class society through eugenics: the breeding of good middle-class 'blood' or, alternatively, the restriction of breeding of the working class, foreigners and other undesirables (Kohn, 1995).

At the same time, the English middle classes were undergoing a cultural revival associated with healthy living and moral rectitude. Movements such as Arnold's 'Muscular Christianity' made an explicit link between the moral fibre of the ruling classes and physical activity, and sport became a way of making men fit to run the Empire and run the capitalist system (Mangan and Ritchie, 2005). The modern sports of the modern Olympics were developed and codified by the ruling classes of Western Europe, and the exclusionary nature of amateurism – enshrined until the end of the twentieth century in the Olympic movement and many middle-class sports such as rowing, cricket and rugby union – was testament to the hegemony of the ruling classes (Dunning and Sheard, 2005).

The invention of modern sports was fundamental to the resurrection of the Olympic Games as an elite, amateur activity. This resurrection was linked explicitly to the survival of the hegemonic, instrumental whiteness of the Western elites. In 1908, reflecting on the increasing importance of the modern Olympic Games in the wider geo-political landscape, their founder Baron Pierre de Coubertin expressed his hope that the Games were having 'an influence, which shall make the means of bringing to perfection the strong and hopeful youth of our white race' (de Coubertin, cited in Carrington, 2004, p. 81).

For de Coubertin, the modern Olympics were beyond nationalism, but not beyond the symbolic boundaries of early twentieth-century notions of race. The Games, as King (2007) has argued, were designed and promoted by an elite section of white European society at the end of the nineteenth century as a means of preserving and promoting elitist ideas of belonging and exclusion. The rhetoric of the open playing field symbolized by the Olympic rings masked the reality of sport's role as the maker (and marker) of racial difference (Mangan, 1981, 1986; Mangan and Ritchie, 2005): sport made white men fit to serve the engines of commerce and empires. The ideology and ethics of the International Olympic Committee (IOC) remained strongly shaped by its founding father's beliefs. The IOC was dominated in the first half of the twentieth century by Europeans, Westerners, white men trained in the national governing bodies of sport of their own countries. These white men tried to keep the Olympics free from 'politics', which for them was a way of preserving the power of the Western hegemony over the rising economies and societies of the rest of the world. They defended amateurism and rules of governance designed in the nineteenth century by European sports governing bodies, and supported the use of sport to protect the interests of the ruling classes. At the 1936 Berlin Olympics, the IOC's white men found a common purpose with the Nazis, adopting the torch race staged by the Germans for future events and praising the Nazis for their determination to preserve 'European' civilization (Keys, 2004). The political struggle in the Olympics movement started after the Second World War, when countries freed from imperial control pushed for greater democracy in the IOC, and for sanctions and boycotts against openly racist regimes such as that of South Africa. But although the struggles brought changes, and the IOC embraced professionalism, the Olympics still remained a Trojan horse for white, Western values and hegemonic power.

NATIONAL MYTHS, ELITISM AND MODERN SPORTS

In parts of the West where there was nationalist struggle, sports became a way of identifying with either the local elite or the oppressed cultural group: in Ireland, the Gaelic Athletic Association allowed Irish nationalists to resist British imperialism through supporting hurling and the Irish version of football (Fulton and Bairner, 2007). In parts of the West where institutional racism was a part of everyday life, such as the United States or Australia, sports were racially segregated through official sanction, and the white-only governing bodies were favoured when it came to money and ownership of sports resources (pitches, fields, equipment). In the United States, so-called 'negro leagues' and 'colored clubs' were run in baseball from the end of the nineteenth century to the second half of the last century: these were partly acts of resistance and autonomy, but also acts of control and subservience – a way to keep mainstream baseball all-American white (Lomax, 1998). In Australia, the dominant football codes and many other sports operated unwritten colour codes to bar the involvement of Aboriginal players (Tatz, 2009). In India, the British sport of cricket (which had managed in its birthplace to allow professionalism for the lower classes while allowing the white, British elite classes to retain power over the game through its arcane organizations) was the site of racial tension and white privilege – it was seen as the sport played by the colonialists and their collaborators in the Indian elite, though it soon acquired a following among the wider population. A similar state of racial segregation operated in cricket in the West Indies and Australia, where formal and informal practices of racism ensured the whiteness of elite clubs and governing bodies well into the twentieth century.

England saw its nationalism and elite hegemony perpetuated through the sports central to physical education in its public schools: cricket and rugby union. In rugby, the debate over the legitimacy over professionalism was a metaphor for the class struggle. The working-class dominated rugby clubs of Yorkshire and Lancashire were by the early 1890s isolated from political power within the Rugby Football Union (Collins, 1999). They split away in 1895 to form the Northern Football Union, which would allow payments to players. This was the precursor of what is now known as rugby league; over the course of a few years the Northern Union changed the rules of its rugby to create a different sport altogether. With the working-class provincial clubs removed from itself, the English Rugby Football Union became even more dominated by the public schools and the ruling elites. The abuses of the amateur rule at its top clubs were ignored, and England and the British Lions became sources of a genteel, elite and smug nationalism when the British Empire collapsed. Rugby league, on the other hand, was marginalized in the press and in government, struggling to get recognition and an equitable stream of income and publicity. Rugby league was viewed with hatred and suspicion: rugby union players who tried a game of rugby league were banned for life from ever going into a rugby union clubhouse, let alone ever playing rugby union again (Collins, 2009). This inequity and injustice continued for as long as rugby union pretended to be amateur. Up until the 1990s, the British Armed Forces refused to support rugby league, and discrimination against rugby league players and teams occurred in dozens of educational and sporting facilities across England (Collins, 2006). Despite disbanding its rules on amateurism, rugby union in England and across the world still uses its association with political elites to keep its rival rugby code from developing: as I wrote this in June 2013, the Moroccan Rugby Union intervened with the Moroccan government to stop an international match between Morocco and Great Britain, and the government was arguing the local rugby league players and teams should only play officially sanctioned rugby (that is, rugby union).

South Africa provided the most egregiously overt form of racial segregation and instrumental whiteness through the institution of the Apartheid regime. The white South African elite were strongly influenced by racist ideologies and notions of white biological superiority that were part of the popular discourse of the twentieth century. This belief in the purity and superiority of the white race(s) was central to the Nazi ideology of Germany, which led to the horrors of the Holocaust. Despite the lack of scientific evidence for white racial superiority and purity, and despite the dire consequences of following that logic in Germany, such ideology continued to be dominant in the West after the Second World War. As Western empires retracted, white people clung to these beliefs, especially so in South Africa. Putting into action across the entire country policies and practices that operated locally in many towns and districts, the system of Apartheid attempted to permanently protect the interests of the white ruling classes against the non-white majority. This was racial segregation as seen in other countries such as the United States, but on a much larger scale, and with national legislative power. White and non-white were given separate spaces, buildings, services, goods and activities – with the white population having the best share of the resources and the power, and the non-white only allowed access to the worst part. Sports played a central role in maintaining Apartheid and the racist power relationships: white South African national teams in cricket and rugby union were celebrated abroad, touring teams visiting South Africa observed and supported racial segregation (and often failed to bring non-white players), and even when formal boycotts were established, white European, white Australians and white New Zealanders continued to find ways to visit the country and play sport with the white South Africans (Booth, 2003).

Rowing, gender and the history of rowing

Schweinbenz (2010) shows that in Europe, women had been involved in the pastime of rowing – and competitions of rowing prowess – for hundreds of years. But as rowing was transformed into a modern sport in the nineteenth century, it became associated in the West with social elites and hegemonic masculinity. Women were discouraged from taking part in rowing as it was considered too manly, too tough for their supposedly frail bodies (Schweinbenz, 2010). Rowing was the sport of Cambridge and Oxford, of

English public schools such as Eton, and the Ivy League colleges in the United States. By the twentieth century the hold of the European elites on organized rowing competitions and clubs was challenged by the growth of working-class involvement in rowing, and the growth of rowing among women. The ruling classes who controlled the governing bodies of rowing in Europe responded to the working-class threat by establishing their status as professionals in carefully controlled (and limited) positions. Women, however, remained formally 'beyond the pale' of the governing bodies of rowing – up to the middle of the last century, they were excluded and forced to find their own ways to get boats and space on waterways to train and race. Schweinbenz (2010) argues that histories of rowing have concentrated on elite men and ignored the fact that women did row, though she shows that these rowers were marginalized.

QUESTIONS TO CONSIDER

How was rowing transformed into a modern sport? What is the status of rowing today?

REFERENCE AND FURTHER READING

Schweinbenz, A.N. (2010) 'Against Hegemonic Currents: Women's Rowing into the First Half of the Twentieth Century', *Sport in History*, 30, pp. 309–26.

Basketball was created in the United States in 1891 and heavily promoted to schools and colleges by various Christian associations (including the YMCA, in which the founder of the game had first come up with the rules) as a healthy and safe alternative to rougher sports such as football. The sport became something associated with white, all-American, small-town life, a part of the rites of passage of American boys becoming men. Girls danced on the side, the best boys played, and the boys who were not strong enough to play for their school were side-lined in the pecking order of school corridor politics. American colleges had their own basketball teams and they offered a route for successful white boys to get college degrees while getting the fame and glory of Varsity. Elsewhere in the world, basketball was adopted as an amateur, white man's sport in European countries and former European colonies such as Argentina. Professional basketball leagues appeared in the United States and soon white basketballers were making money as sports stars – but the professional leagues offered the chance for poor men from different ethnic groups to play. The increase in the number of African American professional basketballers led to coaches, managers and physical education teachers believing in false racial science and seeking out more African Americans, preferring them over their white rivals because they thought (incorrectly) black people were biologically fit to be better than white people at the sport (Spracklen, 2008). White folk then started to think basketball was dominated by black people, and started to encourage their children to do other sports (Hall, 2001). African Americans saw a chance for their own children and encouraged them to play basketball. The effect was a rapid change in the perceived and actual racial formation of basketball at elite level – and a drop-off in participation by white people. The National Basketball Association (NBA) does offer a route to success and fortune for a small number of African-American men, but the price is the exoticization, brutalization and appropriation of their blackness by the white men who dominate the sports industry, as well as the stereotyping of black masculinity in the white gaze of basketball fans and the shattered dreams of the large proportion of rejected athletes (Hall, 2001).

These tensions over community and identity are linked to romanticized, nostalgic elite imaginary and imagined spaces. Historically, being a sports fan typically involved white people of different classes paying money to support their local sports club. As modern sports were designed as spectacles, people got into the habit of supporting local teams or athletes, or gathering at elite events to show their good taste. For the white working classes of the West, this involved identifying with a club taking part in an elite male team sport, whether it was professional or amateur. The most popular sport was soccer, but other codes of football dominated in certain countries and regions, and not all these codes were overtly professional for much of their history. Other sports such as (ice) hockey, cricket, handball and baseball acted as ways for white, working-class communities to create belonging through local pride, local identity and the exclusion of the Other. For the white bourgeois and elite classes, this popular sports fandom was something they could access and engage in (and many sports clubs had stadia in which poor and rich were allocated separate spaces to watch the sports action). But they also had more exclusionary routes to sports fandom – through following and supporting elite sports such as tennis and golf, and through acquiring the cultural capital to understand and follow such sports. These elite sports allowed elite white people to prove their moral worth – or, rather, prove their insatiable snobbery – by rising above the prejudices of the football crowd to become someone attracted to the aesthetics of individual play. These purposes for sports fandom remain today important reasons for white people's continued interest in sports as spectators. White working-class men (and women) define their right to some local area through their allegiance to a particular club or local sport; in turn, bourgeois white people seek to demonstrate their elite status by gaining white cultural capital from bourgeois sports fandom (still expressed through sports such as tennis and golf); and the ruling white elites use elite white, Western sports such as polo to mark out their elite and exclusionary spaces.

As well as local chauvinism and snobbishness, modern sports allowed individuals and other groups to express crude notions of nationalism through this form of leisure and physical culture. The urge to compete and be the best in any sport led quite quickly in the history of modern sport to the creation of national teams and international competitions with athletes representing their countries. This sports nationalism was a product of the nationalism of the late nineteenth century, when European nation-states were using culture and myth to bind their citizens into a common, patriotic cause against the other European nation-states. This was the era of empire building, of popular belief in the supremacy of white, Western European nations – so it is no surprise that the most energetic nationalizers in sport came from this area, or were in former colonies of Europe such as Australia, New Zealand, Argentina and South Africa. For sports fans, supporting the nation took on huge racist, nationalist significance – it was a means of demonstrating the superiority of the nation against its rivals; it was also a means of identifying with the nation as one's homeland, the land which belonged to the collective of white sports fans cheering on the national team (Bishop and Jaworski, 2003). Team sports such as soccer were the most obvious places where this exclusive nationalism was constructed, as they were popular across all (or most) of the classes of modern nation-states. In the twentieth century, international soccer fixtures offered their white, working-class, mainly male fans a chance to escape the uncertainties of their lives and find solace in community and communal identity – if the national side beat the rival side it was an expression of the rightness of the nation and the masculinity of its footballers; if the national side lost it was a disaster brought on the country by players who were not passionate enough when wearing the nation's colours.

As soccer spread through the world, it served as a site for nationalism in new, postcolonial nations and other countries where modernity brought globalization (Rowe, 2003). In the white nations of Europe and the white European diaspora, nationalism, racism and national teams in sports became sites of tension between the old white hegemony and the new multiculturalism of the late twentieth century. Supporting the national side at soccer or cricket or rugby was judged to be a marker of citizenship and belonging by right-wing politicians, even though the sports and the sports grounds remained places for white prejudice and racial discrimination to take place: in the United Kingdom, for example, former Conservative MP Norman

Tebbitt criticized non-white people in the country for supporting other countries such as Pakistan (the countries from which they had come, or from which their immediate ancestors had come) at cricket Test matches. While today there has been much progress in some countries at using national sports teams to promote a diverse, multicultural nationalism (see Bairner, 2001), the suspicion remains that non-white people are not welcome in their own country if they choose not to support that country's sports teams – and in some European countries the fans of national sides in team sports remain exclusively white, and the fan culture remains racist and exclusively nationalist (Sack and Suster, 2000). This white grip on sports fandom can also be seen in countries where white people have lost political power: the South African Springboks remain a national team cheered more by the white people of the nation than their black counterparts, a team where white Afrikaners can pretend for eight minutes that they still control the country (Nauright, 1996).

In the United States, such virulent, racist nationalism has not been so obvious in the history of fandom in its sports scene. This is probably because the nation's biggest spectator sports are ones that do not have well-established international competitions (even if baseball calls its finals the World Series). However, whiteness and parochialism both play key roles in sports fandom in the United States, both in the past and in this century. American fans follow their chosen clubs as a means of demonstrating their Americanness, their connection with the nation-state. American nationalism assumes that the United States of America is a chosen nation, blessed with the favour of God and fighting the good fight against the forces of evil. This creates an inward-looking, parochial nationalism associated with white myths: the importance of baseball and supporting the local teams, the rites of passage of sports in schools and colleges, and the confidence in American power that does not need success in an international sports area to support it. Sports become sites where white Americans fearing their future as a residual, marginalized culture can dream of all-American, white towns, and suburbs with white picket-fences and whitewashed walls mark out white America (Bairner, 2001). Sports fans in the United States can get satisfaction from seeing African Americans bought and sold like commodities in the brutal world of professional team sports: individual athletes are reduced to their physicality and sports are sites where rich white Americans can still exert their political and social hegemony, through sponsorship, ownership, management and merchandizing. And white sports fans cheer on racial myths made flesh to satisfy the white gaze of the spectators.

CONCLUSION

If one reads the histories of modern sports produced by the governing bodies of sports, it becomes apparent that those histories are partial. The contemporary ideology of sport as individual freedom and pure competition is tainted by the ways in which sports and sports histories have been used since the nineteenth century to foster myths of elitism and the exclusion of others. This chapter has shown that physical culture – modern sports, physical activity and physical education – has always been something which is the product of a tension between those individuals who are able to express their passion for physical activity and those who would use such culture as a means to control others. In instance after instance, people wanting to participate in sports have been denied access to those sports, and sports have been used to promote the interests of the elite (or a wider middle class, or men, or white people, or Westerners). Sports and physical culture have been used to train the wider masses into conformity and obedience, while excluding them from real power. The origins of modern sport and wider physical culture, then, along with the official histories of the Olympics and other modern sports, are parts of the apparatus of instrumentality that continues to hold power. We can see in the next chapter that this purpose of modern sport makes identifying the meaning of sport, the task of philosophy of sport, much more difficult.

EXERCISES

1 In what ways did subaltern groups challenge the Western dominance of modern sports in the twentieth century?
2 How were the modern Olympics connected in myth and in reality to the ancient Olympics?
3 In the last century, how did physical education and physical culture more generally limit the political and social freedoms of women?

Chapter 3

Sport, Freedom, Fairness

SUMMARY OF TOPICS

- ▪ *Definitions: freedom, fairness and sport*
- ▪ *Sports as freely chosen leisure*
- ▪ *Sports as fair competitions*
- ▪ *The tensions in the different purposes of modern sports*

Consider the modern sport of cycling. I was never a cyclist, but I did play on my bike as a child. I had to learn how to ride a bike in the first place, which at the time proved very hard. This was probably because I wasn't learning in an official setting: I learned to ride my bike by following the angry shouts and pointing fingers of my older brother and his friends. When I could ride a bike I was fascinated by the freedom it seemed to give me. I could escape down the canal tow-path to woods and fields up the valley from my house, or I could cycle up to the shops to buy ice lollies. But I never took to cycling as a sport or anything beyond a non-serious leisure pastime. My father, however, had been a proper social cyclist. He had grown up in the 1950s in England, when cycling was an important part of northern English working-class culture (Riordan and Kruger, 2003). He had never been a serious competitive cyclist, though he had done some competitions in his teenage years. His real love of cycling as a sport came from the 'rides out' to the Yorkshire Dales from Leeds. On summer evenings and all-year round on Sundays, thousands of men and women would congregate on racing bikes on the edge of cities such as Leeds, Bradford, Wakefield, Huddersfield and Sheffield – then they would cycle out in enormous pelotons to tackle the climbs of the rural hill country. My father did this for most of his teenage years, and even got on his bike and cycled to France and back. Though he had given up cycling by the time I was learning how to ride my bike, he still followed the professional *sport of cycling. In particular, like many English cycling fans, he was (and still is!) obsessed with* Le Tour de France. *What he liked about cycling was its character-building nature, the brutality of the climbs and the distances that could wipe anyone out on a bad day, the fact that cyclists co-operated with each other in the pack and looked after each other. He knew about Tommy Simpson, the English cyclist who died in the Tour on the way up Mont Ventoux after taking amphetamines, but he still believed, when I was growing up, that professional cycling was one of the few sports where the spirit of fair-play – the social rules that bound the peloton together – ensured the sport's integrity. He believed cycling was a great leveller: that it provided a level playing field in which pure talent was tested, and in which people learned to be good citizens.*

In the last chapter I argued that modern sport was constructed in the past with a specific moral and political purpose. This chapter will use the idea about sport's fairness – the 'level playing field' – to explore the meaning of sports in modern physical culture. We will explore the separate (but related) academic arguments about whether sport is based on a philosophy of fair play, and whether sport gives its participants valuable sociological and cultural freedoms. I will argue that sports can be useful in supporting individuals in their desire and need to make free choices about their bodies in modernity – but that the meaning and purpose of sports is morally ambiguous.

DEFINITIONS: FREEDOM, FAIRNESS AND SPORT

This chapter is an attempt to explore and understand the intersections between sport, society and what is called the ethics of sport: the set of values that are claimed to be tied up in the practice of sport. In other words, we are interested in the meaning of the practice of sport as a physical activity (is it some kind of moral or spiritual good, does it give its participants good examples to follow?) and the purpose of sport as part of a wider physical culture (is there a framework within sport such as 'fair play' that might be extended into society to solve some of the problems of wider society?). This is a question about the philosophy of sport that has implications for the sociology of sport and physical culture. To help us think about the ethics of sport we need to pause and think about the wider problems of freedom and fairness. What follows in the next few paragraphs is some quite complicated philosophy defined and discussed in a very simple manner. I have tried to make the issues as clear as possible so that you can understand them even if you are completely new to the ideas. If you have already studied philosophy or ethics, it should all look familiar – and I hope you feel able to raise critiques of your own against my arguments.

The problems of freedom and fairness are two of the big ethical problems of philosophy. The problem of freedom is sometimes called the problem of free will, though it extends beyond that into the wider social realm. In some traditional Christian theologies it is argued that humans have free will, the freedom to act for good or bad under their own agency (the power or initiative within us, what Christians identify with the soul). It is important for Christian theologians to argue that God gave humans free will as this then accounts for the mistakes people make and the journeys they make through life: all of us become responsible for our own salvation (Williams, 2011). In modernity, in the legal codes developed in the West, the idea of free will has been transferred into the secular space of law. The idea of the soul vanished with the rise of science and the expansion of psychological accounts of the mind: the mind became something that was theoretically reducible to the physical interaction of neurons in the brain (Kane, 2011). Classical economic theory constructed the notion of the rational actor, the individual free to buy and sell using their reason to guide them – this free agent is at the heart of modern democratic politics. Modern secular laws assume that individuals have agency, the power to make their own decisions, good or bad, about their actions. It is given that we are responsible for our own illegal actions, and where we are not responsible for our actions we are often not punished at all. In contemporary popular culture and society, we take for granted that we as individual agents are in control of our own destinies. The American dream is strongly tied up with the idea of individual liberty and choice. If I say I prefer the sport of rugby league over the sport of rugby union, we all understand that I am saying I have used my free will, my agency, my freedom of choice (my tastes and preferences), to select one sport over another. But how much of that choice is mine to make? Contemporary scientific research seems to indicate that there is no free will at all, that the choices we make are pre-ordained by the complex natures of our brains, that we are nothing but brains (Kane, 2011). Through a sociological lens, we might argue that our choices are constrained by the structures of the social world – so my choice of rugby league over rugby union can be explained by the complex class-bound nature of England.

The problem of freedom is connected through the notion of agency to the problem of fairness. If we do act as free agents, then, it is argued, we need to establish a society in which each one of us might be able to act without *unfair* constraints (Guibernau, 2013). That is, if we are all acting on our free will then we must make sure the rules of how we behave ensure the greatest good for as many of us as possible. When we think about fairness we think about how societies are structured, how economic goods are distributed among members of that society, and how power is distributed between people in that society. We want to live in a society where we are treated fairly, where people who do good are rewarded, where those who do bad are punished, and where no one has an unfair advantage because of the colour of their skin or their family name. We seem to share with other humans the wish to be free from abuse and harm, the wish for an equal share of the resources at stake. No one today in the West would defend slavery, and no one would defend murder. This seems to be a universal desire, though whenever we look at the specifics of any given culture we find different specific notions of the norms, values and rules. Think about slavery and murder again. In the case of slavery, for a long time many people in the world argued very strongly that slavery was a natural condition for some groups of humans, and even that slavery improved the lives of those enslaved because they were given the chance to interact with 'superior' civilizations (the Greek, Roman, Persian, European and Ottoman cultures). In the case of murder, there is a long history of judicial execution and the slaughter of soldiers and civilians in wars – if murder is wrong, why is it right sometimes?

Some philosophers have argued that there is no such thing as code of ethics, a rule-book, which says what is right or wrong – there is no moral realism, only a moral relativism that makes morals and ethics solely dependent on social and cultural contexts (Harman, 1975; Wong, 2006). This relativist argument is associated with postmodernism, the cultural turn that argues not only is there no way of knowing what the truth is, there are no truths – about the world, about ethics – to be discovered: all we have is a series of texts and interpretations and uses of texts. There is indeed persuasive evidence that different cultures (through history and around the world) have very different notions of right and wrong. Is there a way of establishing the fairness of an activity or relationship outside of the immediate context of the things we are interested in? Moral realist philosophers claim that we can know right and wrong, good and bad: ethical sentences express propositions; that some such propositions are true; and those propositions are made true by objective features of the world, independent of human opinion.

Thus, moral realism presupposes some verifiable, knowable test of right and wrong, expressed in our sense of ethics (Brink, 1989). For Kant (1996), humans have an innate or *a priori* psychological imperative to be aware of the differences: our critical faculty of morality. Kant's work on ethics and morality has been incredibly influential, as it appeals to our 'common-sense' of moral realism, but his solution to the problem of fairness is not the only one to come to us from mainstream philosophy. Rousseau (2008) argued that the primitive state of humanity is completely without morality, but morals are an expression of the sovereign will of the people in society. That will is part of the social contract we make when we make societies. In founding what has become known as utilitarianism, Bentham (2007) suggested the good is whatever brings the greatest happiness to the greatest number of people. This was an attempt to apply a strict set of rules for understanding and exploring the consequences of our actions; as opposed to moral realism, which is based on an *a priori* deontology (that is, a sense of virtue, or duty, or command).

One other possible answer is a theological one: people who believe that their religious rules are binding in society can follow those rules to establish the fairness of society and everything in it. There is no doubt that the modern world owes much of its moral framework to the great world religions. However, these are very different religions with different notions of what is good or bad, right or wrong; also, there are different interpretations of what is a sacred moral imperative within each of those religions. So we are back to moral relativism if we try to use religion as a way of finding a universal ethics.

John Stuart Mill (1998) expanded utilitarianism in an attempt to understand its connection to liberty and free will. Mill was influenced by Rousseau's idea of the social contract, the idea that individuals choose to sign up to rules about how to interact and behave in any community. Mill argued that we need to distinguish between morality and ethics in public and in private. In public, we have to behave in a way that promotes public virtue: where we interact with others there is a responsibility in the way we behave. In private, however, away from the public sphere, we can do whatever we like, providing we hurt no other (or limit no other's freedoms). Mill might be right about private freedoms, but how do we know what is the morally correct way to behave in public? Rawls' (1971) famous model of social justice starts with the question: if we did not know anything about our family backgrounds before our births (their wealth, their power, their place in the world), yet we were able to do a thought experiment about structuring society, what kind of rules would we make for our future selves? Obviously we would want a society in which our freedom to think and freedom to act was protected – we would try to create a society where we could prosper and have liberty. But Rawls says we would also want to build in safeguards about equality and fairness, as we would not know whether we were from a rich, powerful elite or (as is more likely) from a poorer, marginalized background. Fairness, then, is an essential prerequisite for the rules we need to create for our just society, redistributing wealth and power so that everybody has liberty, not just the ruling elite.

We can see from this that modern sports are obviously activities that might have some moral value. They are (usually) voluntary, chosen freely by their participants; and they are also rule-bound in a way that strives to ensure some parity of competition (we do not usually see grossly unequal and unfair competitions, such as a ninety-year-old amateur having to run a marathon against a professional motorbike racer on the fastest motorbike known to modern science). In the next section, I will explore the meaning and purpose of modern sports in more detail.

Freely chosen: youth sports?

In the pursuit of winning medals and trophies, professional sport has become an intensive training and development regime for young athletes, and abuses of young people occur (Burke, 2001). In every professional sport, talent scouts and coaches find younger and younger athletes who look like they might be winners of the future. Some countries have been strongly criticized for the brutal nature of their recruitment and development of young athletes: in the 1970s, East German sports governing bodies routinely used performance-enhancing drugs on young athletes; and in this century, China was the subject of a number of scare stories about its training regimes for young athletes. It is convenient for countries in the West to distance themselves from the authoritarian ways in which young athletes have been used and abused in the pursuit of gold. It is clear that regimes such as the one that existed in East Germany are inhumane, unethical and immoral: this is the routinization of abuse by adults of children, with the children (and their parents) having little say in what happens. However, it is not quite clear that there is a categorical difference between the regimes in East German sports and contemporary elite sports in the West. Adult coaches instruct young children in situations where it is not at all clear that the children have the ability or the power to give consent – and parents all too often let sports do what they want to their children *so* long as there is a chance for some reflected glory for the parents.

QUESTIONS TO CONSIDER

How can children give consent? What are the specific problems surrounding the sport of gymnastics?

REFERENCE AND FURTHER READING

Burke, M. (2001) 'Obeying Until It Hurts: Coach–Athlete Relationships', *Journal of the Philosophy of Sport*, 28, pp. 227–40.

THE MEANING AND PURPOSE OF MODERN SPORTS

Sports have some moral value based on the idea of fairness, and the notion that people freely choose the activity. That is an ideal moral value, of course, evidently broken when professional athletes cheat. But how does that ideal measure up to the meaning and purpose of modern sports? Before we consider the meaning and purpose of modern sports, it is necessary to step back and look at the meaning and purpose of leisure – as modern sport is just a sub-set of the broader category of leisure. Of course if you have read my book *Leisure, Sports and Society* (Spracklen, 2013a) you will have already come across my rough definition of what leisure is. But I am going to give it again here, so we can consider what role sports play, and what an ethics of sport might begin to look like. In Spracklen (2013a, p. 13) I argued that:

> Leisure is part of our human nature, part of humanity's deep history…Leisure, then, is something fundamental to wellbeing for individuals and for the social group in which individual humans live. It is something to do with freedom of inquiry and choice, something to do with the social world, something to do with the trivial and fun, and something to do with relaxing from the everyday chores.

Leisure activities are those we take part in through choice, in contrast to the chores of work. Leisure spaces are those spaces where we take part in leisure activities. Leisure time is the time we spend doing things that we do not have to do to pay bills or run our homes and families. Most people understand this common-sense definition of leisure. There are, of course, lots of problems with this definition of leisure, which I outline in my other textbook (Spracklen, 2013a). For some people, leisure time is limited and constrained: who gets to 'do' leisure is problematic. Leisure activities and spaces are often products of the systems in which we live, such as governments and capitalism, and as such they are constructed as instrumental leisure. Leisure activities are also often transformed into activities that look a lot like work. But the crucial definition of leisure as something that is 'not work' is important to hold, as it is this one that allows us to see that some kinds of leisure – including sports – potentially have a communicative value to those who participate.

Sports and physical culture as leisure: sport and leisure as work?

Sports and physical culture might be seen as leisure pastimes when they are freely engaged in. As you are reading this book you will obviously play one or more sports, or sports-like physical activities. The sports you choose to take part in will have different meanings and purposes for you. You will probably play some sports and some physical activities because they help you relax, or they are a good way to socialize with your friends. These are the types of sports that are most communicatively leisure-like in their meaning and purpose. However, some of the sports you do will not be simple communicative acts. Some of the sports you take part in will have serious meaning for you. You might very well undertake long and hard training sessions for the sport you take most seriously: working in the gym and doing drills just so you can play the sport your best. This sport is a form of serious leisure. It has become for you almost a form of work in the amount of time and effort you invest in it (it may well have become work for you, and you might get paid as a professional for playing the sport). Robert Stebbins' (2009) theory of serious leisure is very useful at explaining the ways in which our leisure and sports pastime can easily be transformed through dedication and motivation into work-like activities. For people sufficiently intrinsically motivated, serious leisure is its own reward, but there is a problem: to be serious about leisure and sports is hard work, and many people are actually dissuaded from playing sports when they become too serious.

QUESTIONS TO CONSIDER

Why is intrinsic motivation better? How does the idea of serious leisure help us understand the ethics of sport?

REFERENCE AND FURTHER READING

Stebbins, R. (2009) *Leisure and Consumption*, Basingstoke, Palgrave Macmillan.

On one level, then, sports and physical activity more generally are forms of leisure that is freely chosen and fairly constructed. Sports become communicative leisure forms, where free agents create their own rules (their own codes of ethics, but also their own sense of fair play that go beyond the actual texts written down). It is difficult to disagree with this simple definition of the ethics of sport. This is the ethical conception of sports that was claimed by the founders of modern sports such as de Coubertin. The founders of modern sports all believed in the civilizing mission of their activities and the usages of sports in promoting healthy bodies and minds. This was, as Elias (1978, 1982) shows, a way of making the morals of the ruling classes permeate through the rest of society. Modern sports were constructed by men who had been educated in the Classical Greek culture that celebrated athleticism alongside modesty, piety and reason (Mangan, 1981). Sport was also a way of instilling Christian notions of obedience and decency in its participants. Rules of fair play were central to this moral agenda, even if they were generally broken more than they were maintained, as many historians show (Collins, 2013a; Vamplew, 2004). It was not enough to merely play: nineteenth-century athletes had to demonstrate they had inculcated a tacit moral code of virtue, honour, integrity and equanimity. This was partly to show they had the same educational and cultural background as other athletes (who had been shaped to behave in this way by their elite upbringing), and partly to teach to others the right way to be a Muscular Christian. For these ethical agents, it was taken as read that sports were a moral good. They proved this to themselves through the construction of rules: sports were fair competitions that allowed athletes to compete in a pure, natural state of being; they were activities where taking part was privileged over winning, where behaving wrongly in the course of the competition (not adhering to the tacit moral code) was the worst social error. This ontological definition of sports continued to hold sway throughout the last century, as we have seen in Chapter 1, and continues to be influential today: people who take part in sports and physical activity still claim there is something about it that is morally good, in terms of fairness and in terms of its freely-enacted nature.

It is not just contemporary participants in sports who believe this – many philosophers of sport believe it, too (Lumpkin, Stoll and Beller, 1999). There is an entire journal (*Sport, Ethics and Philosophy*) where philosophers can argue for and against the moral status of sports and physical culture. There are of course many strong critics of modern sports as well – but a large proportion of the critics of modern sport will argue for a pristine source of the activity that has been corrupted: the argument against contemporary sports, for example, is made by suggesting they are a 'fall' or corruption of some ideal sports activity (Lumpkin, Stoll and Beller, 1999; Morgan, 2005). Only a small number of philosophers take the view that modern sports have no ethical or moral value whatsoever, either in their nineteenth-century invention as amateur pastimes, or in their contemporary construction as professional industries (Young, 2012). What seems to be central to the argument of Morgan (2005) is that modern sport by its ontological definition is intrinsically something based on a fair contest: the concept of fair play is communicative in a Habermasian sense (Habermas, 1987), that is, discussed and debated away from any conception of instrumental rationality (such as the law of the land or even the rules of the sport). We might see this communicative nature of fair play in the way in which it is customary for British soccer players – professionals and amateurs, Premier League heroes and Sunday morning park veterans – to kick the ball out of play if a player from either side is down on the floor seriously injured. This is a custom that many players respect even though it is not a formal part of soccer's written rules.

The problem with the notion of fair play in the context of sport is it is discussed as a normative ideal, that is, an ideal that is identified as the best morality that sport ought to have, rather than the morality of what modern sports are actually like. Is it an actual intrinsic component of contemporary sport? The professionalization and commercialization of sport has changed the way athletes and teams compete against one another. We might think the gold medals of the Olympics are available to anyone who can try, and we might cherish the dream of one day winning trophies and medals of our own, but the way the sports industry has evolved means that for most of this sport is not a level playing field. Professional sports identify their potential future talent through ever-more instrumentalized scouting and coaching regimes – people who want to succeed in their chosen sport are rarely given the chance to do so, because they do not fit the latest biomechanical, physiological or psychological templates: the sports industry has too much money invested in it to give anybody a turn. The sports industry wants winners identified at an early age, discarding the rest of us. Who does succeed at an elite level? The athletes who win are in rich countries with the resources and the scientific expertise to spend on sports (or have access to that resource, for example, through sports scholarships at colleges), or the winners are those professional sports teams who are backed by multi-billionaires. British soccer again provides a harsh example that shows the essential inequality and unfairness of contemporary professional sport (Roberts, 2004). The amount of money the top Premier League soccer clubs have to spend means year on year they win everything between them: that does not make them the best at soccer; it only proves that money wins. These are not fair competitions, and seem categorically different to the athletic tests of character, skill and strength which have been reified and mythologized in popular sporting imaginations.

Another approach might be to argue that sport's moral nature is associated with its rules (Loland, 2002). Rule-following in sports seems to be associated with the kind of social contract ethics Rousseau and Rawls talk about: the rules of sport are voluntarily agreed upon; there is no compulsion to play sport; but if you do play a particular sport, you abide by its rules (though you can take action to change those rules through membership of that sport's community). This is what might be called a common-sense argument for the importance of rules. Rule-following does not give the rules the importance of a divine command. There is no divinity measuring whether we get into heaven or hell depending on how closely we have obeyed the rules of badminton when playing the sport informally (that is, not as part of a regulated tournament governed by the badminton authorities), but we are bound to obey the rules of the sport if we choose to play it in the social and cultural context of a badminton court. If we throw the shuttlecock at our opponent we are obviously breaking the rules of the game, and they are justified in telling us to stop this wrong behaviour; and if we refuse to stop they are in their rights to walk away or call in some other authority (the manager of the sports centre, perhaps) to instruct us to leave. If we cheat in some other way and they do not notice our foul play, it is still foul play. We are not going to be thrown out of the centre, and we might not be banned or sent to hell – but we do have to feel the shame of our own inner personality at our deceitful ways. If our opponent ever does find out we are constantly cheating they might never play badminton with us again: we face personal shame and social pariah status.

The problem with the concept of sports as rule-following, of course, is again the unwritten or tacit rules that govern how the rule-books are understood in various social and cultural practices (Atry, Hansson and Kihlbom, 2012). The game of 'hide and seek', for example, relies on the tacit agreement that the children hiding are not going to get on a bus to the airport and a plane to another country – but there is no formal rule to stop someone doing this, as the British comedy team *Monty Python's Flying Circus* showed in one of their 1970s sketches. Sometimes I might play badminton with a friend where we deliberately disrupt the rules by throwing things at each other to put each other off, and if we both agree what is acceptable in this rule-breaking (throwing a shuttlecock, throwing an empty water bottle) and what is unacceptable (throwing a chair or a steak-knife) then that is fair by our terms – but is it still the sport of badminton?

Ultimate Frisbee

The sport of Ultimate Frisbee has been around since 1967. The Frisbee is a plastic flying disc that can be thrown more or less accurately over long distances when spun and aimed correctly. The sport of Ultimate Frisbee is a team sport that uses the Frisbee as a way of scoring points – each team tries to move the Frisbee into the other team's end zone. There is a clear boundary to the area of play, and with the establishment of governing bodies in the 1970s and 1980s the rules have been codified and controlled. However, Ultimate Frisbee differs from other sports in having no referee officiating matches – foul play is monitored by the players themselves, who strive to be more honest than each other (Robbins, 2004). There is no doubt that Ultimate Frisbee had its roots in the informal games played by American students when the Frisbee was manufactured and marketed. The commitment to the 'spirit of the game' in Ultimate Frisbee owes itself to the anti-authoritarianism of the counter-culture of the American 1960s: there is a strong belief among proponents of the sport that players can monitor their own actions and operate ethically. As the sport has spread across the world, and become more competitive and professional at elite levels, the question is whether it can retain its claim to have ethical agents as players.

QUESTIONS TO CONSIDER

How has the sport's ethos changed over time? What other sports have similar rules?

REFERENCE AND FURTHER READING

Robbins, B. (2004) 'That's Cheap: The Rational Invocation of Norms, Practices, and an Ethos in Ultimate Frisbee', *Journal of Sport and Social Issues*, 28, pp. 314–37.

Finally, some people argue that there is something intrinsic to sports participation that makes it morally good. This question is related to the debates about what sports might teach us as a society – the debate about the ethics of fair play we have just explored. However, though the two debates are related, it is useful to think of them as posing different kinds of claims, so it becomes easier to critique both. The argument about sports and physical activity as intrinsic moral goods is one that many advocates of sport believe: focus on sport, train hard and dedicate yourself to the ethos of sport and you are, it is claimed, a better person. The sportsperson, it is argued, is more likely to live within moral codes and less likely to be anti-social or deviant. There is research that makes these claims: some of it is poorly evidenced nonsense from the margins of reputable academia, but there is much work in sports psychology, sports coaching and sports science that seems to back this up (see later on in this book, specifically the next two chapters, for the references for this paragraph). At first glance, this is something many of the cheerleaders of sport and physical activity take for granted: they say sport builds what is called character, and one achieves some spiritual benefit from imbibing the ethics and ethos of sport. This connects to the notion of physical culture – doing something physical, it is claimed, instils positive values and morals associated with physical cultural capital. Clearly, people who like playing sport enjoy sport (talking about it, watching it, playing it), and feel happy about playing sport in a sporting environment. This is a strong argument about the value of sport in a spiritual (moral, psychological) sense for those who are already signed up to doing sport. But it says nothing about those who might not wish to take part in sport, or those who are positively turned away from sport by sport's elitist ideologies. Sport's spiritual benefits are there for some, but not for others, and the effectiveness of the sporting intervention is not evidenced in the work of the advocates for sport. If sport was so good at solving so many of the modern world's problems, why is it the source of so many problems, and why do so many people feel sport is not for them?

Sport's spiritual, moral and psychological benefit is a product of people choosing to enjoy it, choosing it to define their identity – which is fine for those who do want to play sport and be physically active, but sport is not a solve-all medicine for everything that is wrong with the world. Advocates of sport want it to be seen as a tool for community development, a way of bringing warring nations together, a way of solving racism, health problems, anti-social behaviour, crime, problems in the classroom and global inequalities. Other parts of the leisure and entertainment industry do not feel so concerned to justify their status: Hollywood is proud to be making money through the production of 'blockbuster' movies, and no one pretends that is anything but a part of the instrumental leisure of today's globalized, Westernized society. But contemporary sport continues to be defended as being something that can give us meaning and purpose because of its origins in the moral crises of the nineteenth century and the evolution of the notion of physical culture as being something as valuable to society – ethically and aesthetically – as the arts. When someone chooses to play a sport because they get some personal value from the activity then that is good for them, because it is a communicative choice. But sport in today's world is not intrinsically moral, or extrinsically ethical, and does not necessarily give us anything.

CONCLUSION

Sports and wider physical culture can be useful in supporting individuals in their desire and need to make free choices about their bodies in modernity – but the meaning and purpose of sports is morally ambiguous. Some of the supposed moral, psychological and spiritual benefit argued for sports in the work of the cheerleaders for sport, for example, will come from feeling physiologically fitter and mentally sharper, but some of that benefit will come from being trained to be a hard worker, a follower of orders; and some will come from physical activity diverting us away from supposed unsavoury leisure activities. The moral good argument fails because it is not clear what divides the correct ethos of sport and the amoral or immoral practices and behaviours supposedly condemned: athletes and others taking part in sports and other physical activity cheat, drink, steal, attack others and destroy things just like anyone else; some of their bad behaviour is actually as a result of their sports activities. In other words, the arguments that sports and physical culture are inherently morally good are incoherent: there are a multitude of ethical and moral imperatives within sport and between sport and other parts of society. Furthermore, all kinds of non-physical activities could be viewed as just as morally good for individuals, such as reading a book or admiring a painting. Sports, then, do not have anything special about them. Some forms of physical activity are good for us because we freely choose them and we like them – because they are communicative. Modern sport, throughout its history, has been bad for us when it has been forced upon us as a means of solving something, or a way of becoming something that someone else, the person in power, wants us to be. In the next chapter, I will begin to balance the negative critique of sport so far with a discussion of some of the benefits that sports might bring.

EXERCISES

1 'The notion of fair play in sport is Western imperialism'. Discuss.
2 In what ways could sports competitions be altered to make them more moral and more ethical?
3 In what ways does gender constrain freedom of choice in sport?

Chapter 4

Character and Community Building

SUMMARY OF TOPICS

- *Definitions: doing sports, character and community*
- *Sport and character building, sport and personality*
- *Social psychology of motivation in sport, and self-determination*
- *Community, socialization and sports*

In the last chapter I concluded that the case for sport as a moral good is questionable. This chapter will begin with the popular argument that sports and physical activity are 'character building'. The chapter will explore the psychological benefits of doing sports through a discussion of key research on motivation and involvement. The chapter also discusses academic research that highlights the social benefit of sports participation through its use as a site of socialization and community. These two subjects – motivation and community – are connected in this chapter because community is directly related to social psychological notions of belonging, and notions of belonging are linked to ideas of character. The chapter will argue that sports and physical culture do give clear benefits to individuals and to society – though such benefits are tempered by the problems that follow the distribution and allocation of moral and social benefits.

DEFINITIONS: DOING SPORTS, CHARACTER AND COMMUNITY

As I discussed briefly in the Introduction to this book, there are three important physical categories in which people do sports, and in this chapter we need to consider all three of them as they relate to character building and community formation. They are related, people can move between them, and people can belong in more than one category – but they do have different consequences for what you might think about the subject of this chapter. First of all, we do sports by playing them, by being *active participants.* When someone asks you a question about whether you like sports, this category is usually the one you think of when you reply to that question – we think we like sports when we are participants in a particular sport, when we take part in it as a physical activity. The second physical category in which we might do sports is that of the *spectator.* Sports spectatorship is an important contemporary social and cultural phenomenon. As we have seen in earlier discussions in this book, watching (and talking about) professional sport is a modern invention. In Chapter 12 I will problematize the notion of sports fandom in more detail, but for now it is merely important to note that people increasingly seem to do sports more by treating it as part of the entertainment industry, as something that fills their lives with meaning, rather than actually taking part in any physical activity itself. The final way in which people do sports is through being an active *volunteer or paid worker* in a particular sports role: a coach, or an administrator, or an official. Just through identifying these three categories of attachment to sports, we can begin to see how they might work on the construction (and de-construction) of character and community. Following a professional football club might give you a sense of connection to a particular city or town. Playing a team sport might give you a sense of belonging but no sense of inner peace, while doing a sport such as long-distance running might give you a sense of inner peace but no sense of belonging. And putting in the long hours as a coach volunteering in a sport like swimming might make you feel part of a community of fellow swimmers and a morally correct person who gives time and expertise freely to the swimming world.

Character is something we associate with our inner, psychological states of being; though it is something that always has a social dimension. When we think about character in its popular psychological sense we are thinking about either some quality of personality that is essential to our individual nature, or some quality of personality that we somehow pick up in the course of our lives. Often people use the word 'character' as shorthand for good character, although references to people of bad character are still very common in everyday discourse. Traditional Christianity believed that someone's character was identical with that person's soul, the spirit that animated the physical body. All souls carried with them certain predispositions – so one could be born lucky, or sad, or clever, to name three examples – but human character was also a product of the choices made by individuals on Earth (Paxton, 1996). Traditional Buddhism believed in more fixed individual character associated with the previous lives one had lived through the succession of reincarnations (Ho, 1995). In Medieval and Renaissance Europe, most university-educated physicians and philosophers believed that each individual born had their own unique character, which was defined by a combination of the position of the stars at their birth (horoscopes) and the relative frequencies of four substances (humors) in the body: pneuma, blood, yellow bile and black bile (Kieckhefer, 2000). The dominance of one humor over another defined one's personality, and we still describe people as being sanguine (full of blood) or melancholic (full of black bile) in English today.

In the nineteenth century, as philosophers and scientists debated the relationship between mind and body, and body and soul, the science of psychology emerged as a way of using the scientific method to understand how selves are constructed. Early attempts at psychological theories relied on theorists undertaking thought experiments – attempting to categorize the mind and its states through introspection (Rylance, 2000). As the science evolved, two important schools of thought on character emerged. The first, Freudian psychodynamics, constructed an untestable framework of unconscious and subconscious drives (for a critique see Borch-Jacobsen and Shamdasani, 2012). For Freud and his acolytes, a person's true character is hidden under a number of evasions and deceits to which we are all victims: our primitive id is in conflict with our ego, and we need the help of the psychodynamic practitioner to find resolution (Freud, 1997, 2003, 2005). The second important school, behaviourism, restricted its theorizing to what could be observed and tested – behaviour – rather than the ontology of the mind. John Watson's ground-breaking work on behaviourism led to the rapid expansion of scientific, academic psychology (Watson, 1913, 1930). By ignoring first causes and concentrating on experimental phenomena, behaviourism allowed psychologists to understand and predict behaviours in test subjects (Mandler, 2007). Behaviourism helped explain the importance of early development as children, the influence of externality to the construction of individual identity, and the continuing importance of environment, culture and society on identity. It gave rise to reformations in legal systems, foregrounded questions of ethics and power in society, and allowed advertising to develop its tactics at making us buy things we do not need: every time you buy a pair of sneakers, blame behaviourism for showing how easily we can be tricked, and what tricks work most effectively at fooling us (Pratkanis, Pratkanis and Aronson, 2001). While behaviourism made psychology a serious scientific discipline, its strict refusal to theorize about the causes of things such as character and personality have led to its over-shadowing in modern psychology. Since the end of the last century, character and personality have come to be seen as epiphenomenon of the physical structures of the brain, but also of processes, networks, relationships that can be modelled using a variety of analogies taken from computing and from nature. It is clear from psychology that our character is a combination of three things: things that are essential to our physiological make-up and genetic inheritance; things we learn through our early development as children; and things we adopt along the way, either as acts of learning and development, or from social interactions with others. Community, then, becomes as important as what goes on inside our brains when it comes to shaping who we are.

The meaning of community in its everyday usage is fairly obvious. A community is a group of people who share some common things: a shared locality, a shared culture, a shared interest, a shared history or a shared language. Community gives meaning to those who belong – through shared symbols, myths, narratives and histories – but community can also be used in a prejudicial way to exclude outsiders. This is a sociological and anthropological conception of community, which fits my own research about the sport of rugby league (Spracklen, 1996, 2007; Spracklen and Spracklen, 2008; Spracklen, Timmins and Long, 2010): belonging in a community is based on symbols, structures, objects, texts, shared histories and myths, and rituals.

Another way of defining community is as a social psychological phenomenon. Turner (1969) has been influential in social psychology for introducing and popularizing the notion of *communitas*: a sense of belonging and existential satisfaction in the cold light of modernity. The concept refers to communal identity we construct in our minds, and is analogous to the *Romanitas* that was supposed to bind members of the Roman Empire into one, imagined community. Turner says that with the advent of modernity the old 'natural' ties of communitas are destroyed, so we moderns seek belonging on the margins of modern society – wherever we can. For Turner and other social identity theorists (Tajfel, 1978), the search for meaning and community is a universal impulse, something hard-wired in us culturally and psychologically: every age of history shows the importance of the feeling of being part of something bigger, and the search for meaning and community even seems to be present in pre-history (Spracklen, 2011). This search for meaning and community is a search for authenticity, which Turner, following Weber (1992), suggests was lost in the transition from the pre-modern community of religion and magic to the modern world of rationality, disenchantment and mundanity. Opotow (1990) argues that community identity is the work of a constant internal process of Othering. All of us try to identify who we are (where we belong) through constructing definitions of people who are not like us: the social psychological Other. In pre-modern cultures, the Other was often associated with unfamiliar tribes beyond the reach of our local networks. In modernity, this Other has become associated with other ethnicities, social classes and nation-states.

SPORT AND CHARACTER BUILDING, SPORT AND PERSONALITY

I like to think of myself as a person of good character. When I reflect on my experience of sport and physical activity, there seems to be some sort of correlation between my belief I am intelligent and intrinsically motivated to do the right thing, and my regular regime of running. I even think running does make me able to perform better in my job: I use the silence of running to contemplate research problems, and I'm sure the mornings after I have gone for a long run are the best hours for my critical thinking and academic writing. But do I run to make me a better person, or am I better person therefore I choose to go running? Or is the correlation I believe to be true merely an artefact of my subjective experience? I want to believe that doing sports has some positive effect on my physiology and psychology – but is this belief a false one?

There is strong evidence that running will improve my physiology and make me fitter (on physical activity's benefits to physiology and physical health see the systematic reviews and meta-analyses in Berlin and Colditz, 1990; Blair, Cheng and Holder, 2001; Nocon *et al.*, 2008; Williams, 2001), though there are limits and caveats to be made about that argument (see Chapters 10 and 11). When it comes to the causal connections between doing sports and personality, the evidence is less clear. Sports psychology is one of the fastest growing subject fields in the wider academic discipline of sport and exercise science. There are hundreds of research papers that claim that doing some kind of sports has some positive effect on psychological states, and to engage with all these claims would make this book a sports psychology textbook (see the excellent Weinberg and Gould, 2011) – but there are many other papers (seemingly not so many) that challenge these claims or use new research to say there are no psychological benefits from doing sports that are not figments of the experiment or the selection of participants (see the discussion in the critical review by Scully, Kremer, Meade, Graham, and Dudgeon, 1998). It is claimed in the research that boosts sport's role in developing good character, for instance, that regular exercise makes people more focused (Carr, 2011), that regular exercise makes people more calm (Biddle, Fox and Boucher, 2000), that people who do sports see their educational test scores improve (see the review in Singh, Uijtdewilligen, Twisk, van Mechelen, and Chinapaw, 2012). Such claims are inevitably used by the people who like sports to prove that doing sports is a good thing. However, such claims are open to strong critiques. Much of the research suffers from the problem of induction: how can we generalize across contemporary society from these specific, small-scale research findings? Just because someone has shown that some people in some particular place do get a psychological benefit from doing some sort of sport, it does not necessarily follow that doing the same exercise will lead to the same benefits (Backhouse, Ekkekakis, Biddle, Foskett and Williams, 2007). More sophisticated sports psychologists have tried to account for the problem of induction by having larger numbers of participants and using randomization and other controls (see Chapter 10) – all this makes the truth of claims more reliable. Another way of trying to capture the truth of the claims is by undertaking meta-analyses of all the claims and counter-claims, assigning values to the methods and the samples and the rigour and so on (these are sometimes called Cochrane reviews). What the meta-analysis work says is that there is some evidence that exercise has a number of psychological benefits, but only if the exercise is sustained and sufficiently intensive (Lawlor and Hopker, 2001). There is strong evidence, for instance, that regular physical activity can help people with depression and people with other mental health issues (Carless and Sparkes, 2008; Carr, 2011).

Another way of thinking about sports and character and personality is to explore if there are particular psychological types that are better suited to taking part and maintaining involvement in sports. This is the psychology of sports personality – what brings you to sport, and what keeps you in sport? There are of course a whole range of sports and physical activities, and the idea that one personality type might suit the whole of sport is plainly ridiculous. That said, there is a range of research findings that suggest certain types or traits – for example extroverts, goal-directed individuals – might make participation and continued involvement in sports more likely (see the discussion in Weinberg and Gould, 2011). This research has some of the weaknesses mentioned in the preceding paragraph. Another problem with thinking about types and traits is that it is easy to assume that these things are fixed, essential characteristics associated with characters that are as immovable as the humors of medieval medicine. There are tests that can be used to identify characteristics associated with particular traits, but no general agreement over the number of traits, what makes each trait different from other traits, and the nature of the trait in the deep biology of the brain. Since the work of Allport (1937), trait theory has shaped popular psychological best-sellers and managerial tools such as psychometric testing.

While there seems to be some predictability in models of traits, and some commonality when it comes to those traits that might be useful to begin and stick with a sport as a participant, it is easy to be trapped into thinking the models are true because the findings correlate with other findings. In the philosophy of science, Cartwright (1983) has shown how models are made to work irrespective of the truth or reality of the things they are meant to model. This allows scientists to improve their experiments and refine their models, but does not get to the problem of what the models represent: they are ideal and simplified representations of the real world. Tests that use trait models make simplifications of the messiness of our personalities and our identities – where we are actually all sorts of contradictions and irrationalities, trait theory boils us down to a few fixed, polar opposites. So we become 'natural' extroverts who prefer team sports, or 'natural' introverts who prefer sports where we play alone, when in fact most of us can be a mix of either type in a range of circumstances (and not always in a rational way – so we might end up displaying the behaviour of an introvert when it is not sensible for us to do so).

Motivation is one of the more interesting character traits that have been explored by sports psychologists. In the last century, educationalists were trying to make sense of the different ways in which school children responded to learning and assessments (Maehr and Meyer, 1997). From behaviourism, there was experimental proof of the extrinsic stimuli that might persuade children to change their behaviour and become more focused, more motivated and more task oriented (Cameron and Pierce, 1994). The efficacy of these stimuli depended on the situation and the child, but there were common themes: children responded well to positive praise and sweets, and less well to punishments (Butler, 1987). This demonstrated that humans are not very far removed from animals in how we respond to conditioning. But the best form of motivation, the kind that secures long-term engagement and involvement, is not associated with extrinsic stimuli – these only seem to work so far (Nicholls, 1979). What keeps students committed to learning and performing to their best is intrinsic motivation, a measurable quality that is related to their sense of self-determination, autonomy and task orientation (Maehr and Meyer, 1997; Nicholls, 1979).

Deci and Ryan (2000) have used the notion of intrinsic motivation and self-determination to show what keeps people involved in activities such as sports (Spray, Biddle and Fox, 1999). Those individuals who engage in sports because they like playing sports, because it gives them a feeling of self-worth and gives them a chance to be self-directed and immersed in the moment (what Csikszentmihalyi calls a flow moment – see Csikszentmihalyi and LeFevre, 1989), remain more likely to be active as they pass through the life course. They are satisfied with the intrinsic pleasure of physical activity and their own sense of accomplishment: they do not seek any other motivation to be physically active. Those individuals who do seek extrinsic motivations – the victory and the glory; the prize money; the accolades from one's peers – get satisfaction when they are at the peak of their sporting careers, and elite athletes who are winners get comfort from extrinsic motivation. But extrinsic motivations take athletes only so far. Sooner or later they are not the best, or they lose their professional contract, or they get injured, or their partner leaves them. When these things happen, individuals who are driven by extrinsic motivations are more likely to give up on sports and physical activity; they are not interested in sport for sport's sake, only sport as a short-cut to something else. Deci and Ryan's (2000) self-determination theory might have the same causal and ontological weaknesses as other trait theories, but it does seem to capture some essential truth about motivation. It may seem they are only saying what we all know – if you like something, whatever that is, you keep on doing it. But the theory attempts to explain why that is by building a convincing model of extrinsic and intrinsic motivation, and connecting this to other social psychological theories such as flow and goal theory (Spray, Biddle and Fox, 1999).

Goal setting and achievement in sports

Balaguer, Duda and Crespo (1999) suggest people engage in achievement situations such as sports in order to demonstrate competence. They argue that there are two conceptions of competence or ability, and show how these ways of thinking about goals and ability might be measured through various tests. The first is self-referenced – where ability is conceived as improvement – and this is referred to as task involvement or orientation. The second conception is other-referenced – where ability is conceived as capacity – and this is called ego involvement or orientation. Task orientation is positively related to intrinsic motivation: people doing the physical activity for the sake of the task and the feeling of quiet satisfaction they get when they have mastered the task. Ego orientation is not related to, or is negatively related to, intrinsic motivation. Whereas task-oriented individuals engage in the activity for its own sake, for ego-oriented individuals the activity is a means to an end. The preoccupation of ego-oriented individuals with outperforming others may lead to a lack of concern about justice and fairness. There is a significant and positive relationship between task orientation and the tendency to perceive playing as fun among the tennis players in their research: this has been confirmed in other research projects over the years on a range of participants in a range of sports.

QUESTIONS TO CONSIDER

What might happen to ego-oriented individuals when they lose competitions? How might sports activities be changed to nurture task orientation?

REFERENCE AND FURTHER READING

Balaguer, I., Duda, J. and Crespo, M. (1999) 'Motivational Climate and Goal Orientations as Predictors of Perceptions of Improvement, Satisfaction and Coach Ratings among Tennis Players', *Scandinavian Journal of Medicine and Science in Sports*, 9, pp. 381–8.

The other side to sports and physical activity and character building is the connection between such activity and what we might call 'bad' character. The notion of 'bad' character is itself epistemologically and ontologically problematic, and recalls the essentialism associated with religious arguments on divine salvation and punishment. Badness is culturally relative, and attitudes over bad character have changed over time even in the short history of modern psychology. Just last century, for example, it was assumed and claimed by Freudians and mainstream psychologists that homosexuality was immoral and a sign of some abnormality (Minton, 2002). Today no right-minded psychologist would make such claims, but there are traits that are accepted as 'bad' today but which may be considered good or neutral by the second half of this century. That said, there are some things that most psychologists would agree on when it comes to trying to identify 'bad' characteristics: selfishness, aggression, and lack of control, for example (see discussion in Hamilton, 2012). There are times when these characteristics might actually be good for individuals: we all need to be selfish at times (turning off our phones, closing our doors) so we get our work done; sometimes we need to be pushy to get things done for us; and allowing ourselves to lose control is cathartic, and at times a seemingly natural human impulse.

There are strong associations between all three of these bad characteristics and sports and physical activity.

Sports seem to encourage narcissism and individualism (through excessive concerns with training, self-development and success) at the expense of co-operation: even team sports seem to atomize the relationships in the team, so that each player becomes an individual striving to achieve his or her goals without a care for the individual wellbeing of others (Welch, 1997). Some sports clearly encourage aggression and tacitly condone violent actions – in many sports aggression is valued, especially where it is targeted on the opposing athletes. Sports participants, especially sports fans but also people who actually play sports, are prone to losing control of their emotions: sports seem to encourage a normalization of violence and irrational, emotionally-charged behaviours (Simons and Taylor, 1992). Feminist psychologists and sociologists have identified particularly exclusionary ways in which identity (character, personality) is constructed within contemporary sport – some of this research is problematic in its use of untestable ideas from Freudian theory, but most of it is built on a solid social science critique using empirical research. Sports promote a narrow heteronormativity and hegemonic masculinity, favouring celebrations of traditional manliness over other forms of gender identity (Connell and Messerschmidt, 2005; Messner, 1989; Waldron, Lynn and Kane, 2011; Welch, 1997). Again, there is a problem with the causality of the relationships in all this research. Looking at aggression, for example, is it the case that sports engender aggression as a trait in normally balanced people? Or do sports act as a space for people with aggressive tendencies to have their aggression normalized? Again, is sport a site for the construction of hegemonic masculinity, or the maintenance of hegemonic masculinity? These questions link to the role of sport in community building.

Hazing, initiations and hegemonic masculinity

News stories about criminal activities and other anti-social behaviour associated with the students in sports teams are increasingly common. We hear about this bad behaviour, and see the aftermath, but there is little analysis of the issue. Getting college athletes to be honest to academic researchers about the rituals of hazing, the initiation ceremonies and games associated with being part of a college sports team, is very difficult. Clayton (2013) solves this methodological problem by constructing a narrative of such rituals based on his own experience, and the experiences of the people he interviewed. He gets his male students to be honest to him through his own involvement in university sports, and his own position as 'one of the lads'. The narrative Clayton provides is a composite one, a re-telling of all these collected experiences. He shows how the intensity of the college sports experience translates into the social settings of the night out. The young men perform hegemonic masculinity: they are rowdy, they drink excessive amounts of alcohol, they talk about women, they chat-up women, and they patrol the boundaries of what is considered proper heterosexual masculinity. The rituals and the drinking and the relentless sexualization of the interactions (with each other and with the young women they target in the bars and night clubs) normalizes hegemonic masculinity, initiates the boys into the exclusive community of elite male college sports, and leaves little room for transgression.

QUESTIONS TO CONSIDER

Why do women's sports teams in colleges behave in the same way? Why is this reported differently?

REFERENCE AND FURTHER READING

Clayton, B. (2013) 'Initiate: Constructing the "Reality" of Male Team Sport Initiation Rituals', *International Review for the Sociology of Sport*, 48, pp. 204–19.

COMMUNITY, SOCIALIZATION AND SPORTS

When sports are said to play a role in community building or formation, community is said to be created at the level of the psychological, the social and the cultural. As a student of sport, you will know that for you this reads like something undoubtedly true. When I played team sports as a young adult, I loved the sense of belonging I got from being part of the team: to me, the socializing that went on around the training and playing was more important than the actual matches. I also felt pride from a young age right into my adulthood being a rugby league fan, supporting this sport and my local professional club: being a rugby league fan, I could find new friends anywhere that other rugby league fans gathered, whether that was on a coach to a Great Britain Test match against Australia, or in the *Yorkshire Pride* bar in Benidorm (which is still decorated with rugby league artefacts). Sports are said to be good for individuals because they create strong psychological bonds of belonging: players identify with their team mates, or their club, or their sport (Walseth, 2006). Sports are said to be good for wider community cohesion and society in the way they allow the people who do sport (in those three different ways discussed earlier: participants, spectators and volunteers) to build social capital, a sense of place, bonding capital and bridging capital (Spaaij, 2012). Finally, it is argued that sports create cultural capital and ties of belonging that operate at a symbolic, imaginary and imagined level: so sports are used to create shared senses of history and belonging, shared national identities and narratives. Sports are seen by some academics and writers as activities that are ideologically neutral, open to all and loved by all – and as such, they are offered as the solution for a range of social and political problems (see Houlihan, 2005). Whether it is as an athlete, a fan or a volunteer of some kind, doing sport is the popular prescription for disengagement, alienation, disaffection and the individualism that has supposedly made the world less communal. Huge inequalities of power in Africa, the result of the history of Empire and the more recent neo-liberal interventions in the continent, are now seen as trifling problems that can be solved through encouraging people to play more sport (Darnell, 2007). Enthusiasts and activists naïvely believe that getting young Israelis and Palestinians playing football together will somehow create the secular and democratic state(s) that are the necessary solution to the problem. In countries in the West such as the United States and the United Kingdom, sports policy-makers continually argue that diverting money to sport is necessary as sport is a way of bringing different ethnic communities together, or reducing crime and anti-social behaviour (Coalter, 2013) – the entire sport development industry is founded on the assumption that pulling on a tracksuit and kicking a football is the most efficient way to construct community belonging.

If we return to the three ways of doing sports we can get a more nuanced perspective on the way sports might be good or bad for socialization and community building. Taking part in a sport as an active participant brings with it the positive effects of socialization: team-bonding, feeling part of something bigger than oneself and constructing strong ties of friendship (Weinberg and Gould, 2011). Being an active participant in sport one learns the internal symbols and practices of that particular imaginary community (Cohen, 1985). When I go running, I will say hello to other runners, and if we meet at gates or stiles we follow a code of the first person who reaches the obstacle keeping it clear or open for the second person. I feel a kinship with my fellow runners – we might not know each other's names but we know each other by sight, and we will say hello to each other if we meet briefly on the main street. If I were more serious about running up and down hills I could easily join the local fell-running club, and get access to the cycle of fell races throughout the running season – as well as access to a wider circle of people as friends (fell runners do like a pint of beer). Of course, it would be reasonably easy for me to join a fell-running club: all I would need to do is work a bit harder at my times and my distances. But for many people, joining a sports club as an active participant and taking advantage of the socialization and community building is almost impossible. Most sports activities are hard to do well, and most people are not physically able to keep up with the serious leisure participants who compete at club level in sports: there are few opportunities to play sports badly but for fun. Another reason why people might not be able to become active participants is the inequalities and social structures that constrain most people's agency in contemporary society. Women's involvement in sports clubs has historically been limited, as we have seen in Chapters 1 and 2, and even today there is a hegemonic bias in sport in favour of men (Krien, 2013; Waldron, Lynn and Krane, 2011). There are exceptions to this bias, but in general women are less likely than men to have access, the agency and the power to be active sports participants. This constraint on participation in sports is also seen in minority ethnic communities, in working-class communities, and in people with disabilities: these social groups are marginalized and relatively powerless compared to the white, male elites who maintain control of contemporary Western society, so they are less likely to have easy access to sports clubs (Spracklen, 2013a, 2013b). Furthermore, discrimination and the fear of discrimination, and the lack of cultural capital, magnify the exclusionary effects (see, for example, Long and Spracklen, 2010).

The second way of doing sport is as a spectator, a sports fan. Here the value of sports as sites for community building is more obvious, and there is a large body of research that demonstrates the strong social and cultural bonds created between professional sports clubs and their supporters (for an example, see Serazio, 2013). Big events such as the Olympics and the soccer World Cup also seem to bring countries together in imagined communities, getting behind the nation's athletes as they progress through the competitions (Rojek, 2013). However (and as we will see in Chapters 12 and 13), the problem with arguing that sports fandom provides a strong sense of community is the communities become exclusive ones, defined by symbolic boundaries that exclude others. To be a Manchester City fan one must learn to hate Manchester United, and vice versa. To be a rugby union fan one must be dismissive of rugby league. To follow Germany in the soccer World Cup one must hate France. Sports fans might argue that the loathing and suspicion they have of their rivals is just ironic banter and symbolic (mimetic) violence, but it is exclusionary, and it does, all too often, transform into actual violence (Braun and Vliegenthart, 2008). Sports fandom, especially the form of fandom associated with watching national sides in international tournaments, can also be a way of imposing narrow (elitist, monocultural) versions of national identity, limiting the involvement of minority ethnic communities and making them 'invisible' (Rojek, 2013; Spracklen, 2013b).

Sports fandom has the potential, then, to create community and belonging, and the potential to socialize people into good forms of behaviour and practice – but it is also a form of sports involvement that can create very exclusionary and hegemonic forms of belonging. We will return to the problem of sports fandom and community in Chapter 12.

The third and final way of doing sports is being a volunteer or non-performing worker of some kind. Sports need people to run clubs, committees and leagues. Sports clubs need coaches and trainers, kit-washers and drivers. In bigger sports, there are paid officials from referees to chief executives. Naturally, anyone who gives their time for no reward is intrinsically motivated, and gains deeper satisfaction from their volunteering (Nichols, Tacon and Muir, 2013). But working in any role in sport has the potential to be rewarding, as long as the roles are freely chosen. The problem is who gets to be a worker in modern sports. The same warning about constraints and inequalities in social structures applies to this way of doing sports: people need the right access to power and the right social and cultural capital to establish such positions in sports clubs and associations, so all too often the elite and exclusionary nature of sports is reproduced (Coalter, 2007). People who become volunteers and workers in any given sport will generally only do so after they have had involvement in the sport as a participant or a spectator. The exception to that rule is where people have been socialized into such roles through the participation of family members – typically, parents become volunteers at a sports club if their child is playing sport at that club (Nichols, Tacon and Muir, 2013). Where people do volunteer or work in a sports setting, their sustained involvement and commitment is dependent on them having the right social and cultural capital in relation to others involved in those sports spaces (Kay and Bradbury, 2009; Nichols, Tacon and Muir, 2013). All sports say they openly welcome anyone willing to volunteer and help get things done – sports rely on the people driving cars and buses, washing dirty kit, selling raffle tickets, and so on – but the reality is it is incredibly difficult for outsiders to negotiate the symbolic boundaries that divide belonging and exclusion. The emphasis on child protection issues in the first two decades of this century has exacerbated the suspicion of outsiders in sports clubs where children participate. But if people do overcome the social and cultural barriers, have the right cultural capital, and are able to demonstrate they are not a threat of any kind, then they can sustain their involvement as volunteers and workers. And being an active worker in sports is an excellent way of finding socialization and a sense of belonging: such people feel identity with their sport, their club, the locality, and the people at the club.

Starting the sports habit

Kraaykamp, Oldenkamp and Breedveld (2013) used survey data gathered in the Netherlands to study what effects parental and social characteristics might have had on whether or not people started playing a sport. The survey, which was undertaken by other researchers, was a representative sample across the entire Dutch population. It was undertaken twice, in 1998 and 2003, and generated a large quantitative data set. Kraaykamp, Oldenkamp and Breedveld (2013)'s research paper is a secondary analysis of this data set. They found that people who grew up in families where there were parents or others already playing sport were more likely to take up sport than those who did not grow up in such sporting families. Furthermore, higher class status among parents meant they were more likely to encourage their children to take up high-status sports. Finally, they also found that having a partner who played sport meant it was more likely an individual would also play sport – though they found that in starting a sport it is better to not have a partner at all. Such social bonds at a family level, then, are important when it comes to whether people do sports at all. Social class and status is also identified as an important factor.

QUESTIONS TO CONSIDER

How can this Dutch research be applied in other countries? What other social and cultural factors might be found in a country such as the United States or the United Kingdom?

REFERENCE AND FURTHER READING

Kraaykamp, G., Oldenkamp, M. and Breedveld. K. (2013) 'Starting a Sport in the Netherlands: A Life-Course Analysis of the Effects of Individual, Parental and Partner Characteristics', *International Review for the Sociology of Sport*, 48, pp. 153–70.

CONCLUSION

Do sports and other forms of physical culture benefit individuals both psychologically and in terms of their social and cultural development? The answer is yes, sports and physical culture do give clear benefits to individuals and to society. Sports are places where we can feel good about ourselves, our identity and our community. There is a psychological benefit from participating in sports, both from the perspective of individual character/personality and from the interaction between individuals in social settings. The latter interaction further benefits society through encouraging strong social bonds and shared belonging. Using the theoretical framework of Habermas we can say that sports, like other forms of leisure, can be communicative: they can be activities or spaces where people come together to interact freely and to develop the lifeworld of the public sphere. It is important to note that other forms of leisure have that same social and cultural quality, the ability to be used freely by humans to build belonging and further human development: and sports and physical culture are arguably not the best forms of leisure to be communicative, given their role in perpetuating hegemony and social inequalities. However, it is clear that it is the physicality of physical activities such as sports that make them important in tackling psychological problems and improving psychological wellbeing. Going for a run or dancing works the body and mind in a positive way that reading a book does not, even if reading a book might be something more communicatively free. But if physical activity is potentially so beneficial, the question becomes: who gets to benefit? The confidence and the ability and the power to do sport are limited to those who have cultural hegemony over the practice. This has ethical and sociological consequences. The benefits of sports and physical culture, then, are tempered by the problems that follow the distribution and allocation of both moral and social benefits. In the next chapter, we will continue to explore the claims made about sport's meaning and purpose, around the ideas of embodiment and gratification.

EXERCISES

1 What other ways might sports give a sense of psychological wellbeing? Find the evidence to back up your ideas.
2 Discuss how modern sports differ from, and are similar to, other leisure forms in their role in community building.
3 Who gets to benefit from sports and physical activity in your country? How does this compare with other countries? Discuss.

Chapter 5

Embodiment and Gratification

SUMMARY OF TOPICS

▪ Definitions: embodiment and gratification
▪ Theories of embodiment and the application of these to sports and physical culture
▪ Sports and the work of Foucault
▪ Sports, physical culture and gratification

When I started running seriously, I did not look like other runners. My body shape was not quite correct, for one thing – and even though that might have changed by becoming more conditioned (less fat, slightly more muscular), no matter how much I run, how far and how long and how intense, I will not be able to swap my skeleton for that of a professional fell runner. But I also did not look like a runner because of the way I presented myself: I ran in heavy-metal band tee-shirts and old shorts, and I had long hair and a long, Viking beard tied into two plaits. People did not know what to think of me. I looked like some crazed biker, but there I was running along the road, not driving along on the back of a Harley Davidson. Before the locals in my town got used to the strange sight of a mosher out running, people would stare and point. Now, most people have got used to the idea that someone who looks 'alternative' – and part of some dangerous subculture – might, in fact, be doing something as mundane as keeping fit. I embodied two contradictory identities at once: the rebel and the athlete. I still have my beard and long hair, but these days I run in 'proper' running shorts, and in the winter I will wear a yellow fluorescent hat and top – so as I have got older the ways in which I embody my identity in my running have changed, becoming more conformist and less carnivalesque. As my hair falls out and my beard gets greyer, it will only be a short time before I shave it all off and look like any other middle-aged, white man out for a run.

In the previous chapter, I explored certain sociological and psychological reasons why people choose to participate in sport. In this chapter I will look at the ways in which individuals choose to do certain sports, and not others. In the reflection above, I am considering how I embody the active runner, and how I embody other identities that do not fit the 'look' of the runner. I will show that individuals taking part in certain sports do so because those sports allow them to embody practices, ideologies, power relationships and beliefs about the world. This chapter will introduce and discuss theories of embodiment and theories of gratification to demonstrate two ways in which individual choice and individual participation is fixed by the need to express different kinds of physicality and the need to seek gratification in the practice of physical culture. It will conclude by considering whether embodiment is a reflection of any special circumstances about the age in which we live – whether we live in an age or society that is no longer modern, but something postmodern.

DEFINITIONS: EMBODIMENT AND GRATIFICATION

Embodiment is the way in which sociological, psychological and cultural symbols and ideas – ideologies, myths, boundaries, genders, classes, roles, capital, inequalities, ethnicities, ages, ideas of ability and normality, tastes and ways of distinction, relationships of power – become mapped onto the physical body. Sometimes embodiment operates to permanently re-shape or mark a body, for instance through the cultural accretion of hegemonic power associated with being biologically male. Just having the 'proof' of being a man physically gives one legal rights in many parts of the world that women do not have, and even in countries that have laws that make sex discrimination illegal, being embodied as male gives one more power and advantage culturally. But embodiment can also be something that is temporary, albeit long-term in duration. It is possible to alter human bodies in a number of ways, sometimes voluntary, sometimes under compulsion. When politicians try to promote sports and physical activity, for example, they are trying to coerce their citizens into doing things to re-shape their bodies: the politicians want the citizens to embody healthiness. Embodiment, finally, might be associated with ways in which the human body is modified. In our natural state, humans did not walk around in clothes, in make-up and with other bodily adornments: all these things are ways of embodying identity and belonging. And all these ways of thinking about embodiment allow us to explain embodiment psychologically, sociologically and culturally. Embodiment is both about how we choose to express things we hold dear to us, and about how our bodies are used to keep the status quo of the political hegemonies that rule our lives. In this chapter, we will explore both those ideas: that we 'write' on our bodies what we want others to know about us; and that are bodies are sites for constraint, conformity and hegemonic control.

Embodiment is a concept that has its origins in cultural anthropology. Cultural anthropology is the academic discipline of exploring and understanding the complexities of lived human cultures. Nowadays, the cultures of Western nations and societies are just as much the focus of anthropological research as any other. In its original form, cultural anthropology was an attempt by Westerners to understand cultures 'alien' to their own, ones that might have been 'untouched' by other influences. When anthropologists went out to explore cultures different to their own, they were interested in establishing the rules of these cultures and the myths and symbols they shared. They wanted to know whether there were any universal mechanisms and processes under the diversity of human cultural experience (Ortner, 1984). In other words, they were interested in mapping belonging and identity as they were shaped in social interactions and in people's minds. Cultural anthropologists soon realized that sociological and psychological ideas of belonging and identity in these cultures could be expressed through the use of the body. In other words, the shift to try to find meaning in the symbolic realm returned to an exploration of how the sociological and cultural could be 'read' onto the bodies of individuals (Csordas, 1990). In classic ethnographies of Polynesian island cultures in the South Pacific, for example, we learn the importance to the individual and the community of the practices of tattooing (Mead, 1929). Having a tattoo is not (simply) a lifestyle choice: it is a way for male islanders to identify themselves as belonging to a particular community, a particular family; a way for men to prove their worth as adult men; a way to demonstrate one's place. Getting a tattoo in the traditional Polynesian manner was a painful experience. The traditional tattoo embodied belonging, masculinity, family and place in the social order. And in this century, tattooing continues to play a key role in embodying Polynesian social identities, even if the technology of tattooing has advanced and the styles have become more Westernized and individualized (Kuwahara, 2005).

In contemporary sociology and cultural studies, theories of embodiment have taken a postmodern (sometimes called post-structural) turn. That is, these new theorists believe that society has changed so much that old ways of thinking about sociology are obsolete. These postmodern embodiment theorists believe a number of things about the state of contemporary life. Firstly, they reject the idea that the state or capitalism has complete subjugation of our bodies. Instead, there is a contestation of bodies and spaces in which bodies move (Butler, 2006; Lefebvre, 1991). Sports, then, become ways in which we might express our freedom to move. Secondly, they reject the idea that we can be free from our own bodily biases and prejudices, meaning we cannot understand embodiment in others without understanding our own embodiment (Alcoff, 2000). Thirdly, they argue that the body needs to be re-introduced into critical theories of sociology and the cultural, which they claim has 'traditionally' ignored bodies and feelings/emotions in favour of trying to construct truths based on the social or the material worlds (Alcoff, 2000; Butler, 2006). Fourthly, they say that sociological methods need to be changed to enable us to enter the emotional world of the people we might be doing research on or with (Rojek, 1995, 2010). Fifthly, they argue that the society in which we live has changed so much that it can be best understood as something 'postmodern', where social structures and social identities become fuzzy, or liquid (Blackshaw, 2010; Rojek, 2010), allowing individuals the agency to resist hegemony and move across embodied identities (Butler, 2006). Again, sports and other forms of physical activity are activities in which we might resist the control of elites. And finally, they are strongly influenced by psychodynamic theories of the unconscious and subconscious, drawing heavily on Freud and Lacan, as well as on French thinkers such as Deleuze and Foucault, who in turn draw heavily on psychodynamic theories.

The work of Foucault (1970, 1973, 1980, 2006) on embodiment, commodification, power and governmentality is essential to understanding sports and physical activity. Foucault argues that the capitalist phase that emerged out of the Enlightenment, and in which we still live, objectifies and commodifies the human body. Governmentality refers to both the way in which governments control the public, and the way in which individuals control themselves on behalf of the state. What matters for the modern state, according to Foucault, is the control of its citizens, the removal of those who are not productive workers, and the policing of civilized behaviour. Through the process of embodiment, individuals learn how to read the wishes of the state and modern capitalism into the control of their own bodies by policing illness, body size, appearance, depression and wellbeing; this embodiment makes us into good citizens who are relatively powerless against the manipulations of our rulers. Judith Butler (2006) puts gender identity and gender performativity central to the sociological debates about leisure, culture and embodiment. In sports and physical culture, embodiment is also strongly connected to the idea of gender performativity, though research on embodiment in physical culture also shows how sexuality, (dis) ability, class and ethnicity intersect with gender.

Before we move on to exploring embodiment in sports and physical activity, we need to consider the relationship between embodiment and gratification. The concept of gratification in this chapter needs to be understood philosophically, psychologically and sociologically. Philosophically, gratification means some kind of satisfaction met through some pleasurable activity – Classical Greek philosophers recognized that people drank wine and ate fine food, and had sex, and listened to music, and played games, because they found these activities gratifying. But was it proper, a moral or social good, to pursue these pleasures to excess? Was it a moral or social good to allow people to pursue any pleasures at all? And who is allowed to seek such gratification? Some Greek philosophers such as Epicurus believed the pursuit of pleasure was a moral imperative: we all have to live our lives in as pleasurable a way as possible (Warren, 2009). Others such as Aristotle and the Stoics believed we had to constrain our urge for gratification and live lives of moderation or abstinence, an ethics similar to that of many religious teachings (Inwood, 1985). In modern psychology, theorists have identified individual character traits that might make people more likely to pursue pleasure for pleasure's sake, or more likely to be self-constrained in their behaviour (Huta, 2012). The pursuit of gratification has become the subject of debates in social psychology about our ability to control our emotions and act as rational agents, and our ability to resist taking the immediate 'hit' of gratification over a delayed reward (Sacchetti and Tortia, 2013). Sociologically, gratification might be best understood as some internal desire that becomes externalized: it becomes a product of instrumentality through the operation of modern, capitalist systems of rationality and control. Gratification becomes something that is morally problematic. We believe doing something or buying something makes us happy, and it does, for a brief moment, but the thing (the experience, the activity, the material object) only provides passing gratification. We are never entirely satisfied by the products of instrumentality because we are not meant to be content with what we have – modern,

global capitalism demands that we purchase more things. All three definitions of gratification connect with one another – we need to think in an
inter-disciplinary way about the concept. In today's globalized world, I argue
in the rest of this chapter, the 'con' of gratification is revealed in how such
things that supposedly satisfy become embodied in us.

SPORTS AND THE EMBODIMENT OF DISCIPLINES

All sports demonstrate embodiment in its superficial meaning. But they
all demonstrate embodiment in its deeper, Foucauldian (1991, 2006) sense
too: that is, in the way that embodiment incorporates self-control, discipline and conformity. Sports train bodies to be the right shape for certain
sports, but that training is a way of disciplining ourselves and conforming
to the hegemonies that control us. To become an athlete in any particular
sport one must learn the unwritten rules of practice: how one trains the
body and mind; and how much work one does on one's body to achieve
the right shape and cardio-vascular system. In elite sports development
and coaching, experts from sports sciences will identify individuals who
have the best bodies for given sports to try to find the most 'natural' athletes: so swimming coaches look for people with strong upper bodies, and
long-distance running coaches look for those with thin bodies and long
strides, and those in American football seeking defensive players for the
future look for young men who are freaks of nature due to their size and
physical presence. When these are identified they may not be psychologically correct, or they may not fulfil the potential of their young bodies, but
the elite coaching and development systems will take a tiny proportion
of those potential athletes and shape them even further to become elite
athletes. This shaping is partly emotional, partly physical. Elite athletes
learn to be absorbed in the act of training, to overcome their reluctance to
punish their bodies, to be willing slaves of the sports systems that demand
their time and effort – in the hope that they might be the best when the
competitions come around. Their bodies are pumped up, slimmed down,
tightened, re-shaped, through years of exercises, diets, supplements and
other enhancing technologies. Elite athletes, then, are the superheroes of
our time, genetic freaks with bodies that are hugely abnormal: over-mus-
cular, stripped of fat, trained to be brilliant at one thing over the whole
range of human experience.

For the rest of us, these elite athletes and their freakishly un-human
bodies become the shapes that we aspire to through our own sports

participation. We might not be gold medal winners at the Olympics, or professional football players, but we need to be more like them if we are to be satisfied with our own sports participation. One must take care to make sure one's diet and other work and leisure activities do not hinder the pursuit of embodied efficiency. The assumption is that it is possible to work the body to fit a particular sport in the best way it can possibly be, not just through formal exercises and coaching sessions, but also in the way one behaves in every other aspect of one's life. So when we become serious about our sports activity our entire life becomes dominated by the norms and values of physical culture. So we learn to eat more healthily, or we take supplements to enhance our shapes and body systems. We learn that it is not a good idea to eat fast food and drink lots of beer the night before our weekly sports activities. We start to monitor the speed at which we walk, the way we carry our shopping sacks, the way we sit at our desks, so we get the most added benefit from these mundane situations. We go to bed early at night instead of going out to a bar or a club. We discipline ourselves and regulate our lives. In other words, we are complicit in what Foucault (1991) calls disciplinary power, the modern way in which the state and other hegemonic powers ensure we conform and behave. Markula and Pringle (2006, p. 39) say that:

> [Foucault] suggested that the disappearance of the spectacle of punishment [in the transition from the feudal to the modern state] was linked to the emergence of disciplinary power: a form of power focused on the control of bodies and exercised fundamentally 'by means of surveillance' [Foucault, 1991, p. 104]... These disciplinary techniques focused on the body as the 'object and target of power' [Foucault, 1991, p. 136] in a manner that shaped and trained the body. Yet the techniques of discipline were different from those employed in slavery; they dispensed with the high cost of policing and the risks of violent retaliation, were relatively invisible and aimed to increase the mastery of each subject over their own body.

For Markula and Pringle (2006), Foucault's insight about the importance of embodiment in the maintenance of disciplinary power is particularly apposite in helping understand the formation of modern sport and physical culture. Modern sports are spaces and activities where people learn how to discipline themselves. They are spaces where everybody is keeping an eye on the activity and the bodies of everyone else in the activity. Sports give their participants the illusion of control while participation is strictly regulated and controlled by the structure of sport and the constraints of modern society. Embodiment of disciplinary power in sports becomes something that is expressed not only through the control of bodies, but also in the adornments of those bodies: sporting physical capital becomes a combination of the shape of the muscles and the branding of the shorts. Foucault (2006) argues that power is not simply imposed on individuals by institutions – individuals accept responsibility for their control. The body and mind are places of contestation between individual wills and the power of institutions, and madness is increasingly a label assigned to any mental states or attitudes that are not useful to the state (Foucault, 2006). Bodies themselves become subjectified – defining our status and power (or lack of it). Identity then is corporeal (of the body) as well as social.

In modernity, Foucault sees the power of governments being one or two steps removed from the social world of everyday life. The state is still all-powerful, alongside globalized hegemonies such as neo-liberal capitalism, but it does not need to exert its power in a brutal spectacle. Instead, we conform to its instructions, rules, mandates and policies. We are educated in formal school systems that include sports, ways of proving one's identity as a follower of rules. We learn from popular culture and the media how to behave, how to act, how to belong, how to hand over our communicative freedoms in return for the false security of borders and laws. We carry the mentality of conformity into adult. Disciplinary power is the mapping of governmentality onto the bodies of individual actors in contemporary society. As mentioned in the Introduction to this book, instead of living our leisure lives as communicatively free as possible, we seem to demonstrate our passive compliance to the Habermasian instrumentality of modern capitalism and state hegemonic power (Habermas, 1984, 1987; Spracklen, 2009). In sports, we accept that men and women should compete in separate competitions, and both normative, heterosexual masculinity and femininity are shaped in and through sports: men become men through the shaping of male dominance in various physical sports, and women become subject to artificial debates about how much muscle and how little fat they are allowed to have on their bodies (Shogan, 2002). Nationalism becomes embodied in the exercise of regimes of physical culture, whether the body modification of elite athletes in the pursuit of glory, or the public health policies of European countries trying to stamp out obesity. Access to and involvement in sports becomes something associated with the elites and the middle classes, and the well-tuned, well-toned sporting body becomes a symbol of the 'better' sort – the better class – against the unruly, un-ruled bodies of the working classes (Markula and Pringle, 2006; Shogan, 2002).

Keep-fit body fascism

In the West, and those parts of the world that have lost their local cultures to the rising American cultural hegemony of Disney and MTV, both men and women are subject to images in the media and popular culture of the correct sporting body, and success or failure in social contexts is seemingly connected to the right body shapes. For men, the sporting bodies of professional athletes are the ones they feel obliged to copy. For women, it is the model or celebrity whose gym-formed, cosmetically-enhanced body shape becomes the archetype: female athletes, even fairly high-profile professionals, are infrequently viewed as having the correct female body types. In this world of Foucauldian embodiment, the sporting body is favoured in all social situations, proof that the owner of the body is disciplined, one of us, someone we trust, someone who can join our workplace or leisure space. The body becomes another commodity, something commodified in the instrumentalization of modern society. As Wright, O'Flynn and Macdonald (2006) show, we have to punish our bodies to make them look the right shape, the one that is held up in mainstream popular culture as the correct body: so men struggle to achieve that six-pack look of ripped stomach muscles, and women cover their skin with fake tan and work at the ideal 'bikini' figure (slim and fit but not too masculine).

QUESTIONS TO CONSIDER

How can we change the way bodies become shaped by media representations? Who has tried to resist this commodification?

REFERENCE AND FURTHER READING

Wright, J., O'Flynn, G. and Macdonald, D. (2006) 'Being Fit and Looking Healthy: Young Women's and Men's Constructions of Health and Fitness', *Sex Roles*, 54, pp. 707–16.

Disciplinary power is similar to Weberian (1992) rationality – the way in which modern states and modern capitalism changed the way we think – but Foucault's concept of disciplinary power allows us to see how much of our own agency is at work in this. We choose embodiment. Sporting bodies keep us fit for purpose as docile stooges, keeping the law, paying our taxes, keeping our heads down (Gramsci, 1971). Disciplinary power has become so embodied in modern sports and physical culture that we feel somehow a failure or a reject if we cannot maintain our sports participation and our sporting bodies – and we dismiss those who do not play sports as lesser citizens who have failed to be responsible for their own bodies. Having a sporting body is a measure of social and cultural status, a symbol of success, one we desire and shape because we are fooled into thinking it expresses who we are as individuals – when all we are doing is fulfilling the wishes of those with real power in the contemporary world, who are content to give us an illusion of freedom around sports so we can be distracted from their capture and maintenance of real power. We become, then, both the prisoner and the guard, monitoring our bodies and the bodies of those around us (Markula and Pringle, 2006). In our sports participation we embody the rule-following and discipline of the modern nation-state, the instrumentality and commodification of global capitalism, the assumptions and prejudices and tastes of the ruling elites, and the gendered and racialized hegemonies that restrict our freedoms (Gramsci, 1971; Spracklen, 2009, 2011, 2013b). In the next section, we will look closely at how the pursuit of gratification in sport is an extension of embodiment.

Sporting bodies and disability sport

Sports contests were constructed to measure who had the best body (or body and mind), or a collection of bodies, in competitions between different humans or humans and some other object. The creators of modern sports wanted to find ways of testing strength, skill, speed and so on in ways that the competitors and spectators might agree was fair. When modern sports were invented in the nineteenth century and into the twentieth century, the unwritten assumption was that sports were about able-bodied (non-disabled) participants competing against each other: people with disabilities were written off by Western society as victims of accidents or disease, people who had no place in mainstream society (but who might be cared for in various institutions and charities). The notion that people with disabilities could take part in sports contests would have been laughed at by the first generation of administrators/creators in modern sport. The very idea of someone having a disability is a Foucauldian statement of how inclusion and exclusion are embodied: the power of language divides the world into those who fit and those who do not fit. Disability sport is a response to the exclusion and marginalization of people with disabilities. In this century, elite disability sport events are now seen as being of equal weight as other events such as the Olympics, and there is a growing disability sport culture in many countries. As Smith (2013) suggests, this brings challenges as well as opportunities for embodiment and inclusion.

QUESTIONS TO CONSIDER

How does disability sport challenge marginalization and embodiment in physical culture? How does it perpetuate marginalization and embodiment?

REFERENCE AND FURTHER READING

Smith, B. (2013) 'Disability, Sport and Men's Narratives of Health: A Qualitative Study', *Health Psychology*, 32, pp. 110–19.

SPORTS, PHYSICAL CULTURE AND GRATIFICATION

Sports are obviously activities that please the people who participate in them: as we have seen in the previous chapter, there is a convincing body of evidence to suggest that individuals taking part freely in sports and physical activity get all manner of psychological benefits from doing so. Many of these benefits are linked to the notion of gratification – the feeling of pleasure and satisfaction one gets from doing something physically active. For the individual engaged in the physical activity there is the pleasure of pushing one's skills to their limits, the satisfaction of achieving goals, whether playing in formal competitions or informally competing against one's previous 'bests'. In sports such as climbing, caving and sailing, the thrill of testing oneself against the elements is an obvious source of satisfaction; climbers feel satisfied when they have found a new route up a cliff, or have got up a known route for the first time in their own climbing histories (Heywood, 2006). Where the activity is team sport there is the added satisfaction of working collectively to achieve those goals, the pleasure of satisfying one's colleagues and earning their respect. Even sports spectatorship can be a leisure activity that gives gratification – one's team or nation or favourite athlete becomes a surrogate figure of success or failure, and the sports spectator finds satisfaction in their surrogate's completion of successful tasks. This is a proxy form of gratification, which some people might feel is less pure than the thrill of taking part in sports, but the thrill of victory and the pain of losing is no less felt for the fan as it is for the athlete.

But what is this pleasure we get from sports and physical culture? Is it something good for us? And if it is, can everybody get this pleasure? Let's consider the sports fan again, before we turn our attention to the gratification one gets from participating in sport. For a sports fan, there is a sense of pleasure in seeing their athletes winning. But this thrill can be addictive. Sports fans can develop unhealthy obsessions with their favourites, spending huge sums of money to follow them around. This obsession can result in the sports fan struggling to maintain a sensible work–life balance, and struggling to maintain social and cultural relationships with those who are not fellow sports fans. The obsessive fan will probably say they are having a good time being a sports fan, but we should not take them at their word. It is clear that taking fandom to an extreme is unhealthy psychologically and sociologically, as it turns from healthy support to the kind of worrying determination to be at every football stadium visited by the team (for example), or to know who came third in the 1948 Olympic men's long-jump event. When one identifies so much with sports fandom, one loses a sense of proportion and balance in the pursuit of the vicarious thrill of success. The pleasure of sporting success for fans is real but it is ephemeral. It gives only partial satisfaction, and leaves sports fans wanting more. It does not give lasting satisfaction in the way achieving life goals such as getting a degree or having a child does. But of course, only a small number of fans get the proxy pleasure of victory. Most sports fans follow teams or athletes or nations that fail at major sports events. For them, there is no pleasure in winning because their teams do not win, and the obsession with gratification can lead to dissatisfaction, depression and cognitive dissonance (Sumino and Harada, 2004).

The pleasure we get as sports participants is something that is less easy to problematize and critique. As I have said, in this book and elsewhere (Spracklen, 1996, 2009, 2011, 2013a, 2013b), sports are perceived in general as male directed and male dominated. In trying to develop a theoretical framework to understand the meaning and purpose of leisure, including sports and physical culture, I have combined ideas about the social construction of masculinity with belonging and exclusion in various imaginary communities, through using the latter's role as a place of defining personal and social identity, through contesting and understanding the meaning of symbols (Barthes, 1972). There is obviously a social pressure to define one's masculinity in a certain way which comes from the concept of masculinity developed by the hegemonic patriarchal ideology of the capitalist system (Hearn, 1987): a hegemonic expression of what it means to be a man. Connell and Messerschmidt (2005) and Donaldson (1993) have argued how the expressions of this hegemonic masculinity can change, but the identity it entails is the same. In sports, the structures and symbols that bind the imaginary communities together, that construct identity and belonging, are gendered – hence the ways in which gratification is found are themselves gendered. Gratification becomes something psychosocial, something associated with Butler's (2006) theory of heteronormativity. Satisfaction through taking part is replaced by the valorization of victory, the heterosexual, masculine conquest played out in ritual form. This does not mean that women cannot get pleasure from sports participation, and it does not mean that women cannot be keenly competitive or violent – but that pleasure is limited and constrained by the rules of heteronormativity. Satisfaction comes easy to men in sport, it is deemed natural for them to get enjoyment from taking part and showing off and winning (Messner, 1989). For women, finding pleasure from sports participation and sports competitions is conversely viewed as unusual, something to comment on as if it is an aberration of some essential femininity of some kind (Caudwell, 2007; Scraton, Caudwell and Holland, 2005).

The limits of gratification in sports embodiment

The modern Western cultural norm of the physically fit sporting body has led to the rapid expansion of gyms, private fitness centres and an industry of life coaches, consultants and con merchants selling the latest dieting fad. For some people, the practices of weight-lifting and conditioning are in themselves sources of gratification. People become addicted to beating their own targets for lifting heavier weights or repeating exercises. Some people enjoy the physicality of gaining muscle mass for its own sake. They move from being sports participants or keep-fit fanatics into the world of body-building. The sport of body-building is an aesthetic one: body-building champions win prizes because they are judged to have the right body shapes. There are strict guidelines for the judges about what shapes, sizes and types of muscle mass are under consideration in competitions. The point of a body-building contest is to celebrate the man or woman with the best muscles in their category, which is supposedly a celebration of the amount of work in the gym that body-builder has done. However, body-building athletes use a large number of unhealthy practices, over-the-counter supplements and (illegal) shape-enhancers to get those bodies (Monaghan, 2001). In the pursuit of what is considered to be an ideal sporting body, these body-builders all too often make their bodies unhealthy. Furthermore, in seemingly using a range of performance enhancers, body-builders may be making their success, and their gratification, of less value to their inner selves.

QUESTIONS TO CONSIDER

How is body-building truly aesthetic? How would you reform body-building?

REFERENCE AND FURTHER READING

Monaghan, L. (2001) 'Looking Good, Feeling Good: The Embodied Pleasures of Vibrant Physicality', *Sociology of Health and Illness*, 23, pp. 330–56.

I showed in Chapter 2 that historically, modern sport acted as a site for the expression and maintenance of hegemonic masculinity, but that the expressions of that hegemonic masculinity were contested between different groups inside sports: so working-class masculinity might be defined and limited in ways different from those associated with the construction of elite masculinity; and black masculinities might be constructed differently to white masculinities. In team sports there still is a conflict between more traditional expressions of masculinity such as bravado, fighting and heavy drinking, and expressions of masculinity associated with increasing professionalization (Kidd, 2013). It is a crucial point that this contest over how masculinity is expressed, and what it means to be a man, is not one between conflicting masculinities (Connell, 1987, 1995; Connell and Messerschmidt, 2005). Rather, it is a contest over defining how a normalized definition of 'man' – white, hegemonic, heterosexual, competitive – is to be expressed within particular spaces of sports and physical culture. In other words, what shapes the spaces where gratification is found are rules of expression within the particular language game (Wittgenstein, 1968) concerning hegemonic masculinity and its relationship with modern sport and modern physical culture.

So people might get some kind of gratification, but it is not a healthy form of gratification: it is the creation and normalization of a narrow form of hegemonic masculinity over any other psychosocially formed gender. It is an exclusionary and divisive form of embodiment. This form of gratification, then, cannot be inclusive. And this ties in to the other problem with the idea that sports give gratification, the exclusive nature of sports themselves and physical culture more generally. Access to most sports, and the cultural and physical capital needed, is limited to white, Western elites as well as to hegemonically masculine men. It is impossible to get satisfaction from sports experiences and physical culture if one does not have access to a sports facility, or one does not have the money for membership fees. It is doubly impossible if one belongs to the majority of the world's population that is structurally constrained by class, gender and/or ethnicity from accessing the privileged leisure spaces of the people in power. Even if gratification in sport was not something unhealthily connected to hegemonic masculinity, even if it was something that was good for people, it would still be something unattainable for the majority of the world's population.

CONCLUSION

We have considered two ways in which individual choice and individual participation in sports is fixed by the need to express different kinds of physicality, and the need to seek gratification in the practice of physical culture. Such choices and opportunities are limited by the social structures that constrain most of us in today's world. We might think we make choices about the physical culture we do, and how we construct our identities through embodiment and gratification. After all, this claim about physical culture is made in much of the sociological and cultural analyses of embodiment and gratification to be found in the academic literature. There is an argument that the world has changed sufficiently for identities to become fuzzy, and for belonging and exclusion to be associated only with questions of lifestyle. Embodiment is held up as proof of this dissolving of identity and structure, this shift to a new freedom of identity-making. Gratification is held up as proof of our freedom as agents to pick and choose the things we like, that the world has moved on from the world that created sports in the first place. This is the claim that the world, and leisure and sports, have become post-modern: that social structures and constraints have been removed enough for people to make choices about who they are, and what they do. This is a persuasive claim. After all, the world has changed dramatically in the last one hundred and fifty years or so: many Western societies have become post-industrial economically; political power has shifted with the rise of globalization; political freedoms and (gender and racial) equality have both been on the increase; and the internet and other technologies have changed the way many of us behave in our work and our leisure lives. Postmodernity seems to be something that is happening, at least to some of us. Is embodiment, then, a reflection of postmodernity? Is gratification postmodern? Is physical culture something postmodern? The answers are no, not necessarily. There are elements of embodiment, gratification and physical culture that might be viewed as postmodern, but the substance of sports, of gratification and embodiment remains fixed firmly in the instrumental, hegemonic structures that still constrain most of the world. Postmodern choice in sports and physical culture is only for the elites who have the power. In the next chapter we will look at the final set of claims about sport and well-being, and how they relate to the other positions on what sport is today, and the argument running through this book.

EXERCISES

1 How might sports-like activities have been a form of embodiment before the modern age?
2 What is the connection between body image, fashion and popular culture played out through sports celebrities?
3 Why is the gratification from playing tennis different to the gratification you might get from reading a poem?

Chapter 6

Sport and Wellbeing

SUMMARY OF TOPICS

- *Definitions: debates about wellbeing*
- *The problem of wellbeing*
- *Wellbeing, modern nation-states and policy-making*
- *Sport and policies for physical activity and health, and wellbeing*

If you have read this book from the beginning you will know by now that my chosen physical activity is running up and down the hills outside my home town. When I go for my run up onto the moors, I do it because I like it. I also run because I have been enculturated into this middle-class leisure activity. At the same time, the British government has spent millions of pounds encouraging people to take part in regular sports and physical activity. Part of the government's reason for this policy to get people doing sport is to reduce the cost to the National Health Service (see Chapter 7). But the government is interested in improving individual and social (what they call societal) wellbeing. When I reach the top of the hill and run past the cairns that guide me back down, do I thank the government for encouraging me to run? Do I even note the government's policy? And when I get back down the hill, do I write to my local Member of Parliament asking for a tax rebate, because I am helping the government meet its targets on regular sports participation? The government's policies on sport, physical activity and wellbeing are far from my mind when I run, and I don't think their advertising campaigns have influenced me at all. But I do think running is good for me.

In the last chapter I discussed embodiment and gratification, with a focus on the idea that we embody the policies and demands of the state when we do sports and other forms of physical activity. My reflection highlights the difficulty in identifying actual chains of logic between the cause of promoting sports and physical activity, and the effect of people doing such activity. This chapter begins with the well-aired claim that sports are good for people and that people should be encouraged to take part in sports because it will improve their wellbeing. This has already been explored in this book, particularly in the previous chapter (Chapter 5) on embodiment and gratification, but also in Chapters 3 and 4. In these other chapters I have discussed the moral and social benefits said to come to individuals and society from sports participation. This chapter builds on some of the discussions in those other chapters, but focuses on the debate about wellbeing. The chapter will explore debates in policy and community development about the value of sport as something that improves wellbeing. Sport's moral good and social good are again examined from a number of perspectives – from the evidence of sports and exercise science, to the claims made by politicians and philosophers that sports are good because they fix a number of moral, spiritual, social and political problems – to understand the wider debate about the role of the state and the role of the individual in improving wellbeing. The chapter will argue that wellbeing is a problematic term in itself, and it is impossible to say that sports improve it, but as we have previously seen, some people get some satisfaction from some sports and physical cultural activities. Before we explore what politicians and policy-makers might say about sport and its role in promoting wellbeing, it is necessary to understand and define wellbeing.

DEFINITIONS: DEBATES ABOUT WELLBEING

Wellbeing (or 'well-being' or 'well being', depending on which dictionary or custom you follow – I am following the Oxford English Dictionary spelling) is a neologism that owes its early twenty-first century popularity to the conflation of a number of contradictory trends. The first trend is the fashion for re-naming things that previously existed through the invention of meaningless terminology. Wellbeing is clearly what people in previous generations might have called mental and physical healthiness: the state of being where individuals feel they are well and happy, and where society is constructed in such a way as to promote happiness and quality of life for the greatest number of people. The second trend is the quantification and instrumentalization of modern nation-states. Wellbeing becomes something equated with happiness, and something that can be measured objectively inside and between nation-states. The third trend is the focus on individualism and spirituality implied by the 'everyday' use of wellbeing. Wellbeing is linked to my pleasure and happiness, my psychological state. So the term wellbeing becomes something to do with health and healthiness. It becomes something to do with policies, measurements and analogies with economic wellbeing (which is easily measured through profit and loss). And it becomes something about individuals and their mental states of being and their individual feelings.

Wellbeing in children: the benefits of active leisure

One of the ways in which wellbeing might be measured is through the construction of multiple survey tools that ask batteries of questions about what respondents feel about a range of topics. Typically, this might involve using a standard questionnaire around happiness that has been used in many other research projects and which is recognized as having some sort of rigour, alongside a questionnaire that gets respondents to respond to specific activities and how they feel about them. In this way researchers can correlate responses and test the probability of statements such as 'sports improve wellbeing'. Holder, Coleman and Sehn (2009) explore wellbeing in children through asking the young people in their research to fill in the Piers-Harris 2 questionnaire, which measures self-concept (what individuals feel about themselves), as well as the Faces Scale that measures happiness, alongside a separate questionnaire about their involvement in and feeling about different types of leisure (they also ask parents to fill in a questionnaire). Holder, Coleman and Sehn (2009) show that active leisure – physical activity, sports – is positively correlated with the wellbeing of the children in their study, whereas passive leisure (for example, watching television) is negatively correlated with wellbeing. The value of active leisure and sports to the children in their research is clear.

QUESTIONS TO CONSIDER

How would you design a project to see if active leisure could improve the wellbeing of children not engaged in these activities? How important is age in this?

REFERENCE AND FURTHER READING

Holder, M., Coleman, B. and Sehn, Z. (2009) 'The Contribution of Active and Passive Leisure to Children's Well-being', *Journal of Health Psychology*, 14, pp. 378–86.

Historically, in pre-modern cultures, wellbeing was the responsibility of kinship networks (Durkheim, 1997). Individuals had close relationships with others and there was a family interest in looking after each other as much as possible – at the expense of strangers and outsiders, or those who transgressed the norms and values of the culture. These networks were extended to the level of tribes in many pre-modern cultures, and the analogous family tie remained. As pre-modern cultures grew in size, the relationship between members of the cultures and the emerging rulers of those cultures evolved and changed: religions were established with clear rules about how to behave in the culture; and secular laws emerged that organized the obligations of the ruler(s) to those in their control. Wellbeing became measured through the number of adherents to sacred rules that guaranteed access to some after-life, or through the number of people who swore oaths or paid taxes. By the time of the Ancient Greek philosophers, it was taken as axiomatic that good rulers cared for the gods by building temples and taking part in sacred rites, and that the same good rulers proved their moral goodness by providing public works and fair laws for their citizens. The sacred and the secular were inseparable: the wellbeing of the state and its citizens was the outcome of acting properly in the sight of the gods. The idea of rulers acting according to divine instruction to bring about wellbeing was a powerful one, and still exists in many countries. In other countries, however, claims about the divine nature of rulership were diminished by the slow separation of the sacred and the secular: this is most apparent in the West, where modern nation-states have abandoned the notion that governments act in the name of God for the idea that they act on behalf of the people, or the constitution, or the rule of law. With the decline of the idea that God is keeping an eye on things, secular politicians have had to appeal to others to prove their worth and earn the right to stay in power: major corporations, other nation-states, established elites, the military and the citizens.

Why has wellbeing become so important in this century? Since the development of economics as a social science at the end of the eighteenth century, economists have built models of the success of different economic policies enacted by governments. Modern polities supposedly eschew warfare and violent confrontations for economic success. Since the end of the eighteenth century politicians and policy-makers have looked to economics to help them measure the success of particular fiscal policies. The financial impact of raising a particular tax has been modelled and reasonably successful predictions have been made. In the last century the development of global capitalism, and trans-national frameworks such as the United Nations and the World Bank, gave economics a central role in measuring the success of governments and nation-states. Countries are lined up in league tables of success against indicators such as the Gross Domestic Product (the amount of stuff produced per person). This economic model of wellbeing is well-established, and even now governments are said to be failing if they do not produce the expected financial results – their policies are judged to be a failure against the economic measures of prosperity.

The problem with economic measures of prosperity is they do not capture the overall fitness or wellness of a given population. The classic example is the mean annual salary in Western countries such as the United Kingdom and the United States. Look those indicators up and it seems like the 'average' annual salaries look quite good for most people. But this is a mistake. These salaries are mean values – they include the small proportion of people who earn huge sums of money, people like merchant bankers, movie stars, professional football players and the like. When you take out those very untypical high earners you see that the vast majority of the population in those countries live on very small annual salaries, with a significant number of those people struggling to pay their bills and get enough money to pay for the weekly food costs (Wilkinson and Pickett, 2009). A government following an instrumental ethics would not care about this fact – for governments pursuing narrow goals and objectives, the wellbeing of its citizens may well be low on its list of priorities. But most governments are interested in some citizens' wellbeing, and interested in the wellbeing of the masses, because this often serves the interests of those in power (governments interested in the wellbeing of the masses in such a way are also being instrumental, for instance believing happy citizens equal more economically productive citizens). Economic indicators of wellbeing do not translate easily into how good a government is doing, and how well the lives of the majority of the population might be.

In a dictatorship or a feudal monarchy or oligarchy, especially those where there is no urban middle class to challenge the elites, the people who have power might not actually care at all about the impact of their policies on the masses. But modern, democratic nation-states do have urban middle classes, elections and public spheres (newspapers and other media free from state control) where policies are challenged (Beck, 1998). Demonstrating the efficacy of policies, then, is more important than ever in modern nation-states. Policy-making becomes an exercise in utilitarianism, where governments try to demonstrate to the citizens that they are acting *in the interests of the citizens* rather than in the interests of the state. This means they need to show that their actions have positive consequences in a utilitarian sense: ensuring the most benefit to the most people. This is where we come back to wellbeing. In modern nation-states, people can judge the success of government policies that have an impact on them directly, but they can also investigate – through the public sphere – and find out the success of policies on the nation as a whole. In turn, policy-makers can use wellbeing as a measure of the success of their policies. How happy are the citizens, as a result of a particular government policy? How healthy are the citizens? How satisfied are the citizens? These three questions touch on facets of wellbeing as we understand it today. While there are attempts to agree models and mechanisms to survey happiness and satisfaction, and some research is underway, these two indicators of individual and social wellbeing are subjective (Thin, 2012). There is a problem of the ontological status of happiness, just as there is for satisfaction (which was discussed in Chapter 5). It is not clear whether subjective reporting of feelings of happiness can be aggregated and compared to build up a notional, national picture of happiness. Furthermore, even if we could agree on a standard model and unit of measurement of happiness, and we solved the problem of subjective reporting, how could we be certain that an increase in reported happiness was the result of a particular policy?

The third measure of wellbeing is health. Here we might feel we are more secure in making claims about the impact of policies on wellbeing. Modern, scientific medicine has been a huge success story, and has improved the lives of millions since the advances in techniques and technologies in the nineteenth and twentieth centuries. Alongside improvements in patient care and survival rates in hospitals, public health was transformed in modern nation-states in the nineteenth century with the construction of systems that brought clean water to the majority of citizens and took away waste water to be treated (Schultz and McShane, 1978). As scientists and doctors found cures for some diseases, populations were inoculated against these diseases through enormous, often compulsory programmes; and some foodstuffs were fortified by nutrients to ensure children and others at risk of malnourishment got the things they needed to live healthy lives (Bishai and Nalubola, 2002). All these public health policies resulted in diseases and other illnesses disappearing or diminishing. In short, these interventions in public health resulted in huge improvements in the biological wellbeing of individuals and populations.

That said, there are reasons to be cautious about assuming biological, physical healthiness always results in an improvement in wellbeing. And we should be wary of accepting the myth of the success of modern medicine too easily. Foucault (1991, 2006) has shown how the medicalization of madness was a strategy by scientists and doctors to take control of a range of forms of human expression. Medicine has become part of the instrumentalization of modernity, an industry and system that dehumanizes individuals and exists to make profits and keep power, while maintaining a veneer of independence and objectivity. Until the end of the twentieth century, public health interventions routinely took place whether people consented to them or not (Cross and Carton, 2003). In this century, pharmaceutical companies have inordinate influence over doctors and patients, and hundreds of things that are just part of being human – feeling unloved, feeling confused, feeling tired – have been medicalized and turned into disorders with pills we can buy to supposedly cure them (Goldacre, 2012).

Paralympism, medicalization and the negation of wellbeing

The 'common-sense' view of the Paralympics is that it promotes wellbeing – it encourages the inclusion of people with disabilities in sport, it provides sporting success, it provides role models for people with disabilities, and it reduces exclusion and marginalization. Peers (2012) uses Foucault to examine the rhetoric and discourse of the Paralympic movement through history. She shows that the foundation of the Paralympic movement was predicated on the medicalization of disability and the social construction of disability through the 'freak show'. As the Paralympic movement struggled for credibility and recognition it was shaped by elitist notions of class, gender and visibility. Paralympic sports were places where abnormality could be viewed and savoured, where body shapes that were deemed to be 'freakish' could be viewed alongside the technologies of wheelchairs, prosthetics and other devices. As Paralympism gained recognition from the wider sports world it created new ways of testing, monitoring and classifying athletes, objectifying and dehumanizing them. Rather than promoting people with disabilities and athletes with disabilities as being equal in worth to others, it has normalized the view that they are worth less: athletes with disabilities perform in separate competitions, and the Paralympics becomes a spectacle where people can gasp with a mixture of horror and sympathy at the poor victims. This is a negation of wellbeing: it is bad for the athletes who provide the spectacle, and bad for us who indulge in the charade.

QUESTIONS TO CONSIDER

What is the role of commercialization in this? What is the role of the media?

REFERENCE AND FURTHER READING

Peers, D. (2012) 'Patients, Athletes, Freaks: Paralympism and the Reproduction of Disability', *Journal of Sport and Social Issues*, 36, pp. 295–316.

The medical model of wellbeing leads politicians and policy-makers to pump more money into public health and medicine and to cheer when the population lives longer. While there have been successes in modern medicine, there are limits to its knowledge and skills. We might be able to make our populations older, but is that good? Do we want to live a hundred years, with the last thirty in the fog of dementia and the pain of physical breakdowns? Are we truly happier if we follow that path – or are we happier if we die at the age of sixty after a life spent smoking cigarettes? The fact that the medical model of well-being is the one that is dominant is demonstrated by the debate in the public sphere: you might prefer to smoke and die young, but no politician would dare to say something like that on the news, because the pursuit of improving our health means we must do everything the doctors tell us to, even if it means we live a mean, un-lived life. Medical ethics tells us all lives are sacred and we must do everything to keep people alive – here the medical ethic follows the religious one – so even where people would prefer to be killed than to suffer a long, drawn-out, terminal illness, there is public anger and legal challenge. Wellbeing, then, has been hijacked by a medical hegemony that reifies physical biological wellbeing – which is easy to measure – over any other form of mental, social or cultural wellbeing – which is not readily quantifiable.

SPORT, POLICIES FOR PHYSICAL ACTIVITY AND HEALTH, AND WELLBEING

Modern nation-states all have some feeling of obligation or duty to their citizens, enshrined in constitutions, laws and other contracts between the rulers and the ruled. All nation-states provide public services and regulate services that exist in the private sector. In most nation-states, health and welfare (like education and defence) are the responsibility of the state, delivered or commissioned directly by the government (Baldwin, 1990; Coalter, 2007, 2013; Houlihan, 1991; Jacoby, 1997; Thin, 2012). Some nation-states such as the United States have a minimalist approach to health and welfare, leaving the wellbeing of most citizens to the voluntary and private sectors, and funding only basic welfare for those who slip through the net of the insurance industry – though of course at times in its history the federal government of the United States has been more 'welfarist', such as the era of the New Deal (Jacoby, 1997). In Eastern Europe and the Soviet Union in the twentieth century, the communist state-systems planned and supported a plethora of sports and leisure activities, and promoted state control of services (Riordan, 1991). In Western Europe in the twentieth century (and in places such as Canada, New Zealand and Australia), a consensus emerged among politicians that the state needed to take a more direct role in the health and welfare and life of its citizens – this was the era of the formation of the British National Health Service, and the social democratic compact in Sweden and Germany (Baldwin, 1990). Sport, leisure and recreation were seen as activities that needed to be supported, delivered and funded by the public sector, along with arts and culture. This interest in welfare and wellbeing in the second half of the twentieth century was related directly to the articulation of human rights in the United Nations' Universal Declaration of Rights, which states that welfare and wellbeing are rights that everyone should be entitled to expect from national governments, alongside education and equality and such like. Written by a committee chaired by Eleanor Roosevelt the text has thirty articles, among which are the following (http://www.un.org/en/documents/ udhr/, accessed 10 May 2014):

> Article 22. Everyone, as a member of society, has the right to social security and is entitled to realization, through national effort and international co-operation and in accordance with the organization and resources of each State, of the economic, social and cultural rights indispensable for his dignity and the free development of his personality.
>
> ...
>
> Article 24. Everyone has the right to rest and leisure, including reasonable limitation of working hours and periodic holidays with pay.
>
> Article 25 (Part I). Everyone has the right to a standard of living adequate for the health and well-being of himself and of his family, including food, clothing, housing and medical care and necessary social services, and the right to security in the event of unemployment, sickness, disability, widowhood, old age or other lack of livelihood in circumstances beyond his control.

Article 22 gave nation-states the responsibility of providing welfare and resources to enable people to develop as individuals; Article 24 specified leisure as a key human right; and Article 25 made nation-states responsible for ensuring the rights of individuals around health and wellbeing. In France and the United Kingdom, local councils became key providers of sports programmes and facilities (Houlihan, 1991). Sports participation was promoted alongside the construction of sports and leisure facilities – which had already been happening in modern nation-states at the height of modernity (Spracklen, 2013a). In the late nineteenth century, local councils and officials in the West started a global trend of building parks for recreational use. These parks would have bowling greens, children's play areas, walkways, gardens, green fields for sports, ponds for bathing, and bandstands. The people who built these public parks believed in the positive power of recreation – they believed everybody had a right to enjoy what was called rational recreation, civilized forms of leisure that had an uplifting function (McDonald, 1984). This belief that leisure and rational recreation had a useful function led to the construction of public libraries, public baths, and local stadia for team sports and athletics. Making this infrastructure available for public use, went the argument, would make people undertake proper recreation: activities that would make them better people.

Sports were seen as one part of a wider sphere of leisure activities that were good for the welfare of citizens: playing sport was as important as reading a book, or going to a museum. Leisure itself was as important for citizens in the plans of policy-makers as going to school or being cured of some illness (Henry, 1993). National sports organizations were created and funded by government grants to promote sports participation, and national governing bodies of individual sports were funded by governments in return for delivering state priorities (Houlihan, 1991). There were controversies over the amount of money used to fund sports, and debates over how to spend the money fairly – and whether you got more people taking part in sport by funding elite sports and success at big events, or funding grassroots provision (the debate about whether sporting success generates more interest) – but there was a consensus that sports were a key part of leisure that needed to be provided for by the state. Sports and physical activity were seen as key ways to improve public health, and policies were created to promote both formal sports participation and involvement in other forms of physical activity such as walking (Coalter, 2013; Henry, 1993; Houlihan, 1991).

By the first decade of this century, however, such state-funded sports provision, and sports delivery by local councils, was under threat from funding cuts and an emerging neo-liberal view of the role of the state (which argues that the state should not deliver services, and should only be a commissioner of services from organizations in the private sector). This neo-liberal trend collided with the global financial crisis that started in 2008, which brought more funding cuts in many nation-states, with sports and leisure services targeted as particular 'marginal' activities compared to things like hospitals and schools. While sports and leisure services continue to be funded in some countries such as Finland, in others public sector sports delivery and funding has diminished (Coalter, 2013). In this new world of neo-liberalism, how do sports providers, workers and policy-makers demonstrate to governments that their funding should not be cut? Wellbeing seems to be the way to make the case for maintaining funding for sports.

Many nation-states, following the lead of trans-national organizations, have started to measure the wellbeing of their citizens using a range of measures and indicators. Sports participation is being used as both a proxy indicator of wellbeing (feeling happy and secure and having free time to be able to participate – wellbeing leads to sports participation) and a direct indicator of wellbeing (sports participation makes you physically and mentally healthier – sports participation leads to wellbeing). The Office for National Statistics (ONS), which works for the government of the United Kingdom, was commissioned by politicians early in this century to define and measure 'societal well-being'. The indicators and measures used to assess wellbeing were identified across a broad range of categories, and relied on self-reporting of satisfaction and security and leisure and how much sense of community people feel they have, as well as objective measures such as healthiness, financial status, employment status and the environment. Some of these statistics were collected specifically for the survey of wellbeing but others were already present in other surveys managed by the ONS or other government agencies. In a review of the measures it uses to assess wellbeing in 2012 and 2013, it was decided to include sports participation as a key indicator of the likelihood of 'wellbeing'. In the explanation for including sport, along with arts and culture, the ONS also explained why it was removing one of the measures about leisure it had previously used. It is worthwhile reading this explanation at length (http://www.ons.gov.uk/ons/rel/wellbeing/measuring-national-well-being/domains-and-measures---may-2013/review-of-domains-and-measures-of-national-well-being.html#tab-What-we-do, accessed 10 May 2014):

> The measure, 'Percentage who were somewhat, mostly or completely satisfied with their use of leisure time' has been removed as this question is not asked on the Understanding Society, the UK Household Longitudinal Study (UKHLS), which replaces the previous source, the British Household Panel Survey (BHPS). It is also considered to overlap with the 'satisfaction with amount of leisure time' measure. The most commonly requested additions during the consultation were measures to reflect arts, culture and sport. ONS had previously excluded these measures due to lack of UK data for these topics. However, ONS have been convinced by the weight of evidence in favour of including measures to reflect these areas... Consideration was given as to whether the measure should separate arts and culture or combine them and whether a combined measure would prove too broad a measure to be meaningful. Another consideration was whether the measure should cover engagement or participation... It was also acknowledged that the measures of well-being were incomplete without some measure of sports participation. The proposed measure is the percentage of respondents who had done 30 minutes or more of moderate intensity sport at least once a week in the last four weeks of being interviewed (note that recreational walking and cycling is excluded). The measure selected was based upon the advice of the DCMS and Sport England.

The ONS argues that the measure assessing satisfaction about the use of leisure time overlaps with the measure assessing satisfaction at the amount of leisure time. This can easily be shown to be an over-confident claim. The measures are two completely different things. One might be over-worked but one might have the money and cultural capital to do something meaningful in one's leisure time. One might have an enormous amount of leisure time because one is unemployed, underemployed or retired from work – but one still might be unhappy about the types of leisure activities one pursues. This is actually a real problem for the wellbeing of a significant proportion of the population, but it is not difficult to see why the government wants to drop the measure: the increasing number of underemployed people is an effect of the neo-liberal economy, people on flexible contracts (zero-hour contracts) on minimum wages, and waiting around all day and filling in here and there at short notice means the use of that leisure time will never be satisfying.

The introduction of a sports participation measure shows that the ONS believes the arguments made by the Department for Culture, Media and Sport (DCMS) and the quasi-government agency Sport England that regular sports participation improves health and wellbeing. There was a strong lobby during the review stage from the sports world and supporters of sport in the media and in politics (Coalter, 2013). It was argued that sports and physical activity improved wellbeing; it was also argued that sports participation was a strong *indicator* of wellbeing (making sports participation its own cause and effect, and making the problem of causation disappear with a flash of semantics). The inclusion of arts and culture is also problematic in this same way – is it a measure of how many people are satisfied enough with the rest of their lives to be able to enjoy something artistic or cultural? Or is doing something artistic and cultural something that creates wellbeing? There is no doubt that arts and culture, like sports and physical culture, have some transformative value. But all these leisure activities need considerable amounts of social, economic and cultural capital to be able to appreciate them and gain benefits from partaking in them: it is those who are already satisfied with their lives – because they don't have to struggle to pay their bills, because they already have access to knowledge and skills and the right symbols and networks – who get the benefit.

The sports participation measure itself is the one that Sport England already collects through its Active People Survey (participation rates for Scotland, Northern Ireland and Wales are collected through other surveys). This measure sets the participation rate and involvement quite low – one short session per week of something self-reported as moderate intensity. It is arguable that such a low participation rate, at such a potentially low intensity, might not actually make much difference to the health of those taking part (biological benefits from physical activity seem to come from sustained, intensive and frequent participation), and it is doubtful whether the psychological benefits of such physical activity would be long-term (see the references in Chapters 4 and 5 of this book). Strangely, recreational walking and cycling are removed from this measure, even though there is evidence that regular participation in both these things has clear health benefits (see discussion of both in Pucher and Dijkstra, 2003). So it is not altogether clear what use the measure serves, other than a proxy indicator to measure sports participation against other countries (rivalry between nation-states on such measures is quite common, and as I have already mentioned, every modern nation-state is interested in wellbeing, and every nation-state's sports lobby has put sports on the wellbeing agenda) and an indicator to show who feels 'well' enough to engage in sports. The things that might improve wellbeing in physical culture are not actually being measured: the psychological states associated with any sustained physical activity and the biological benefits associated with intensive and frequent activity.

Sport, health and wellbeing policies in Australia

Fullagar's (2002) study of the recent history of policies towards health and wellbeing in Australia shows the shifting priorities of the country. In the 1960s, and into the 1970s, the Australian government became concerned with rising rates of cardio-vascular diseases, and promoted physical activity as a direct solution to this health problem. Funding was invested in physical activity programmes because the government was fearful about the risk of Australian men being less fit than their Asian counterparts. The panic about national fitness was a reflection of the wider political panic about immigration and the rise of Asian countries as economic rivals to Australia. In the 1970s, the policy focus around physical activity shifted to promoting such activity as part of an individual's quality of life. Individuals were seen as choosing to be healthy or unhealthy. The government's task became that of instructing people to take control of their own lives so that they would become proper members of the healthy nation. This was a neo-liberal agenda that reified choice and individual responsibility, and which negated the role of the state in providing healthy activities and regulating the food industry. Fullagar (2002) uses Foucault's concept of governmentality (see the previous chapter) to show that this shift made individual citizens responsible for the embodiment of the state's policies, monitoring their own behaviour and the behaviour of others.

QUESTIONS TO CONSIDER

What other factors were at work in making and changing these policies? How much influence does the state have in shaping our lives today?

REFERENCE AND FURTHER READING

Fullagar, S. (2002) 'Governing the Healthy Body: Discourses of Leisure and Lifestyle within Australian Health Policy', *Health*, 6, pp. 69–84.

CONCLUSION

The problem with using sports participation as a way of improving the wellbeing of individuals is partly the result of the problem with understanding wellbeing itself. Governments and policy-makers want to demonstrate that they care for their citizens; or that their policies improve the lives of their citizens – wellbeing then becomes a utilitarian ideal, where the greatest good of the greatest number is sought out. But how do you measure that goodness or happiness? Wellbeing is a problematic term in itself, and it is impossible to say that sports improve it. It could be that the people who already feel they live 'well' lives are the ones who are likely to take part in sports and other forms of physical culture: the measurements then become a way of confirming that those with most power, wealth and freedom are the ones who are taking part in sports. If you feel secure in life, you will feel happy, you will do more constructive leisure activities, such as sports, the arts and communicative leisure; if you are insecure in life, you will feel stressed and possibly unhappy, and you will not engage in meaningful leisure activities, nor will you use your leisure time productively. As we have previously seen, some people do get some sort of satisfaction from some sports and physical cultural activities – and physical activity is something that can improve people's biological, physical health. Sports and physical activity can be a great solace and a great source of enjoyment for people who participate. So perhaps the people who benefit right now from physical culture, the ones who get the improvement of their wellbeing, are the elites of our nation-states, the people with power – and the overall wellbeing of humanity is left unaltered as those with limited power (or no power at all) derive no benefit from physical culture. In the next part of the book, we will consider some problems in understanding sport, and exploring sport in society. We will begin, in the next chapter, with a subject related to wellbeing and sport's role in it: the obesity 'epidemic'.

EXERCISES

1 How is wellbeing in Islamic nation-states grounded in Islamic ethics? How has religion informed wellbeing in India, Japan and China?
2 What sports might be bad for personal or societal wellbeing? Explain why.
3 Which is more important – a long life or a good life? Discuss.

Part II

Problems

Chapter 7

The Obesity Epidemic

SUMMARY OF TOPICS

▨ Definitions: *fat, weight, mass, overweight, obese*
▨ *Obesity as a modern-day moral panic and claims made about the extent of the problem*
▨ *The evidence for obesity*
▨ *Obesity as a policy issue and the social construction of obesity*

If I did not go running, I would put on weight. I don't eat anything with too many calories in it, I'm actually a vegetarian and I'm quite fussy about the things I like to eat. But I do like to drink real ale and whisky, two alcoholic drinks that are notoriously bad for causing their drinkers to develop paunches. In the past, when I played rugby and went running, I didn't need to worry about the calories in all the social drinking that went on around me. Now, even with my regular physical activity, I have a little bit of a beer belly. In my family, on both my mother and father's side, I have had relatives who have been medically assessed 'overweight' or 'obese' and who have suffered poor health because of that weight (there is a 'medical history', to use the jargon). So I know there is a real potential of health problems of my own if I am not conscious about the exercise I do and the things I eat and drink. We all know people in our lives who we think are overweight, fat or obese, or we have seen people on our streets, at our universities, or on our television screens, who we think fit the image of someone who is fat.

In my reflection, I confess to worrying about my weight. Many other people in the West seem to feel the same anxieties. In the last chapter I discussed sport and wellbeing in general, and government policies aiming to improve lives. This chapter will use the 'problem' of obesity as a starting point for a wider historical, philosophical and sociological analysis of sport and physical culture. The obesity epidemic is supposedly a problem in the West that some academics claim is due to falling rates of sports participation. The chapter will explore the evidence for the obesity epidemic, and introduce critical analyses of the epidemic from sociology and philosophy. The chapter will argue that the obesity epidemic is an example of how moral panics and myths combine with prejudices to establish scientific research agendas. It will be argued that sports and physical culture lose their communicative value when they become mixed up with the politics of blame.

DEFINITIONS: FAT, WEIGHT, MASS, OVERWEIGHT, OBESE

Fats are naturally occurring chemical compounds that play a variety of roles in biochemistry, and which have also been used in the modern chemical industry. Fat is part of life for mammals. Fatness is just a measure of the amount of fatty tissue (adipose tissue) an animal might have in its body. Some parts of the body might be predominantly made of fatty tissue, some might be partially fatty and some might be considered to be fatty on a temporary basis. Humans as animals have bodies that can be described in exactly the same way: humans have layers of fat that act as energy storage and protection against the weather, and have lots of other vital functions (Trayhurn and Beattie, 2001). There is a range of genetic variation when it comes to the amount of fat individual humans might have in their bodies, and a range of environmental factors that might decrease or increase the amount of fat. So people might be genetically more likely to be fat or thin, but also the things we do – the foods we eat and the activities we do – have an important bearing on whether we are fat or thin. The more we eat, the more calories we consume, the more likely it is we will create fat deposits; and the more we exercise our bodies in any way, the more we burn calories, the less likely we will have fat deposits.

Fat becomes something other than a fact about the human body when humans decide that fatness beyond some given level is a medical, social and cultural problem. In contemporary Western popular culture, and in the public sphere of political discourse, there is a prevailing opinion that says everyone has an 'ideal' body weight – and people who are over that ideal are deemed to be 'overweight'. The number of people who are overweight has become a problem to be solved. Obesity has become another name for being seriously overweight, and it is used in popular discussions about diet, health and exercise in ways that differ from its clinical definition (Gard and Wright, 2001, 2005). When people are described as being obese there is an assumption that they are seriously overweight to the point that they have all kinds of health problems. When weight is used in this popular definition of being fat, it is of course body mass that is being measured and judged. People who are overweight or obese are also often seen as having abnormal body shapes (Gard and Wright, 2005; Wachs and Chase, 2013).

There are philosophical problems in this 'lightweight' account of obesity, all of which will be returned to throughout this chapter. The first problem is the problem of definition, what has been described in other chapters of this book as a problem of ontology. Everybody knows what obesity is, and everybody knows it is being overweight in some way. There have been medical definitions of obesity, but these have not always captured the sense of being dangerously overweight, and the sense that obesity is something that is dangerous. Furthermore, when scientists, politicians and people in the street talk about obesity, they do not always seem to mean the same thing. Scientists with a direct research interest in the matter, like medical practitioners, have strict definitions of obesity. Other researchers might use the term more loosely, and politicians and people in the street might use it completely erroneously and egregiously when in fact they mean something else. The second problem is one associated with causation. There is a consensus that being obese somehow causes ill health, and doing physical activity causes bodies to become less obese. Both these assumptions about causes and their effects are not necessarily the case, and certainly not as simple as the claims might suggest. Obesity might be a factor in ill health, or a symptom of ill health, but it might not have a necessary causal link to ill health. Similarly, doing regular exercise might improve elements of health but might not in itself reduce obesity or ill health overall. The third problem is related to that of causation, and is the epistemological problem of proving something to be the case, demonstrating some theory or claim to be true in all possible cases. This is the problem of induction or generalization. The famous eighteenth-century Enlightenment philosopher David Hume (1978) said that no matter how many times we might make an observation about something being the case, it is logically invalid to say that something is true for all people at all times (including the future). So, for example, if we have observed that the sun rises in the east every morning of our lives, and we have read that other people have made the same observation, we might think it is easy to predict that the sun will rise in the east tomorrow. But Hume says we cannot make that claim without assuming the regularity of the universe. Scientists may have found some correlation between obesity, (lack of) exercise and ill health in some people; but there are potentially insurmountable problems in finding valid reasons for truth-claims to be extended to the human population at large. Scientists try to solve the problem of induction by developing statistical analyses of probabilities (another way to solve the problem might be designing experiments that show some truth-claim to be false, which is what Popper says is the core of scientific method – see Popper, 2005), but the caution of risk and chance in scientific findings is often changed in the translation from academic research to policy and the media. The final problem is that of representation and modelling. What is obesity meant to represent? What is the relationship between fat, mass, ill health, body measurements and models of obesity?

Healthy eating and sport and exercise science

Sports science has taken an interest in nutrition for many years, but this interest was fuelled by elite sports and their search for the best diets for their athletes. Scientists discovered optimum combinations of various vitamins, sugars and other substances; explored timings for loading carbohydrates, proteins and fats for training and for competition in particular sports; and explored the importance of hydration. A significant proportion of research on nutrition in sport and exercise science remains focused on elite athletes. However, sport and exercise scientists have started to take an interest in healthy eating among the wider population, and research has taken place exploring how best to encourage healthy lifestyles – a combination of increased physical activity and better diet – among groups that are perceived to be most at risk from ill health associated with inactivity and poor diet. In applying sport and exercise science to the wider population, the confident knowledge-claims about nutrition and obesity in the artificial setting of elite sport are tempered by a more cautious approach to understanding how the real world works. Elite athletes routinely accept the instructions of scientists and coaches, eating and drinking whatever is given to them, but in the wider population people are suspicious of scientists and other professionals. Archbold, Richardson and Dugdill's (2009) research has explored how to get families involved in healthy eating through involving them in the process of research and the process of designing interventions. The research eschews the lab-based, quantitative research of elite sports science for qualitative research methods: ethnography, pictures, diaries and conversations.

QUESTIONS TO CONSIDER

How would you design a programme to improve diets? How else can public health programmes benefit from sports science research?

REFERENCE AND FURTHER READING

Archbold, V., Richardson, D. and Dugdill, L. (2009) 'Looking beyond Parametric Measures to Understand Children and Families Physical Activity Behaviours: An Ethnographic Approach', *Journal of Science and Medicine in Sport*, 12 (Supplement), S77.

OBESITY: WHAT THE PAPERS SAY THE DOCTORS, SCIENTISTS AND SPORTS SCIENTISTS SAY, AND WHAT THE RESEARCH ACTUALLY SAYS

It seems like a new media story about the increasing obesity epidemic, the crisis of ill health plaguing Western countries, appears every day. It has become taken as true that young people are not exercising and becoming obese. There is a crisis now, or just on the horizon. The populations of the USA or the UK or Australia or any other rich, Western nation-state are said to be a nation of inactive couch potatoes, with levels of physical activity at a dangerously unhealthy level. Children and adults alike are chastened for being obese or overweight, and it is always predicted that this will become a huge burden to the state in future years, as all sorts of chronic diseases emerge in later life. For instance, my daily newspaper here in the United Kingdom told me that 'Doctors sound alarm on child fitness and health' (*The Guardian*, 22 August 2013, p. 3). The story cited research published in a medical journal about the amount of exercise undertaken by the young people in the study. Almost half of the participants in the research were found to be 'sedentary' for six hours *per diem*. In a two-month period following the story, there were eighteen similar stories posted on the newspaper website.

The first new report mentioned is a classic story of its type – a conflation of one report's findings about the amount of inactive time spent by children in one piece of research, inflated into a story about the epidemic of obese, unhealthy children being 'glued' to their computers and televisions. Modern life, modern families and modernity itself are blamed for ruining children's future lives, even though these children will almost certainly live far longer on average than their parents and grandparents. You might think this is just tabloid journalism by an irresponsible newspaper, but *The Guardian* is a well-respected, liberal broadsheet that is known for its award-winning investigative journalism. All newspapers, news channels and websites are guilty of reporting in sensational terms on obesity: the media in general has a poor record at understanding scientific research and reporting on it accurately (Goldacre, 2008).

These stories have been popular in the media since the 1990s, but the panic about obesity really took hold in the first decade of this century. There are too many to mention any but a couple of illustrative examples. In *The Guardian* again, a story in 2005 combined the newspaper's liberal critique of cuts to the British National Health Service (which should in theory provide its free services equitably without moral judgements about who is worthy of help) with the obesity crisis – in the story, we are told that in one area there are no free new hip-joints for the obese, or those who have a Body Mass

Index (BMI) of more than 30 ('NHS cash crisis bars knee and hip replacements for the obese', *The Guardian*, 23 November 2005, p. 4). In the right-wing newspaper *The Daily Mail* the obesity crisis has become almost a daily ritual of wailing and bemoaning the state of the nation. The newspaper campaigns against political correctness, Europe, immigration and sexual freedoms. It too has tried to find ways of connecting the fear of obese teenagers doing unhealthy (and immoral) leisure activities with the fate of the country's position in the world. In a 2006 story we find out unsurprisingly that the newspaper thinks that the obese 'couch potato' generation is not fit for the army, but also that 'political correctness' is forcing the British Army to accept overweight recruits ('Army forced to admit clinically obese because of recruiting crisis', *The Daily Mail*, 2 November 2006, on-line at http://www.dailymail.co.uk/news/article-414154/Army-forced-admit-clinically-obese-recruiting-crisis.html, accessed 10 May 2014).

The BMI mentioned above is the way in which obesity is most often measured in doctors' surgeries and hospitals, and it has been the most common measure used in much of the health and sports science research. Body Mass Index is calculated by dividing body weight (kilograms) by height (metres) squared. An adult BMI of between 25 and 29.9 is classified as overweight and a BMI of 30 or over is classified as obese. When it is used in children BMI has to be modified to take account of differing growth-rates. BMI is a model that provides an indirect measure of fatness. In this it is similar to measuring the ratio of waist to hips. There are direct measures of fatness that can be used in scientific research and medical tests: skin-fold thickness, measuring the waist circumference, and bio-impedance (which uses measurements of conductivity of human body tissue to estimate the proportion of lean tissue against fatty tissue). While it is reasonably clear that these latter measures do actually provide a reliable indicator for fatness and obesity, the BMI is much more problematic (Griffiths, Gately, Marchant and Cooke, 2012). It is possible to be assessed as clinically obese by the BMI measure through having a body shape that is muscular, stocky and short. Many athletes and people doing sports and physical activity that increase muscle mass will be obese on the BMI measure, which is clearly ridiculous (Gard and Wright, 2005). But the measure also claims people are clinically obese where they might not look like the stereotype of the enormously fat person sitting on the couch. BMI creates an epidemic or crisis that might not exist: people who measure as obese under the BMI test might not be leading unhealthy lives, and might not be at risk of illness and early death in later life (the evidence suggests that people are in fact living longer in most Western countries).

However, there is a prevalent consensus in science and medicine that people (at least, those in the West) have been getting fatter since the last century (increasing in overall mass and increasing in the proportion of fatty tissue), with an increase in the proportion of people who are clinically defined as 'obese' (Rokholm, Baker and Sorensen, 2010). It is generally agreed that this is a modern phenomenon, linked with changes in diet and lifestyle in the West (that is, it is not 'people' who are becoming obese, but the relatively affluent people of the developed world). People in the West are consuming more processed foods, and eating more calories and fat in their diets (Poston and Foreyt, 1999). People are relatively richer so they eat more food, but have less time to prepare their own food, so they buy calorie-rich products in supermarkets. People walk less than their grandparents or great-grandparents did, as driving cars has become the normal way to move from place to place in Western countries. At the same time, Western societies have become post-industrial: strenuous work in factories has been replaced by employment where people sit at their desks. There may be other causal factors behind the increased incidence of obesity, such as genetic or biological factors – but these are not primary causes of the fact that people do seem to be larger. It is the structure of the society in which we live, and the decisions we make (or are able to make) about how many calories we consume, and how many we burn, that are the primary causes of the phenomenon.

Drivin' along in my automobile: how the West became a car park

At the end of the nineteenth century, the internal combustion engine had been invented, and automobile and trucks were being produced for markets around the world, but it was not clear that they would become the undisputed winners in the twentieth-century struggle over roads and transportation systems. City roads were still being built for pedestrians and horse traffic or trams, cross-country roads were poorly maintained and suitable only for horse-drawn coaches, and inter-urban transport meant steam trains and ferries. Automobiles were an expensive luxury, driven only by the trend-setting elites who could afford to pay for the rare and expensive petroleum oil that powered the engines. Many cities created policies that banned private automobiles from their streets, or carefully regulated their use; most governments legislated to force cars to drive at very low speeds (Norton, 2008). After the First World War, thousands of ex-soldiers returned to their home towns with the knowledge of how to drive motor vehicles, which they had learned in the military as drivers of trucks. These military vehicles were sold cheaply on the market. Finally, cheaper sources of oil were discovered, and became key elements of the British and American economies. In the first half of the twentieth century, the automobile and truck industry lobbied intensively to challenge policies and laws that restricted their use. They were successful at making city planners and legislators make streets primarily for motor vehicles, with pedestrians forced to move to the side. After the Second World War, owning an automobile became a mass-market dream, a key moment in the lives of American teenagers, and other countries followed this fashion, abandoning their trams and trains and building huge, multi-lane roads.

QUESTIONS TO CONSIDER

How has automobile culture worsened public health? How is this culture being challenged in this century?

REFERENCE AND FURTHER READING

Norton, P. (2008) *Fighting Traffic: The Dawn of the Motor Age in the American City*, Cambridge, MIT Press.

Sports scientists and physical educationists are playing a key role in arguing that the rise in obesity is linked to an associated decline in sport and physical activity (Gard and Wright, 2001). In the literature and in the media, sports academics and advocates have continually argued that obesity can be tackled by sports and recreation programmes, just as they have argued for the importance of physical activity in promoting health and wellbeing (as we have seen in the previous chapter). Promoting the use of sport and physical activity as a 'cure' for obesity is popular among politicians, journalists and sports administrators, who eagerly publicize any sports science research that makes such a causal link (Sallis, Carlson, Mignano, Lemes and Wagner, 2013). My own university is at the forefront of tackling child obesity through targeted intervention and physical activity – Professor Paul Gately's high-profile Weight-Loss Camp has managed to achieve both short-term and long-term targets about reducing weight and making the children who have been through the course more active and more aware about diet (Griffiths, Gately, Marchant and Cooke, 2012). What the science actually shows is that tackling obesity is not as easy as might be supposed. There are many factors that make an individual obese, and many ways in which that individual might lose that excess mass. Close, targeted coaching and mentoring about a good diet and sustainable and enjoyable physical activity do seem to work for some people. But this intervention at the level of the individual does not tackle the real causes of 'obesity'.

OBESITY AS A POLICY ISSUE: THE SOCIAL CONSTRUCTION OF OBESITY

Obesity, then, is increasingly seen as 'epidemic' in the West, a problem of modern society: too many children doing nothing but drinking pop and watching television. Obesity is linked to supposedly increasing chronic health problems, and the increasing costs of the health services in Western nation-states. For the United Kingdom, the health service – funded directly through taxation – is perceived as being 'at risk' from this so-called 'lifestyle' problem. Politicians from both wings of British politics have claimed to be doing things to tackle obesity and to encourage children and adults to be responsible for doing more physical activity. When Labour were in control from 1997 to 2009 (under Tony Blair, then Gordon Brown) the prime ministers were keen to see a healthier nation because they believed in the morality of physical activity (Perkins, Smith, Hunter, Bambra and Joyce, 2010). But they were also bound by their policy commitment to keep taxes low, and the public sector borrowing requirement to a minimum, so they had to look at ways of lowering the cost of the health service. More charitably, it could be argued that the Labour government was serious about the nation's health because they believed good health is a key to social inclusion and good citizenship. So the government put tackling obesity at the centre of *Our Healthier Nation*, its Green Paper on health. Similar strategies to put tackling obesity at the heart of public health and physical activity policies can be seen in other social-democratic, welfarist countries, and even the federal and state governments of the United States are working towards or have passed legislation to promote physical activity as a means to reduce the levels of obesity (Mello, Studdert and Brennan, 2006). In the policy-making arena, just as in the reporting in the media about the science, we can see the social construction of obesity at work (Gard and Wright, 2005). Obesity could be seen to be a result of the commodification and commercialization of society. We have become victims of the hegemony of fast food and processed food. Families eat at McDonald's because children want the plastic toys, and parents want some place the children will be happy and the food is cheap and pleasant enough; and the adverts tell them to go, so they go. We could blame capitalism, and modern commerce, and the power they have over our governments – but we generally do not blame the food and hospitality industry.

We could argue obesity is a symptom of postcolonial capitalist relationships between the West and the rest of the world. We are literally consuming the planet because we have got the power and the wealth to be able to do so for the first time in history. But that argument is rarely heard. We could claim obesity is a symptom of postmodernity. As everything has become virtual and instant we have lost the link between time and space, mind and body. Obesity could be about status, and how men in particular might show off their beer bellies to flaunt their masculinity; anthropologically speaking, fat was and is a marker of wealth and power (Connell, 1995). Our concern with obesity could be gendered, linked with male-produced images of perfect women and control over women's bodies (Butler, 2006). Gender, masculine hegemony and heteronormative ideals of feminine bodies might be important in debates over acceptable body shapes: certainly, men have less pressure than women to conform to ridiculously underweight, slim body forms that still have fat deposits in the right places.

However, there are other inequalities and structures of power and control at work in the social construction of obesity. When we think of the obese, who do we think of? We inevitably think of the less well-off, people living on bad diets in socially excluded neighbourhoods (Jones, 2012). We do not seem to think of overweight politicians. In the United States, for example, reality television programmes and other forms of popular culture perpetuate a myth that the only fat Americans are 'white trash' living in trailer parks, or African Americans in Detroit or some other half-derelict city. So these concerns about the 'problem' of obesity could be linked with class. As we saw in Chapters 1 and 2, most sports have grown out of middle-class or elite activities and are still participated in by the middle classes and the elites. Physical activity is seen as something done by the middle classes. Over the last thirty years, the class-based nature of sport and physical activity has become a problem to be 'solved': how to get the working classes 'active'. This concern with inactivity has increased with the increase in social exclusion and long-term unemployment – how to keep the 'work-shy layabouts' from getting into trouble (Nichols, 2004).

But what is social class? Social classes are in all societies, and have existed at all times. But their meaning and purpose in social relationships have changed over time. Marx was one of the first sociologists to examine and identify the dynamics of the modern class system (Marx, 1992; Marx and Engels, 2004). In the Industrial Age and place in which he wrote (nineteenth-century Western Europe), he identified a tiny ruling class that owned the land, a small middle class that owned capital, and a large working class, the proletariat, that only had their labour to sell. Most sociologists now agree that class has at least four different dimensions: economic – life chances, work, production (occupational classifications, the jobs you do or the jobs your parents do); political – interests, issues, commonality, power, hegemony, distribution;

social – status, prestige, lifestyle, leisure, consumption; and cultural – identity, community, tastes. In this century, people have argued that classes have disappeared, that we have all become middle class, or we have all become consumers (see Jay, 2010). This of course is nonsensical. Social class exists in all societies. Humans have a learned capacity to discriminate and build belonging and exclusion (Spracklen, 2013b). Class is alive and well today: there are still people whose choices in life are limited by their social class.

How, then, does class limit choice? How is social class made by society and the individuals in it, and how do the classes with power use that power to shape and control the other classes? How do people feel part of a class, and how do others impose class on them? French theorist Pierre Bourdieu developed the theory of 'habitus', the tastes and habits that we adopt through our upbringing and life choices (Bourdieu, 1986). Habitus, which shapes class culture and consciousness, is defined by a number of things: language; child-bearing and family; schooling and reading; work; community networks and volunteering; leisure and culture; and sports, recreation and outdoor pursuits. We move through life limited by our upbringings, but our circumstances and access to economic, social and cultural capital provide ways in which habitus might be changed. The ruling classes have the power to define certain forms of culture as literary or high-brow, and they also have the power to dismiss certain forms of culture as low-brow or trashy (Jones, 2012). Even though high-status individuals today seem to be more omnivorous in their consumption of popular culture, the elites still exert their power to label things and social groups they do not like as deviant or marginal, such as playing computer games, or eating fast food, or going on holiday to Florida (Emmison, 2003).

Historical concerns about the working classes have continued into the present. It was in the late nineteenth century, following industrialization and the growth of the urban working class, that class became a major 'problem'. As we have seen earlier in this book, British, French, German and American policy-makers and commentators were afraid of 'degeneracy', of moral decline, of being 'swamped' by the working classes: they feared the decline of Western political power. Muscular Christians saw sport as a way of improving the working classes: moral improvement through physical activity (Mangan, 1981, 1986). Physical improvement of the lower classes through physical activity became a decisive factor following the Boer War, when recruits to the British Army had to be rejected because of poor health (Judd and Surridge, 2013). Spectator sport, as we have seen earlier, was a problem for the promoters of sport as a means of improvement. On the one hand, it was 'bread and circuses' keeping people in their place, but it also encouraged gambling, drinking and absenteeism. These themes have fed into contemporary debates about physical activity and obesity. There is the moral imperative in the need for social welfare – social democracy, the dominant theme in postwar European politics. There is the New Right and neo-liberal debate about the cost of social welfare. And there is the increasing authoritarian trend in democratic countries around the need for social control (Gard and Wright, 2005).

What we are witnessing in the construction of the obesity epidemic is the construction of folk devils and a moral panic. The working class, particularly young working-class men, have been perceived as a social problem to be contained since Victorians first coined the word 'hooligan' (Scraton, 2004). The working-class layabout has become a folk devil for our times, socially excluded, and participating in anti-social behaviour. What to do with them has been an expressed aim of modern governments, following hysteria and 'moral panics' about them through the years. Sport has been seen as a way of controlling these young people. Stanley Cohen (1972) was the first social theorist to identify the process through which folk devils are created – the moral panics that build up from hot air, speculation and stereotyping. He observed that there was no real or violent Mod/Rocker split in youth culture in the sixties, and most of the trouble was either isolated or blown out of proportion by public fear, police over-reaction and press hysteria. The obese working-class youth, watching porn on the internet, eating a burger, has become an acceptable way of middle-class and elite people expressing their disgust at the lower classes, and imposing their power on the lower classes through the process of demonization. The fear of the working classes visible in the debates about obesity shows that a moral panic is potentially building (Gard and Wright, 2005; Jones, 2012).

So what about obesity itself? Does obesity exist? There is a philosophical problem associated with the reality of obesity. We all 'know' what overweight people look like. But the concerns about obesity relate to people who may not fit our stereotype of the overweight. Furthermore, different people might have different understandings of what obesity actually is. The scientists interested in obesity measure it using the BMI. But how reliable is the BMI as an indicator of health? How does the BMI indicator represent obesity? Is the indicator a model of obesity or somehow the 'real thing'? In the debate from 2006 about the obese being not fit for the army, *The Sunday Times* ('Army to call up a bigger body of men', *The Sunday Times*, 8 January 2006, on-line at http://www.thesundaytimes.co.uk/sto/news/uk_news/article210867.ece, accessed 10 May 2014) reported that professional sports stars from rugby union such as Jonah Lomu would have been disqualified.

Is there evidence for the problem? Obesity is understood as a health problem. But the evidence for the link may not be so clear cut. BMI may not be an accurate indicator (Griffiths, Gately, Marchant and Cooke, 2012). Bad diet and obesity may not be the same thing. There is a problem of inductive logic at work here: when people are living longer, perhaps being overweight or obese might not be something that creates problems for most of us, just for some of us (perhaps just the most extreme cases, or ones where genetics might have an important causal factor). There is also still the problem of causation – in what way does obesity cause ill health? Perhaps the causal link is in fact the other way round, and people become obese when other things are affecting their health. In fact it is likely that there are multiple causes, multiple effects, and multiple explanations for obesity and ill health supposedly connected to it.

Portion sizes and 'big' food challenges

Two possible cultural causes behind the higher rate of obesity in America compared to European countries are increased portion sizes and the big food challenges (Schlosser, 2001). The average American portion in restaurants is much larger than the equivalent dish in Europe or other parts of the Western world. This is not just a problem with burger chains or fried-chicken joints: the larger portions are found in all types of American restaurants, from diners to elite establishments. Big portions are also found in the supermarket, where processed food and ready meals generally come in larger measures than their European equivalents. This is a product of consumer demand, cheap production prices and competition between suppliers. When portion size is combined with a lack of legislation against unhealthy saturated fats, high sugar content and processed oils, it is easy to see why Americans, despite their wealth, have poorer diets than Europeans. Also, there is the culture of big food challenges. Many restaurants have special dishes that come in enormous portions, which customers are challenged to eat to win some sort of prize. This legitimation of excess eating and gluttony normalizes huge portions and unhealthy diets – especially when it becomes the subject of laudatory television programmes. Big food challenges are treated as entertainment and a legitimate sports contest to which every American can aspire.

QUESTIONS TO CONSIDER

Why hasn't this unhealthy culture being legislated against? How do gender and class work in this culture?

REFERENCE AND FURTHER READING

Schlosser, E. (2001) *Fast Food Nation*, Houghton Mifflin, Boston.

Gard and Wright (2005) are concerned about the nature of the scientific evidence presented as proof of the problem of obesity, ill health and lack of physical activity. They have doubts about the claims that being 'obese' leads to health problems. They have concerns about the confusion between the clinical definition of obesity and the popular definition, and concerns about the validity of the BMI indicator. Is obesity a social problem? Gard and Wright have argued that the 'obesity problem' is an example of the creation of a moral panic of the sort first discussed by Stanley Cohen. The folk devil is the overweight working-class consumer of burgers, not the overweight politician drinking whisky. In other words, obesity is not a social problem, or even a health problem. It is a problem created by the media, by policy-makers and scientists with vested interests, and is part of a continued attack on difference by the established social and cultural elites.

CONCLUSION

The obesity epidemic is an example of how moral panics and myths combine with prejudices to establish scientific research agendas. Sports and physical culture lose their communicative value when they become mixed up with the politics of blame. The myth-making and hyperbole of the obesity epidemic, and the pushiness of policy-makers and politicians, is evidently a means of keeping the working classes in their place. The obesity problem plays on elitist unspoken revulsion at contemporary working-class culture, and the elites' fear that these people are causing the West to 'degenerate' – in other words, the concern over obesity may well be evidence that we are as socially Darwinistic as our nineteenth-century ancestors. But then again, billions of dollars, pounds and rupees are spent each year on advertising food with poor nutritional value. We are all victims of coca-colanization and instrumentalization: our communicative leisure choices are constrained by the power of instrumentality to change the way we live, rest, play and eat. Perhaps, then, the real issue about obesity is one about power and hegemony: how the people with power use their power to keep the rest of us stupid but content (Gramsci, 1971; Spracklen, 2009, 2013b). In the next chapter, the pressures on sports performers, and the instrumentality of elite sport, will be the subject of an analysis of performance enhancement.

EXERCISES

1 What is coca-colanization, and how has it shaped the obesity epidemic?
2 How is the obesity issue linked to feminist struggles over embodied power?
3 Why are we living longer if we are getting bigger?

Chapter 8

Performance Enhancement

SUMMARY OF TOPICS

- *Definitions: the world of drugs and drugs in sports*
- *Understanding performance enhancement and the nature of elite sport*
- *Drugs, performance and sports science*
- *The ethics of enhancement versus the pressure to win, and the meaning of sport*

In the previous chapter I discussed the limits of understanding obesity, and the connection between the obesity 'epidemic', wellbeing, sport and the wider industries of sport. In this chapter the spotlight is on doping. Just as I started to put this book together in January 2013, Lance Armstrong, seven times the winner of *Le Tour de France* and a sports superhero admired by fans for overcoming cancer to become the best professional cyclist of his generation, admitted in an interview with celebrity broadcaster Oprah Winfrey that he had been systematically using performance-enhancing drugs, that he had colluded with his team mates and his coaches and managers to hide the fact they were all involved in this practice, and that he had lied consistently when he had denied taking performance-enhancing drugs (Sparling, 2013). Armstrong's confession came after years of denials and threats of legal action by Armstrong's lawyers against journalists and writers who tried to investigate the truth, and after a long formal investigation into his (and others') use of performance-enhancing drugs by the United States Anti-Doping Agency (USADA) (Poplak, 2013). That investigation found Armstrong had used drugs and the USADA recommended Armstrong was stripped of his medals and titles. This led to Armstrong taking the USADA to court, but the judge ruled that the USADA were right. Armstrong continued to publicly defend his innocence but from August 2012 onwards more and more of modern sport's ruling organizations turned against him. The public confession came only after the evidence of his guilt had convinced the sports world to act. It might be easy to see why Armstrong took the performance-enhancing drugs – but why did he fight so determinedly to keep his name and his record, and why did he go to Oprah to confess? This story tells us a lot about the high stakes of professional sport, where sports stars are celebrities and the public face of big profit-making systems.

This chapter will look at performance enhancement in sport, beginning with the evergreen issue of doping in elite sports. The philosophical arguments for and against doping in sports will be explored, together with sociological explanations for the use of performance enhancers. Performance enhancement will be identified as a central element of sports participation (in this chapter, those who do sport, not those who watch it) in modern physical culture – all sports participants want to get better at their sports, and all coaches want their athletes to improve their performance. Doping in sport, it will be argued, is one end of a continuum of performance-enhancing strategies, but one end that is confused by the hypocrisy of modern, professional sports and their instrumental practices.

Before we look at the sociology and the ethics of doping in sport, we need to consider performance enhancement in sports and physical activity more generally. In Ancient Greece at the time of Plato, athletes competing in the various sacred games were trained beforehand to improve their performance, following strict regimes of physical activity in their city's *gymnasia* to make them better at the actual games which they were expecting to compete in (Young, 2005). This physical training was often accompanied by particular diets – abstaining from certain foods and drinks, eating and drinking an excess of others. The Ancient Greeks at the time of Plato saw their athletes as being representatives of the pride of their home city, so they were marshalled and trained by older men. As well as improving their physical potential, the Greek athletes and their trainers and supporters would pray and make sacrifices to the gods to try to improve their spiritual potential. So the ideal of amateur athletes competing on an equal basis, representatives of different cities seeking to find out which city had the best man, did not hold: training, and the use of other performance-enhancing practices, was all part of a series of legitimate interventions in preparing athletes for the games.

Today, in most of our sports and physical activities, we do things other than the activity to help improve our performances of that activity. It is seen as a normal and everyday practice to work out at a gym if we are involved in a team sport or track and field. We do repetitions and put in long hours during the week honing our bodies so that we can be the best physical fitness for the performance at the weekend. We follow the guide of coaches and trainers, obeying their instructions about how we move our bodies, what we do with our bodies, what we eat and drink – or, if we do not have a coach or trainer, we follow the advice of our fellow athletes or search books and the internet for advice on regimen (diet and training). We take pills and energy drinks and other potions with claims on the tin that the magic inside will make us faster, stronger. We trust that there are best ways to improve our performance, and easy ways to success, if only we do our exercises and diet in the correct way (Duncan and Klos, 2012). Even though there is no evidence that it works, many of us still seek divine favour through prayer or the wearing of lucky charms or the completion of lucky rituals: wearing our favourite running shorts, or kissing a cross, or drinking our energy drink using our left hand only, or something else equally irrational. Nearly everybody, then, who takes part in sports and physical activities of any kind seeks to improve their performance through the application of diverse practices based on what we think is truth – it seems to be an accepted matter of fact that we can all improve our bodies (and our minds) to reach an optimum performance, through the application of some kind of knowledge.

DEFINITIONS: THE WORLD OF DRUGS AND DRUGS IN SPORTS

We do not have to travel far across the internet to find examples of the harsh words used by policy-makers, politicians and people in the sports industry about the use of drugs in sport. Here is a British politician, a government minister in charge of sport, responding to the news that the United Nations had adopted a code against doping in sport (this is an example I used in my own seminar classes when I taught sports science students some philosophical issues; I am sure you can find a story from your own country and from this decade):

> Sports Minister Richard Caborn has welcomed today's announcement that the International Convention Against Doping in Sport has been adopted unanimously by the UNESCO General Conference meeting in Paris. This is the first time a legal instrument aimed at eradicating doping is both binding and universal...'I'm pleased that I was able to use our Presidency of the EU to generate support for the Code, which will make

sure drug cheats everywhere face the same tough sanctions irrespective of their sport or the country in which they train or compete.'

(Press release from UK Sport, http://www.uksport.gov.uk/news/2173, 19 October 2005, accessed 8 December 2005)

The politician's words are clear: there is no room anywhere in sport for drugs, and people who use drugs are 'drug cheats' who will face tough sanctions if they are ever caught. This wording and tone is the same used for other illegal drugs (and their users and their traffickers) in Western nation-states, such as heroin, cocaine and cannabis. The harsh language appears in the International Convention Against Doping in Sport itself, for instance:

Article 8 – Restricting the availability and use in sport of prohibited substances and methods

1. States Parties shall, where appropriate, adopt measures to restrict the availability of prohibited substances and methods in order to restrict their use in sport by athletes, unless the use is based upon a therapeutic use exemption. These include measures against trafficking to athletes and, to this end, measures to control production, movement, importation, distribution and sale.

2. States Parties shall adopt, or encourage, where appropriate, the relevant entities within their jurisdictions to adopt measures to prevent and to restrict the use and possession of prohibited substances and methods by athletes in sport, unless the use is based upon a therapeutic use exemption.

(International Convention Against Doping in Sport, UNESCO, http://portal.unesco. org/en/ev.php-URL_ID=31037&URL_DO=DO_TOPIC&URL_SECTION=201.html, accessed 11 May 2014)

The use of the phrase 'trafficking' is the tabloidization of anti-doping policy. This part of the Convention asks nation-states who sign it to treat perform-ance-enhancing substances and activities that have been prohibited under the rules of sport (the list of prohibited substances and methods maintained by the World Anti-Doping Agency (WADA) and other international sports organizations) as something exactly equivalent to an illegal drug such as heroin. So performance enhancers are trafficked, and governments are encouraged to legislate against possession and use of performance enhanc-ers. The moral consensus (or moral panic) becomes 'drugs are wrong'; so say the tabloids, the celebrity commentators and the politicians (Ben-Yehuda, 1989). Drug is just a word used to describe some chemical compound that can have an active impact on human bodies, and it came to be used to gener-ally refer to types of compound that were developed in the chemical industry for the benefit of modern medicine (even though there are many drugs to be found in 'nature', and many herbal remedies have such compounds as active ingredients). Illegal drugs that are used for pleasure are seen as unethical and tainted with sin; their users are seen as immoral. Drug itself has become a marked word with immoral and dangerous connotations, so that people who take various forms of drugs for medical reasons often avoid using the word (van Ree, 1997). Drugs used for pleasure, then, have become a shorthand catch-all expression for everything wrong in society. They are described as a 'stain' on modern society, politicians go to war on drugs, and in popular culture the drug pusher and the drug users are folk devils, the junkies and crack-heads of a thousand episodes of police dramas (Ben-Yehuda, 1989). Drugs such as heroin, cocaine and cannabis are associated in the Unites States and other Western countries with the evil Other, strangers from beyond the borders of the nation or from minority groups, outsiders who have invaded and infected innocent young minds with these harmful substances (Provine, 2008).

Drugs used for pleasure were not always a social and moral evil. Historically, many cultures have used mind-altering substances for pleasure and for community building, with coffee a favourite in the Muslim Ottoman Empire, and alcohol the drug of choice in Christian Europe. Heroin, cocaine, cannabis and opium were all sold as medical cures for a number of ailments through the second half of the nineteenth century, when modernity and the medicalization of society allowed a capitalist market in medicines to emerge (Musto, 1991). But gradually these drugs were prohibited by a combination of moralizing politicians, public health 'experts' and journalists stirring up public outrage at the dangers of allowing young people too many freedoms to associate with each other and with the feared Other (Opotow, 1990). Drugs became the subject of a *tabu* – not only were they legislated against, they were represented as dangerous to body, mind and soul, things that offended the divine and polluted the body.

Drugs in society used for pleasure are the subject of moral panics on the front pages of tabloid newspapers. The consensus view from the back pages, in the public sphere of contemporary sport, is that the great evil is the performance-enhancing drug and the athlete who uses performance-enhancing drugs. The journalists line up with the people who run modern sport to say it is the work of cheats. Anyone found to have used performance-enhancing drugs is seen to have cheated other athletes from a victory. The cheats are said to have cheated their supporters and their teams and their countries. The cheats are said to have cheated the particular sport or the nebulous notion of sport itself, some sphere or space or cultural form that exists somewhere out in the world independent of the people who create it. In this sense, sport has become another form of the divine, a god who sets examples, punishes wrong-doers, and favours the righteous, and who is worshipped through the prayers of athletes and supporters alike. Using performance-enhancing drugs, say journalists and sports administrators and those others with a vested interest in the divine god of sport, is 'unsportsmanlike' (Magdalinski, 2008). In that sense, those who are caught using these performance-enhancing drugs become pariahs, thrown out of the temple and the boundary of the tribe, cast out into the wilderness of demons and snakes, which is all they supposedly deserve.

As we have seen, Lance Armstrong, who was the *epitome* of the righteous athlete, was found guilty of the sin of using performance-enhancing drugs, and has had his medals and titles removed, expunged, as if he never existed. His name no longer appears in the list of winners of *Le Tour*, and now there is only a blank space between the winners in 1998 and 2006. Armstrong's punishment also reflects the consensus view in sport and the sports media about the nature and extent of the problem of the use of illegal performance-enhancing drugs, that it is seen as the work of rogue coaches and athletes (Klein, 2012). The occasional pariah can be expunged from the record because they are only ever few in number, and the doping is never something that everybody does in elite sport because of the culture of elite sport. If everybody was doping then potentially everybody would have to be expunged, and if that was to happen there would be no elite sport left from which to make money. So the sports advocates continue to say it is the work of those nasty rogues, a handful of bad apples, and they turn away from the truth that is right before their eyes: performance enhancement is a logical consequence of the money invested in elite sport and sports science and coaching, and the culture of hegemonic masculinity that elite sport represents (Hanstad and Waddington, 2009).

Le Tour de France

Professional cycling is a gruelling sport, especially the multi-stage road events exemplified by the Tour de France. In the world of professional cycling, there have been a number of scandals about top athletes using illegal performance enhancers or using performance enhancers that were so new to the black market that the governing bodies had not made them illegal. In its early years, the Tour de France saw cyclists try all kinds of drugs and potions to stay on the road. By the second half of the twentieth century, various amphetamine-type substances were in use. Towards the end of the last century blood-doping became the favoured way of seeking illegal advantage among professional riders on the road circuits. Blood-doping is a way of artificially increasing the number of red blood cells in the blood of a rider, through the use of certain drugs that increase the density of such cells in the plasma, or through regular injections of blood that has a high red blood cell count. Such effects – an increase in the density of red blood cells

– can easily happen through training harder or training at high altitude, or using oxygen tents to recover after training, so it was impossible to prove illegal blood-doping from counting red blood cells. The cycling authorities responded by trying to introduce rules to suspend riders who had 'abnormal' red blood cell counts for their own wellbeing (Zorzoli and Rossi, 2010). Only the arrest of a number of riders and support team members in possession of illegal performance enhancers proved the widespread use of blood-doping.

QUESTIONS TO CONSIDER

Were the rules to suspend riders fair? What sociological pressures were at work on the riders?

REFERENCE AND FURTHER READING

Zorzoli, M. and Rossi, F. (2010) 'Implementation of the Biological Passport: The Experience of the International Cycling Union', *Drug Testing and Analysis*, 2, pp. 542–7.

DRUGS, PERFORMANCE AND SPORTS SCIENCE

Since the second half of the last century, in the West and in other emerging economies such as China, sports science has been funded extensively to produce success. Government policies have officially promoted investigations into substances and practices that might be defined as performance enhancers. Historically, sports science was the key to the development of elite sports and elite sports performance in the twentieth century (see the work of Park in Mangan and Vertinsky, 2013). Performance-enhancing drugs became used routinely in professional sports before the Second World War, where there was no attempt to ban their use and the practices went unregulated and unremarked upon (Beamish and Ritchie, 2006). In the Cold War, success in elite sport became a proxy indicator for victory in actual conflict, and both Western and Communist governments invested huge amounts of money in sports science to find drugs and activities that would give their own athletes a winning advantage. Sports scientists, then, played a crucial role in developing and producing these performance-enhancing technologies, whether the drugs such as steroids and amphetamines, or the practices such as improved diets, or training at high altitude. As elite sports and professional sport became dominated by athletes who were using performance-enhancing drugs, stories started to emerge about some of the consequences to the health of athletes and the abuse of children in elite sport regimes in places such as East Germany (Dimeo, Hunt and Horbury, 2011). Young people were being forced to take performance-enhancing drugs by coaches and officials, and they were consuming huge amounts of substances that had not been tested for their long-term effect on health. Governments and international sports organizations were slow to act, and many people in positions of power in elite sports tried to resist the creation of anti-doping policies, but eventually opinion in the public sphere had turned so much against the 'doping culture' that there was a real fear that people would stop watching elite sport and spending money, and sponsors would walk away (Beamish and Ritchie, 2006). As various substances were made illegal, and as officials set up global responses to doping in sport such as WADA and the International Convention discussed earlier in this chapter, it became clear that one of the key issues was research into performance enhancers as a means to understand their impact, and also as a means of finding reliable ways to screen athletes to find out who was actually taking anything banned.

In many countries sports science has offered itself as a solution to the use of illegal performance enhancers (Dunn, Thomas, Swift, Burns and Mattick, 2010). Sports scientists are investigating both the use and misuse, trying to provide ways in which coaches and officials and athletes might get clear advice on risks to health, while coming up with new ways to track and test the use of known, illegal performance enhancers. Being educated to understand the dangers of using performance-enhancing drugs is obviously a good thing, and the scientific research allows us to balance claims and counter-claims in the media about whether certain substances are harmful, and whether they actually work to improve performance. There is, though, a tension between sports science's need to find out what the levels of risk and efficacy actually are for particular performance enhancers (science is on the surface a systematic attempt to find out the truth about things without being swayed by subjective biases and opinions), and the anti-doping advocates in the public sphere who have already decided that these drugs are terribly harmful but cleverly effective in improving performance.

However, despite the public disavowal of illegal performance enhancers in the work of learned societies in sports science, and the work done by many sports scientists in trying to establish tests and knowledge about risks, sports science remains defined and fixated by the quest to improve the performance of elite athletes (Beamish and Ritchie, 2006; Miah, 2007). In sports science, most of the research is still focused on providing the winning margin in certain sports and at certain levels from elite youth sport through development programmes into international competitions and professional sports leagues. Most of the money that comes from grants and sponsorship into sports science is predicated on finding out the value of some technology for the makers of that technology or for a certain elite sports organization. Not all sports scientists engage in this kind of funded research, but a significant proportion of sports science is assessing the usefulness of something for performance enhancement, and this is the kind of work that is generally funded by some organization or corporation. In the contemporary world of higher education, where university departments are ranked for their ability to bring in grant or sponsorship income and consultancy fees for their research projects (and where individual careers depend on generating this money), there is an additional internal pressure on sports scientists to go where the money is.

In the performance-related sciences of physiology, biomechanics and psychology, especially, there is a vested interest of sports organizations and corporations who create technologies (new kit, new drinks, new pills), the instrumentality of research assessment exercises, and politicians and policy-makers seeking better results for the nation's elite athletes. This has led to the actual cultural practices of elite sports performance, where athletes become dehumanized and passive, obedient recipients of whatever their coaches and managers tell them they need to do. The cost of failure is enormous – for athletes who fail to get professional contracts, for those who fail to win gold, for athletes nearing the end of their careers or coming back from injury, and for all the other people in the sports system who rely on the performance of athletes for their own profits: coaches, managers, agents, officials, shareholders and owners of corporations, media tycoons and politicians. Why this focus on performance? Sports science does not have to be about improving performance. But decisions made in the community of sport, the sports spaces and networks, the sports systems, all favour performance: it seems like 'normal science' and 'common sense' to use sports science in the aim of making athletes bigger, faster, stronger. Funding and sponsorship depend on results. The government and the press want results. An athlete's career depends on results and the difference between success and failure is very marginal at an elite level: getting results means finding a way of going one better than every other athlete in the competition. Is it any wonder sports science is expected to help provide those results?

The result of all these tensions and pressures is the existence of a Pandora's box of performance enhancers available for athletes and their coaches: some legal (such as putting athletes in oxygen tents or training at high altitude) and some illegal (such as injections of erythropoietin (EPO), a hormone in the body that controls the process of red blood cell production), even though the effect of the enhancement (in this case, a higher proportion of red blood cells in the athlete's blood) is often the same. The incoherence of anti-doping policies might be seen to be evident by athletes and coaches when they approach the Pandora's box – it is not the pursuit of performance enhancement that is wrong, nor an intervention or technology to improve performance, nor the effect of the technologies. If the harm of an illegal enhancer is perceived to be as low as or lower than one that is legal, it is easy to see why an athlete or coach might think the illegal substance is okay to use. Furthermore, the Pandora's box will contain things that the anti-doping organizations have not yet made illegal, and things they do not even know exist: the 'cutting edge' of performance-enhancement sports science is always one step ahead of anti-drugs testing and rules. This is why the sports authorities have found it difficult to prove drug use: the scientists advising the athletes and coaches know how to fool the testers, and they are quick to develop new variants of the performance-enhancing drugs that are not on the banned list and off the radar of the anti-doping scientists.

The illegal industry or 'black market' of performance-enhancing drugs is predicated on science and scientists. It is an applied science that needs trained professionals with the right skills to develop drugs and other performance-enhancing technologies. As the scientists work to find new ways of improving athletic performance, some of the technologies become legitimate and others are put on the prohibited list – the distinctions between the two are not always clear, and some scientists will continue the work on illegal performance enhancers in private laboratories. This science is the product of an uneasy power relationship between sports science and those with a vested interest in success: politicians, policy-makers, coaches, athletes. Even where sports science is used to fight the use of these drugs, there is a question of contested knowledge. First of all, known users of illegal performance-enhancing drugs have been caught by tests or by chance finding of drugs or by the confessions of others, yet these same athletes have passed many tests while being active users. There are ways and means to fool the testers, some involving taking masking substances, others simply associated with handing over another person's urine for testing (Cooper, 2012). Some illegal substances are impossible to test for, and can only be measured through proxies, and some new drugs are not found because the official testers don't know about them. Who gets to test for drug use? WADA and national anti-doping agencies have taken it upon themselves to do this work, and it is not clear that the relationship between the people in these agencies and the sports organizations and athletes is as objective as we might think. If we do think they are completely objective, can we still trust their findings? Hartley (2013) has shown how the nature of the tests and the evidence they supposedly provide is subject to legal appeals and judicial rulings on what counts as scientific proof – all too often, athletes can claim the test results are tainted, or are false positives, or an artefact of bad practice in the labs, or a result of athletes taking legal performance enhancers, supplements and medication. Put simply, there is too much at stake in elite sport for athletes not to use any and every means possible to achieve success. But why is that the case?

Another way of examining this obsession with bigger, faster, stronger, is to look at how sport constructs, and is constructed by, hegemonic (that is, dominant) symbols and norms of masculine behaviour and identity (Connell, 1987, 1995). As discussed in previous chapters, sport as we know it is historically and geographically specific – it is not a universal activity (although some of its aspects may be). Modern sport as we have seen owes its origins to nineteenth-century England and its development to the growth and dominance of the West (America and Europe) in the twentieth century. Modern sport is a means of people with power using their power to stay in power, and to keep the working classes, minority ethnic groups and other marginalized groups in their place. Sport is linked to what Connell (1987, 1995) calls the gender order, the historically constructed power relationship that privileges the power and interests of men over women, and heterosexual men over homosexual men, and elite heterosexual men over subordinate heterosexual men. This gender order is not static, and it can be and is challenged in all sorts of ways, but the gender order reflects the actual distribution of power in the West in modernity, and historically in what we might call the 'Abrahamic' tradition, that is the cultures of Judaism, Christianity and Islam. These belief systems used (and to an extent, still use) divine law to support the power of men over women and the ostracism of homosexuality. Other pre-modern cultures and societies also legitimized the gender order in their laws and customs, such as the Romans and Greeks. It was assumed by these cultures that men were naturally superior to women, and the best sort of man was strong, tough, and virile. The Classical man combined with the Christian man in Western Europe (who was perfected in the Middle Ages) to produce the modern version of hegemonic masculinity (Spracklen, 2011).

At the same time that modern heterosexual, hegemonic masculinity was being constructed, modern sport was invented. Modern sport, as we have seen earlier, was a deliberate attempt to combine the ethos of medieval Christian masculinity with a Classicism removed of its homosexuality. Modern sport became a way of making boys and men tough and virile, but pure and chaste. Sport, then, became associated with a particular type of masculine behaviour, a particular sort of masculine identity: one that pursued glory, attained victory, but remained morally pure. Sportsmanship was equated with the chivalry of medieval romances and the pursuit of glory, winning trophies was celebrated as knights on the Quest for the Holy Grail celebrated seeing that cup in the final castle:

> Steel that he was, his courage never failed him, his conquering hand seized many a glorious prize when he came to battle... Thus I salute the hero. – Sweet balm to woman's eyes, yet woman's heart's disease! (von Eschenbach, 1980, p. 16)

In the thirteenth-century poem *Parzival* cited above, the aspiring knight is given an image of what it means to be a man, to be a knight. The hegemonic masculinity portrayed is one of nobility, courage and prowess in battle. However, the site of developing and reinforcing this masculinity is not found in war: instead, it is the tourney ground where the allegorical character of the perfect thirteenth-century noble man is found. In the nineteenth century, the medieval tales of Arthurian knights loving women in a chaste manner, serving God and playing fair in battles and jousts, became the template for Muscular Christianity, so much so that the new Houses of Parliament in England became a mock-Gothic castle complete with statues and paintings of Arthur and his knights (Mangan, 1981, 1986). Sportsmen were expected to be as hard as steel, full of courage. They were conquerors and winners. And when they won, they won the heart of their women, who would do anything for them. Sports became ways of promising the fulfilment of heterosexual desire and proof of the sportsman's own heterosexuality and normality, and his rightful position in the gender order.

Masculinity and professionalization

With the maintenance of the gender order and hegemonic masculinity at stake, the pressure to perform, and the pressure to succeed, has become normal practice in elite sport, and in other levels of sport, too. This masculine imperative has become so much a part of modern sport that it distorts women's sport and puts pressure on female athletes, too (the imperative is socially constructed as masculine but it is not a biologically or psychologically masculine trait). Over the last century, the code of honour associated with sporting masculinities diminished as sport professionalized and societies became more individualized (Kidd, 2013). Sports became a way of demonstrating the superiority of individual men or teams of men. The contemporary masculine imperative linked to heterosexual, hegemonic masculine identity is to win at all costs, respect the coach, support the team/country/sport, and to bond with comrades. Athletes are meant to suffer for the cause, playing through injury and using pain-killers. This becomes a way of normalizing abnormal behaviour – training patterns, diets, and obeying the strange and abusive instructions of coaches. Performance-enhancing drugs are then a logical extension of the masculine imperative to win at all costs. Sports science itself has become a 'masculine' science: making men bigger, faster, stronger, since men's sport (athletes and teams) and men's performance counts more in global, elite sport than the performance of women athletes or teams.

QUESTIONS TO CONSIDER

How does this work in different sports? How can this culture be changed?

REFERENCE AND FURTHER READING

Kidd, B. (2013) 'Sports and Masculinity', *Sport in Society*, 16, pp. 553–64.

The long-term effects of performance enhancement in elite sport are commercialization and commodification, and a struggle over the bodies of athletes and the rules of sports (Miah, 2007). The commercialization comes from the global industry and control of sports science research. There is a tension between the needs of science and the needs of coaches, managers and athletes. There is a tension between benefits to health and benefits to performance. Science does not operate in a value-free bubble; its aims and activities are a part of society. Scientists have an imperative (their internal moral framework) to be guided by ethics, informed consent and balances of risk and benefit. There are two discourses in sport about performance-enhancing drugs: drugs as moral evil, and drugs as an unmentioned, out-of-sight means to an end. Is this hypocrisy? Perhaps what is needed is a mature debate about why the drugs are used, and what pressures to abide by masculine norms athletes and scientists may be under.

Should they be banned at all? Another way of investigating this issue is philosophically, analysing the arguments made for and against bans. In particular, we can view the issue as an ethical one. Philosophers of sport and law have challenged policy-makers in sport to come up with rational, logical arguments against drug use, and to have consistent, coherent policies about drug use. Parry (1987) summarizes and critiques the main arguments against the use of drugs in sport (and for the banning of drugs). Against the claim that drugs should be banned because they enhance performance, Parry says that even if the claim is true, is it an argument against the use of drugs? Intensive training, new technologies and better nutrition also enhance performance. Against the claim that drugs should be banned because they allow athletes to train harder, Parry (ibid., p. 33) says 'So does living next door to the swimming pool, or having access to the best facilities, but they are both allowed'. And why is it wrong for athletes to take steps to train harder? That is the purpose of sports medicine! Against the claim that drugs should be banned because they are illegal, Parry points out that there is an ontological problem about the meaning of natural: some legal products are made in laboratories, and if testosterone isn't natural, what is? And isn't sport itself an unnatural activity? Against the claim that drugs should be banned because their use forces others to use them, Parry says we are all rational human beings with the ability to make free choices. Not every athlete does choose to use them (but it could be argued that all modern sport is about competing with rivals). On the argument about drugs being harmful, Parry wonders if that is actually the case: how can we know this? It is the problem of induction again. And even if it was true, in all cases, isn't sport itself hazardous through over-training and its physicality? Why be concerned with one type of harm and not others? On the argument that drugs are illegal, Parry counters by reminding us that only some drugs are illegal. Some drugs that are illegal are not used as performance enhancers. There are contradictions between legal positions in society, moral positions in society, and the balance of harm and effect. Why ban marijuana and not tobacco? Why do sports policy-makers collude with breweries, tobacco companies and fast-food chains to promote their products, while at the same time worrying about drugs? So what does that leave us? Parry returns to the idea of rules in sport and the concept of fair play. Athletes choose to compete because they agree to abide by the rule of the game, and they assume that the officials will ensure that everyone abides by those rules; this is the contract we enter. Any attempt to evade these rules for advantage is cheating. If things are prohibited in the rules then they are wrong according to the rules, and to break those rules is to cause harm. It is an attempt to undermine and destroy the whole social contract of sport.

Authenticity, honesty and performance

One of the claims made in favour of banning performance-enhancing substances is that such drugs create an inauthentic performance (Magdalinski, 2008). It is argued that sports contests should be understood as competitions that measure the authenticity of a performance – when that authenticity is questioned by the use of technologies that enhance the performance that might otherwise have been, we can see why those technologies should be banned. Sports certainly feel like they are meant to be an authentic performance and test of authentic ability, strength or skill. Sports spectators might be assumed to expect authentic performances in return for the money they pay to see sports events. In other parts of the leisure and entertainment industry, people do seem to desire the authentic over the artifice of enhancement. In live music performances, people pay to see the musicians play and sing live, and where artists have mimed along to backing tracks or hidden musicians there have been strong claims that this is a form of deception and cheating. We want to see for ourselves how good the musicians actually are at performing; we do not want to see an inauthentic performance, and where we do we feel within our rights to ask for our money back. Most fans of music genres such as rock, folk and jazz would prefer a rough, live but authentic performance over a polished, inauthentic backing track.

QUESTIONS TO CONSIDER

What else might happen with live music to limit its authenticity? What is the ontological problem with authenticity?

REFERENCE AND FURTHER READING

Magdalinski, T. (2008) *Sport, Technology and the Body: The Nature of Performance*, London, Routledge.

CONCLUSION

Sports science responses to drug use in sport raise questions about transparency, power and objectivity. The pressure to win at all costs comes from the history of sport and its link with hegemonic masculinity – and the pursuit of celebrity and profit in contemporary sport. Understanding epistemological, ontological and ethical questions in philosophy can help us unpick most arguments against the use of drugs – but the argument by Parry from the social practice of rule-following seems to be sound. So even if there is no coherence to the bans, where bans are in place they need to be policed and maintained. If bans are lifted, even though this might be logically more coherent, the commodification of modern sport will be complete. In the next chapter, I will look at physical education in schools and the debate about making it compulsory.

EXERCISES

1 How have performance-enhancing drugs become part of popular culture?
2 Why does the argument about athletes being role models fail?
3 'The Olympics should consist of competitors drawn randomly from the population to reduce the unfairness of performance-enhancing technologies'. Do you agree? Discuss.

Chapter 9

Compulsory Physical Education (PE)

SUMMARY OF TOPICS

▪ *Definitions: education and physical education*
▪ *The historical development of physical education and its link with certain social and cultural values*
▪ *The problem of what to teach in schools and policies in favour of physical education*
▪ *The tension between the communicative value of physical activity versus the forced, compulsory nature of physical education*

In the last chapter, I explored how the high stakes of modern, instrumental sport leads to performance-enhancement strategies, because sports competitions are all about winning at whatever cost. This chapter looks at the debate about making physical education compulsory in schools and the relationship between physical education and the same instrumental moral politics of sport. Physical education and school sport are an established and compulsory part of the curriculum in most countries in the world. Politicians fight to demonstrate in their campaigning material that they will increase the number of hours dedicated to physical education and school sport. Policy-makers and the sports industry work together to try to persuade politicians and the wider voting public of the importance of physical education and sport more generally, and are vocal in their dissatisfaction when funding is threatened – as the Coalition in control of the

United Kingdom found out when it targeted school sports programmes in its wider austerity campaign against public spending (Collins, 2010; Phillpots and Grix, 2014). This chapter will challenge the notion that physical education and school sport are necessarily social or moral good things. This chapter will argue that compulsory physical education and school sport even fail to achieve what their advocates want them to achieve around sport and physical activity – compulsory physical education puts young people off from playing sports and being physically active, and encourages sports activity only among those already engaged in sport. It is suggested that the future of sport and physical activity is actually threatened by the instrumentalization of activities that should by definition be voluntary.

DEFINITIONS: EDUCATION AND PHYSICAL EDUCATION

In all human cultures and societies, young people have been trained to become effective adults. In many pre-agrarian cultures, such training was closely linked to the roles of men and women in the tribe (Mead, 1929). In agrarian cultures emerging in the Bronze Age in the Middle East, Eastern Europe and Asia, class distinctions between farmers, warriors and the ruling classes became fixed in social relationships, so the training for boys and girls changed according to the position in the class structure (Kristiansen and Larsson, 2005). For the children of farmers, boys and girls, the training was hands-on in the family unit. For the ruling classes, formal education systems emerged for the boys who would be the leaders of the next generation. These varied from culture to culture, with the main focus being martial skills. In Egypt, China and Greece, other forms of education emerged for the priests and scribes, bourgeois functionaries who ran religions and bureaucracies, and the ability to read and write came to be valued by those below the ruling warrior class but above the rural, farming classes (Williams, 1972). By the time of the height of Ancient Greece and Rome, it was considered normal for all boys from the ruling classes to receive formal teaching in various subjects considered proper for an elite man: rhetoric, literature and philosophy. Roman boys from the Senatorial class were educated at home by private tutors, but gradually schools emerged around famous teachers where other urban elites could send their boys (Bloomer, 1997).

Roman education and Roman virtue

In the second half of the fourth century, in the reign of the Christian Emperor Theodosius, an ex-soldier wrote an account of the history of the Empire. This soldier, Ammianus Marcellinus, was writing in a classical historiographical tradition. Ammianus' history is partly an account of the last pagan emperor (Julian), but also a rhetorical rage at the incompetence of the emperors that followed him. These restored Christianity, and encouraged corruption, indolence and a suspicion of the learning and the serious leisure lives of the Roman elite (Friell and Williams, 1998). Ammianus despises the immorality of the leisure activities of the Romans of his day. The ruling classes are vain, lecherous and prefer dancing, bathing and fashion to philosophy or improvement of any kind. Ammianus is a believer in the traditional Roman values of virtue: of piety to the gods, respect for learning, and celebration of martial courage. In this sense, he is following the work of earlier critics of Roman vices, such as Juvenal, Seneca and Cicero, who all mock trends in Roman culture that promoted dancing, gambling, drinking and sex at the expense of learning and military training. His history, then, preserves an ideal about the role of education in the Roman Empire: it was for elite men only, and gave such men skills to make laws, write histories, lead armies and make arguments.

QUESTIONS TO CONSIDER

What other evidence is there for Roman beliefs in manly virtue? What forms of physical education existed in Classical Rome?

REFERENCE AND FURTHER READING

Friell, G. and Williams, S. (1998) *Theodosius: The Empire at Bay*, London, Routledge.

With the advent of Christianity in Europe, secular schools struggled to compete with Christian schools, and the classical pagan education system disappeared altogether when the Emperor Justinian closed down the schools in Athens (Watts, 2004). Formal education was replaced by private tuition in war and diplomacy for elite boys, and reading and writing Latin for novices in monasteries, who needed to know Latin to be monks (Innes, 1998). In the Islamic world, formal education systems lasted longer, but were limited by the needs of religion. In Europe, formal schools started to re-emerge in cathedrals at the end of the first millennium of the Common Era, and these were limited to boys and to the elite and urban classes. By the nineteenth century, education had become more secular, and much teaching was done in vernacular languages, but education in most nations remained limited to a few basic subjects such as reading and writing, a bit of classical literature and scripture, and was limited to a few elite boys. The British public school system (the private, fee-paying schools) was re-invigorated in the nineteenth century through the gradual adoption of a Classical curriculum (the teaching of Greek and Latin), along with history and formal sports (Auerbach, 2010; Mangan, 1981, 1986). This curriculum was supposed by its founders, men such as Arnold, to provide the best of ancient and modern along with the moral physicality of Muscular Christianity. Other Western countries such as France, Germany and the United States adopted similar models for their elite classes.

Physical education, then, was initially a means of promoting Muscular Christianity among the ruling classes and the new urban bourgeoisie, who could afford to send their boys to be educated. The second half of the nineteenth century, however, also saw the growth in the West of the idea of universal education, education for all (including girls), with state-sponsored legislation on the construction of new schools combining with an impetus to provide schools for the poor that came from local councils, charities and religious groups. Because the people creating the schools and designing the legislation were all educated in the private school systems, it was natural that they would see the value of physical education. So schools were built with playgrounds attached to them, then eventually formal playing fields where sports, physical training and gymnastics could all take place (Auerbach, 2010). Initially, physical education was seen as something extra-curricular – sports would take place after formal teaching had taken place, in the evenings or weekends, or they would be informal forms of play and physical activity that were encouraged whenever the children gathered. In the last century, school sport in the West became something associated with the success and pride of schools, and formal sports competitions emerged along with the creation of sports facilities, specialist sports teachers and coaches. Most of these sports teams were for boys, even in schools that catered for both boys and girls, as girls were not encouraged (or expected) to be sporty. At the same time, proponents of physical education (sports enthusiasts, sports governing bodies and organizations, health officials) convinced school governing boards, local councils and national governments of the need to formalize physical education within the public (state) curriculum (Tinning, 2012). Without much evidence of the efficacy of physical education, or much understanding of the history of education in private schools (where sports were still seen as a means of making men fit to run the world), these advocates of physical education in state schools argued that physical education and physical culture were as important as moral education or artistic culture in the training and development of young people (Kirk, 2010).

Nation-states were interested in making their future citizens healthy and ready to become soldiers or reliable, dependable workers. In Germany, physical drills were seen as a means of protecting and promoting Aryanism through sublimation of the individual to the governance of the nation-state (Hardman and Naul, 2002). In the United States, school sports became a way for the capitalist belief in the primacy of the individual to become normalized in the struggle to be picked for teams and the struggle to win (McComb, 2012). Physical education was seen as a way of creating morally fit, obedient, content citizens, ready to fight and die for the country and, in the West, ready to fight communism and unionism in the factory (Collins, 2013a). As other nation-states gained independence or modernized through the twentieth century, under the influence of either the Soviet Union or the United States, they adopted models of education that were based on the idea of universal, tertiary education developed in the West. This meant they also adopted school curricula that included physical education and school sports as compulsory elements of an 'all-round' education. Physical education and sports were meant to instil in the students both healthiness and moral rectitude, an understanding of the importance of physical culture in society and a strong belief in competition (Collins, 2013a; Kirk, 2010).

PHYSICAL EDUCATION, PHYSICAL ACTIVITY AND PHYSICAL CULTURE

Physical education and school sport are so taken-for-granted in (Westernized) modern education systems that the main debates in policy have been about the lack of time children spend doing physical education and sport and about the quality of the activities and curricula provided in schools. As we have seen earlier in this textbook, physical activity (such as physical education and school sport in particular) is viewed as a social and moral good that will equip children with important skills as they grow into adulthood. In this period of crisis in late modernity, physical activity has become a solution to the perceived dangers amongst school children of obesity, ill health, indiscipline, anti-social behaviour, poor learning and engagement, lack of social cohesion and lack of moral responsibility. This is probably a good thing for governments and policy-makers to do: there is evidence (as I have demonstrated earlier) that doing physical activity is a good leisure habit, with some benefits to our health and wellbeing, though the strong claims about its use in tackling a wide range of modern problems are over-stated. There is also the danger that doing physical activity as a communicative leisure choice becomes a means of imposing the moral and social inequities of contemporary physical culture, that urging people to do more exercise leads to the glorification and legitimation of bodily strength and prowess (which leads to the legitimation of hegemonic power and the governmentality of self-surveillance and the surveillance of others, as we measure ourselves against the norms imposed on us by the state – see Gramsci, 1971; Foucault, 1991, 2006). However, physical activity is probably a good thing if people choose to do it of their own volition, and if marginalized people have the same opportunities as those with power and money to have fun picking the activities they like.

The problem comes when physical activity (a communicative leisure activity, which people get value from because they freely choose to do it and engage with it) is then conflated without any justification with physical education and school sport (Coalter, 2013). People who vote on the right respond to scare stories and moral panics about juvenile delinquency and moral degeneration, so Conservative politicians are quick to use physical education and school sport as benchmarks of their own moral probity through making claims that they will increase the number of hours in the curriculum dedicated to such activity. In the 1960s and 1970s, many left-wing politicians and voters were dismissive of physical education, seeing it as a way of making young people conform and learn bad habits about discipline and hierarchy (Kirk, 2010). With the rise of the neo-liberal compact in the West, left-wing politicians have become centrist politicians chasing votes by pursuing what they think are popular policies, so they have promoted more physical education and school sport to be more populist and right-wing than their rivals.

Most educators and academics in sports pedagogy and sports science would say that physical education is so obviously a right thing to do that to suggest it is not compulsory is dangerous and stupid. This is because these people have gained enormous value from physical education and school sport, and still get much value from their continued involvement in sports and physical culture. All teachers would argue that their chosen subject is worthy of inclusion in the curriculum; they are passionate defenders of their subject and that is why they teach that subject. Many academics of sport are also involved in sports away from the classroom or the laboratory, either running sports clubs or coaching elite athletes or helping develop and organize active recreation programmes. This is no different to other academics who have specialist subjects, especially those with an applied nature: academics who teach film production, for example, will have a passion for the technology and the art and the culture of film, and will probably retain some professional link with production companies or be involved with film as an amateur artist. Even most philosophers, historians and sociologists of sport (and physical activity) agree that physical education and school sport is ultimately something of value (social or moral), even if their support is tempered by strong critiques about physical education and hegemonic masculinity, the practice of elitism and the lack of inclusivity and diversity in the types of activity offered. It is rare that these voices from the humanities and social sciences take up a critical analysis of sport without having some love for one sport or another, even if that love is tempered by measured reflection.

I challenge the notion that compulsory physical education and school sport are inherently socially or morally good things, and I suggest it is the compulsory nature that it is the biggest problem with them. At best, I suggest the arguments about the value of physical education and school sport fail because these activities have nothing about them that could be a social or moral good apart from the communicative value of leisure, and the feeling of wellbeing associated with physical activity; at their worst, they are socially and morally problematic, and philosophically incoherent. Physical education and school sport even fail to achieve what their advocates in the public sphere want them to achieve around sport and physical activity, and physical culture: compulsory physical education puts many people off from playing sports, and encourages sports activity only among those already engaged in sport. The future of sport and physical activity is actually threatened by the institutionalization of activities that should by definition be voluntary.

In the sociology of physical education, this concern about the compulsory nature of physical education and its problematic meaning and purpose is not the primary point of debate or consensus. Sociologists of physical education are extremely critical of particular practices and policies, and many will suggest that traditional sports are best replaced by other forms of physical activity, but there is little call for the removal of physical education from the (compulsory) curriculum – even if that should be the logical consequence of their research projects. The journal *Sport, Education and Society* is one of a number of sociology journals devoted to critically examining the importance and relevance of physical education. Often the academic papers in this journal and others like it draw on philosophical themes, or historical analyses, or theory from cultural studies. Papers in the academic sub-field of 'physical education and sports pedagogy' typically critique existing or historical practices within physical education and wider sports education. David Kirk and others influenced by the work of Foucault and Bourdieu have shown how physical education was used through much of the twentieth century as a tool in a Foucauldian regime of governmentality, which involves controlling and commodifying bodies (Foucault, 1991, 2006). Kirk (1998, 1999, 2010) is keen to map the genealogy of physical culture as an exclusionary and hierarchical practice, which legitimizes the power of the elites over others. Feminist sociologists such as Anne Flintoff and Sheila Scraton (2001) have shown how physical education practice and policy in the past – and in many cases, in the present – has promoted male, team sports and hegemonic masculinity. Physical education teachers have favoured the strongest and the fastest, ignored boys (and girls) who do not fit the jock/sporty stereotypes, and marginalized or ignored altogether alternative masculinities and femininities.

Other sociologists have shown that physical education is a site for the construction of racialized and sexualized hierarchies, or a place where the disabled are unable to freely participate in the practices (Fitzgerald, 2005). Much of this is associated with the compulsory nature of the activity. Once physical activity becomes physical education, a compulsory part of the curriculum, it becomes a tool of the state, of the gender order, of hegemonic power. Young people no longer take part in physical activity because they enjoy it and choose to do it; instead they are forced to take part in physical education and school sport and told it will make them better. The compulsion is seen to come from higher up, and the finger-wagging in the public sphere sends a strong message about what people with power think physical education should be: school sport, winning and losing, discipline, keeping the young people off the street, off drugs, off the problem list, in their place. Young people are not stupid, they know when something is instinctively wrong, and many of them choose to quietly disengage from this vicious, instrumental practice (Habermas, 1984, 1987). Schools, teachers and coaches then become complicit in allowing the activities to become sites of domination, exclusion and humiliation, promoting winners and mocking losers.

However, sociologists of physical education themselves seem reluctant to embrace their own research conclusions and argue that physical education should be abolished. Rather, they argue that their research only demonstrates the failure of current physical education policy and practice, which is, to be fair on these sociologists, quite true. The *status quo* of physical education policy in every nation-state is woefully old-fashioned and geared to promoting elite sports development rather than inclusion and healthy, active lifestyles, with only little policy development and systematic cultural change here and there. The sociologists of physical education who critique the practices then litter their conclusions with recommendations about how physical education should be changed at policy level and in practice: through moving away from team sports, through embracing different kinds of activity such as dance and disability sports, or through schemes targeted specifically at girls to encourage them to keep involved in physical education, school sport and physical activity. It would be an interesting research project to map the previous careers and degree paths of strong proponents of physical education in sociology of physical education: how many would turn out to be former physical education teachers or graduate students from a physical education degree? Whatever their motivations, they remain critical but friendly with the notion of compulsory physical education and school sport. Kirk (2005, pp. 251–2), for instance, concludes a review of the problems associated with the British government's policy on school sport and physical education (PE) with a recommendation about how to improve participation in physical education:

> I began this article with the suggestion that there are some structural problems in the delivery of PE and youth sport that the PESSCLS [PE, School Sport and Club Links] strategy in the UK may fail to identify due to the lack of a research agenda to inform policy development. I suggest that the review of research evidence carried out in this article does reveal these structural problems, and also provides us with some possible ways to resolve them. I argued that quality early learning experiences are of crucial importance to continuing participation in physical activities for elite performers and so, we might infer, for the majority of young people also ... The weight of evidence from this modest review in itself suggests a radical reconceptualization of current UK government policy as it is expressed in and through PESSCLS. I propose that the review and development of further research studies would permit more finely tuned and targeted adjustments and refinements to the PESSCLS strategy.

So for Kirk, the problem becomes how to inform policy-makers about the best way they can achieve their targets, and the argument about the real problems with the assumption that physical education should be compulsory and every child should be made to do some is set aside. Kirk also makes a mistake in assuming that the good practice and learning techniques that kept elite performers interested in physical activity can automatically be applied to the 'majority' of young people. Those young students who do enjoy their physical activity and their sports, and their physical education, do so because they believe they have autonomy and control over the activities (Beiswenger and Grolnick, 2010). The best way to get young people physically active is to give them the choice to come to it themselves.

What Kirk's work shows is the danger of coming to the conclusion that compulsory physical education is a good thing before one begins to examine the impact of policies and strategies. Everyone who likes sports and physical activity, or who took part in such things at school, makes the critical error of arguing from their own experience to generalizations about the whole of education or society. This does not happen to the same extent with other activities. Playing a musical instrument is definitely good for children who learn how to play one, the practice helps them learn other valuable traits and qualities, but no one would suggest that playing an instrument be made a compulsory part of a school education. Some people can play, some can learn, some will never have a musical ability. It is a mark of a good school or a good national curriculum that values music education and finds the resources to give students the opportunity to learn to play music. But forcing young people to play a musical instrument against their will would rightly be seen by music educators as counter-productive. Why should sports and physical activity be any different? There is an intense lobbying system at work that combines ruthless positioning, the use of supportive academics, and the irrational nostalgia of adults. Barrie Houlihan and Mick Green (2006) have examined the ways in which physical education and school sport were lobbied for by professionals and academic advocates in the United Kingdom. As they suggest, the success of that campaigning relied on supporters of physical education convincing sceptics that it should remain a compulsory part of the curriculum (Houlihan and Green, 2006, p. 89):

> The promotional commitment and lobbying activity of the key individuals was supported by a steady accumulation of evidence that was persuasive to the more sceptical politicians and senior civil servants in the DfES [Department for Education and Skills]. The evidence was of three types: the first, produced by a variety of organizations, including the National Playing Fields Association, the Secondary Heads Association and PEAUK [Physical Education Association of the United Kingdom], demonstrated the continuing erosion of opportunities for PE and school sport through the selling of school playing fields, the reduction of curriculum time allocated to PE and the lack of trained PE teachers in primary schools; the second was evidence from adjacent policy areas which documented, for example, the growing health problems among young people; the third, commissioned largely by the YST [Youth Sport Trust], but also present in OfSTED reports, was evidence of the educational, social and health benefits of sport. The lobbying activity of individuals was, over the last 8 years or so, supported by an increasingly well-established network of organizations, including not just the YST, but also the network of specialist sports colleges and the PESSCL board, all of which helped to embed school sport and PE-related policies in the decision processes of the DfES in particular and of the government more generally. While the first two types of evidence were important in raising the profile of issues associated with school sport and PE and thus providing a focus for concern and complaint, it was the activity of the third group of actors that provided a focus for action.

Arguments in favour of physical education are never made in an entirely coherent manner. The case is too often stated rather than demonstrated. For politicians, physical education and school sport make good campaigning strategies, demonstrating they are trying to solve some mythical problem about the youth, some anti-social behaviour or obesity, while also defending the traditional school curriculum. For sports managers, sports governing bodies, sports policy-makers and physical education teachers it is a simple case of defending the thing they value the most. Academics researching physical education, however, have to come up with some cogent reasons why physical education should be retained as a compulsory subject within the curriculum.

One argument in favour of compulsory physical education is a utilitarian one: physical education serves a function, encouraging young people to take up the habit of physical activity, so they become in later life physically fitter (and perhaps psychologically happier and mentally better equipped). This utilitarian argument is not concerned with protecting physical education and school sport in its current shape. It recognizes that there are many things wrong with the way physical education encourages hegemonic masculinity and elite competition and the exclusion of people who do not make the teams. For people who make the utilitarian argument, schools and policy-makers need to look at what works: what actually helps people keep the active habit of physical culture, or what ensures people live healthier lives.

Another argument comes from the belief that schools have a duty of care for their pupils. Schools are training grounds, but also serve as places where young people are protected from making the wrong decisions. The idea of state-sponsored national curricula comes from a belief that some subjects need to be compulsory and taught to all children in schools that are influenced by the state's policies. There are private schools in various countries where children are given complete control over what they learn, but most schools share an understanding that there are some things that all children in modern society need, whether they like it or not. Schools are places where adult guardians make decisions on behalf of children that the children themselves would not make if they had a choice: so schools drill students in maths and science, topics that are deemed to be vital to the economy, to society and to the individual, even if they are painful (at times) to learn. Physical activity, sport and their school equivalent physical education are judged to be equally as important to the state, society and the individual as maths and science: physical education might not be something a child would freely participate in given the choice, but we make them do it because it is believed the importance of the subject outweighs any dissatisfaction with the subject. Children cannot make informed decisions about their own education, this argument goes, and choice should not be extended to them on physical education or they might argue that science should be voluntary, or attending school might just become an option. This argument is made most strongly by the advocates and academic cheerleaders of sport; those who themselves have had positive experiences of physical education, school sport and physical activity. For people who love sport and enjoyed sports and physical education at school and university, it is as important to the balanced curriculum of a school as history, music, art or literature (Kirk, 2005, 2010).

American college sports

In the United States, sports have become a powerful and significant part of the cultures of its schools and colleges. Sports teams have become big business, and athletes have become untouchable heroes, lauded for their successes and given easy rides through the system. Svare (2004) argues that colleges and schools have colluded in promoting a system of professionalization and marketization of school sports. Svare's concern is the way in which schools and colleges have accepted the argument that success in sports contests is good for the athletes involved, good for the students who cheer on the winning athletes from the sidelines, and good for the learning culture of the institution. Because competitive sport has become essentially professional at college level – in terms of the marketing material, the hours spent training and the appointment of highly-paid professional coaches – college sport has become a minority pursuit for those talented enough to win sporting scholarships. Getting sports scholarships has become touted as a way to success and a potential professional sports career, a short-cut to fame. The pressure then is on faculty to ensure that scholarship students pass their grades while working full-time on their training and sports activities. Svare argues that sports success is promoted above academic success as the way in which students are measured.

QUESTIONS TO CONSIDER

What would happen if college sports lost their status? What gender biases are at work in American college sports?

REFERENCE AND FURTHER READING

Svare, B. (2004) *Reforming Sports: Before the Clock Runs Out*, Delmar, Sports Reform Press.

As we have seen in earlier chapters, physical activity is probably good for us but only where it is freely chosen and communicative in nature: its goodness is associated with its value as informal, voluntary leisure, far removed from the hegemonic powers that shape late modern society. The idea of communicative action and rationality comes from the work of Jurgen Habermas

(1984, 1987). He shows that all humans have an innate desire to discuss and socialize, and act freely. Communicative rationality was given space in modern society in the Enlightenment, when feudalism, autocracy and irrationality were replaced by the belief in reason to solve problems. This led to the construction of the public sphere and the lifeworld, that part of human civilization where we debate and discuss free from the structures of nation-states and modern capitalism. In my own theorizing on leisure, I have shown how leisure spaces and leisure activities contributed to the lifeworlds in the past, and how they continue to bolster the lifeworld against the dangers of instrumental rationality, the systems and structures that threaten to swamp the lifeworld (Spracklen, 2009, 2011, 2013b). If physical activity is to be meaningful to us as rational human beings, it has to be something that is freely chosen and freely engaged in, individually or socially.

As physical education and school sport are particularly modern examples of compulsory, structured physical activity, then it is obvious that there is a problem in making a claim about compulsory physical education and school sport as a moral or social good. They are part of the instrumental leisure structures of this moment in late modernity (Spracklen, 2011). People who are strong advocates of the value of physical education based on their own positive experience are naïve or misguided, or dangerously optimistic. There is no evidence to suggest that physical education or school sports have any unique and intrinsic moral or ethical value when they are made compulsory. And there is no evidence to suggest it is a social good – in fact, there is lots of evidence to point the other way. Instead, there is an incoherent rhetorical argument made based, on the one hand, on a hidden instrumentalism, and on the other hand on romantic benevolence. The things that should be compulsory in schools do have clear moral and social goods. It is impossible to be a functioning adult member of the lifeworld without having the ability to make critical judgements, express yourself and balance evidence. In our liberal democracies, then, we have to make sure that all children are taught subjects that will make them critical thinkers: they need to be able to read, they need to be able to write, they need to be able to understand mathematics and science, they need to have a grounding in humanities and social sciences, they need to know some other languages to help them get by in the global society we live in. These enable children to become members of the lifeworld. Physical education is not one of those kinds of subject. It is nice to do for those who want it, but not essential. Against the teacher-knows-best attitude, it is clear that the case made is purely subjective: you had a good physical education experience, maybe I had a bad one, but at least I have not made my case against compulsory physical education on the back of my own experience. Actually I like physical activity, and I do think it's good for me, and good for people who do it – I just do not want to extrapolate from my happy experiences to a universal law about what young people should be doing in school.

With regards to the utilitarian argument for physical education, it is in fact difficult to make because the evidence suggests that participation rates in physical activity among adults are actually dropping or flat-lining, not rising, despite the amount of time and money spent on compulsory physical education, school sport and sports development (Coalter, 2013). This evidence that adult people do not continue any physical activity beyond education tallies with the research evidence gathered by sociologists of significant proportions of class cohorts being alienated from compulsory physical education, school sport and physical activity (Svare, 2004). If we want people to do more physical activity, then, we have no option but to strike compulsory physical education off the curriculum. If we really think sports and/or physical activities are good things we should allow young people to choose to do them willingly, to find out about them through a voluntary search. That way, they are more likely to stay involved, and less likely to drop out of physical activity altogether. Keeping physical education on the curriculum as a compulsory subject, then, is harmful to individuals who have bad experiences; harmful to sport when participation rates continue to drop beyond school-age; and, perhaps, harmful to the wellbeing of society.

Instrumentality and physical education in China

For the elites of pre-modern China, leisure sites divided into the formal rituals of the court and temple, and the informal and private domestic activities of the home. In both sites, men and women were expected to conform to their gender roles, and to respect the hierarchies of class and caste. Sports and physical activities were seen as not be-fitting proper, elite gentlemen. Instead, leisure for these elites involved contemplation, reading, and listening to recitations and music. In the public spaces of the court and temple, men could become involved in strenuous activities such as archery and hunting, but these were linked to military training and instrumental obeisance, and were not free choices made for the love of physicality. China first modernized under the Nationalists, who encouraged Westernization and urbanization. Under the reign of the Communists, nationalist festivals and ceremonies were (re)created for mass participation and in-strumental conformity, some traditional Chinese plays were judged to be educational because of their correct themes, and Chinese youth were encouraged to take part in sports and physical recreation, such as gymnastics and physical training, through con-trol of the school curriculum (Riordan and Jones, 1999). The Communist Party is able to make physical education compulsory because of its complete control of the state.

> **QUESTIONS TO CONSIDER**
>
> *Why did the Communist Party take so much interest in physical activity? What moral panics exist in contemporary China?*
>
> **REFERENCE AND FURTHER READING**
>
> Riordan, J. and Jones, R. (1999) *Sport and Physical Education in China*, London, Taylor and Francis.

CONCLUSION

It has been argued here that compulsory physical education puts some young people off from playing sports and being physically active. The future of sport and physical activity is actually threatened by the instrumentalization of activities that should by definition be voluntary. Just because we have had physical education and school sport on the curriculum for the past hundred years does not mean it should stay there. Some traditions are good, some are bad, some make no difference to people's lives, some are deeply harmful. The curriculum of today is actually very different to that of thirty years ago. What schools should teach should not be based on what the teachers and policy-makers were taught: schools should teach what teachers, parents, communities, governors, councils and nation-states believe are the subjects most important to individual and social wellbeing (and possibly economic, too). There is no reason to keep compulsory physical education and school sport because of habit or subjective experience. In the next two chapters the exclusionary nature of sport and sports science will be explored through a discussion of the limits of sports science, and the role of sport and sports science in constructing myths about biology and essentialism.

EXERCISES

1 If physical education became voluntary, how could provision be made fair?
2 'School sports should be replaced by informal play sessions'. Do you agree? Discuss.
3 What role should sports clubs have in promoting sports for young people?

Chapter 10

The Limits of Sports Science

SUMMARY OF TOPICS

■ *Born athletes and definitions of epistemology and ontology*
■ *History of coaching and sports science*
■ *What can we know? The difference between natural science and social science*
■ *The development and status of sports science*

In the last chapter a critique was made about the ways in which people in sport have tried to use schools as a way of making athletes. This chapter begins by asking the popular question – are athletes born or made? This will introduce the issue of the limits of sports science, the extent to which it is possible for science to continually provide modifications and improvements to sporting bodies. The history of coaching and sports science will be examined, along with philosophical debates about the limits of science, the connection between the natural and the social, and the uses of science. Academic research will show that the success of sports science is ultimately connected with socio-economic factors such as the wealth of nations, the budgets given to the governing bodies of sports, and the economic interests of corporations that own brands, patents and technologies. This chapter will argue that sports science has proven its potential in the domain of elite sports, but this only proves the economic power of rich nations to buy sports success – and it is not clear that this will continue indefinitely. It will be argued that sports sciences, with the exception of psychology, have not provided any sustained way of improving other aspects of physical culture, though such benefits may well be possible.

BORN ATHLETES AND DEFINITIONS OF EPISTEMOLOGY AND ONTOLOGY

Are athletes born or made? Despite the weakness of the arguments about biological essentialism when it comes to 'race' and gender, it seems fairly safe to say that some people have the right biological characteristics to do well at some sports and not others. My childhood dream of playing professional rugby league evaporated when I realized I was never going to be big enough or strong enough to compete. Most people can play any sport to a greater or lesser extent, but elite, professional athletes have to have the right basic shape and internal systems (there are exceptions of course, where elite athletes have become successful despite their unconventional bodies, because they have exceptional mental abilities, psychological strengths or other unlikely biological characteristics). But the bodies are not enough to succeed. To become the best, an athlete has to be identified by the elite sports systems: sports coaching and sports development programmes. Then they have to undergo high-performance training and development to become elite athletes. So while it is true to say that biological differences limit the opportunities to be a successful athlete, elite athletes in modern sports today are made by the sports science technologies that develop and nurture them. But what are the limits of that sports science technology? What does it mean to say we know what makes successful elite athletes? What are the limits to our knowledge about sports science and other technologies that shape the modern sports competition? And how can we be confident that such knowledge-claims tell us something about the nature of things? When we ask questions about how we come to know things, these are called epistemological questions (Bird, 1992; Papineau, 1996).

When we ask questions about the nature of things, or the reality of things, we are asking ontological questions (Psillos, 1999). Both kinds of questions are important in understanding the role of science, its history and philosophy. Why should we consider truth-claims to be true? What is special about science? And do the epistemological and ontological claims in sports science match the standards set by 'mainstream' sciences such as physics or chemistry? Before I try to sketch out the deep philosophical problems and how they might help us understand the limits of sports science, we first need to explore the history of coaching and sports science.

HISTORY OF COACHING AND SPORTS SCIENCE

In the early years of modern sports, competitors tried to gain advantage over each other through superstitions, trial and error, irrational beliefs about clothing and times of the day, prayer and training of the body. All these things were haphazardly applied to improving performance, as we have seen in the chapter about performance enhancement (Chapter 8). As sports contests became more important, and players started to become more professional, sports clubs and teams started to retain coaches or trainers, usually ex-players, who could attend to the preparation of the athletes (Vamplew, 2004). That preparation initially consisted of teaching athletes the skills of the particular sport, though some trainers and coaches put their athletes on special diets (alcohol was famously used to stimulate rugby players before a match – see Collins and Vamplew, 2002). This was a form of folk science (Keil, 2010), taking a combination of half-understood popular science claims in the newspapers and magazines and combining them with the practical knowhow of how one might improve one's performance – what Polanyi (1958) calls tacit knowledge. For the athletes and clubs of professional and elite sport in the late nineteenth century, this folk science was enough to satisfy them that they were doing all they could to get winning athletes.

The initial development of sports science in the early twentieth century was fuelled by the rapid growth, and increasing importance, of collegiate sport in American popular culture. Backers and fans demanded the development of 'proper' scientific knowledge about the best diets, the best regimes of training and development, and the best ways in which 'natural' performance could be improved through the creation of various technologies (Beamish and Ritchie, 2006). Being based in elite American universities, these sports teams found scientists in labs nearby who could give them practical solutions to their coaching and development problems, using the latest scientific knowledge and methods. So there was a swift development of the discipline of sports science as the application of existing scientific disciplines (mainly biology but elements of chemistry and physics as well) to solving coaching and performance problems (Wrynn, 2003). In the period between the two world wars, sports science struggled to be accepted as a proper scientific discipline in science departments, but it did become something that sports governing bodies, clubs, coaches and athletes started to accept as an important technology of improvement (Ivy, 2007). That said, sports science struggled to distinguish its findings and recommendations from the folk science and tacit knowledge that continued to shape sports coaching philosophies and techniques (Twietmeyer, 2012) – a problem that still plagues debates on sports coaching even today (Taylor and Garrett, 2010).

Pioneers and mavericks: the professionalization of sports coaching

Bodnar and Perenyi (2012) explore the socio-historical frameworks that legitimized the sports coach as a professional in Hungary from the nineteenth into the twentieth century. Following the work of Allen Guttmann on the emergence and structure of modern sport, they argue that sports coaching pedagogy in Hungary was not recognized as being of much importance to Hungarian sports governing bodies and committees until the 1920s. Bodnar and Perenyi show that modern sports spread rapidly from Great Britain to the elites of the Austro-Hungarian Empire, and in the nineteenth century members of an athletics club and a rowing club sought advice from Britain about how to prepare and play modern sports. But these attempts to understand the sports were not precursors of formal, professionalized coaching. The people who acted as conduits of knowledge transfer were all players or ex-players, who provided *ad hoc* support and advice on an amateur basis. Sports clubs in Hungary remained committed fully to the ideology of amateurism, and while they took preparation and training as important, this was left to the devices of individual gentlemen who swore oaths to one another to train in their leisure time. Following the break-up of the Empire and the emergence of Hungary as an independent nation-state, sporting success of the country at the Olympics became a source of shame, as Hungarian athletes failed to compete against their better-trained rivals. So Hungarian policy-makers established a number of schemes to improve elite sports performance, and professionalized coaching regimens, with professional coaching techniques, were adopted.

QUESTIONS TO CONSIDER

What else was happening in the 1920s that spurred on professionalization in sports coaching? How did Hungarian sports policies change in the second half of the twentieth century?

REFERENCE AND FURTHER READING

Bodnar, I. and Perenyi, S. (2012) 'A Socio-historical Approach to the Professionalisation of Sporting Occupations in Hungary during the First Decades of the Twentieth Century: The Coach', *The International Journal of the History of Sport*, 29, pp. 1097–124.

The growth of sports science was appropriately linked to the growth in the importance of sports and physical activity, as mass practices and professional industries. In the period following the end of the Second World War, the boom in professional sport in the West encouraged scientists to try to assist athletes and coaches to find that 'winning edge'. Professional sports clubs and sports governing bodies employed professional coaching staff and advisers from university kinesiology and physical education departments. The Cold War struggle between the American West and the Communist East led to countries on both sides investing money in sports science and professionalized training and development regimes. In the West, this led to the establishment of sports science departments, learned societies, academic journals and systems of grants and sponsorship for applied research. In Eastern Europe, the performance focus of sports science to make Communist athletes bigger, faster and stronger than their Western counterparts led to the creation of huge systems of performance-enhancing technologies. While the West lacked the internal power of the Communist elites to dictate policies and strategies, huge amounts of money were invested in sports science in the expectation that ways to make Western athletes beat their rivals would be found in the lab (Riordan, 1991). The Eastern European model of sports science and elite sports coaching and development was adopted by many other countries around the world, especially after the fall of the Iron Curtain led to the migration of Eastern European coaches and sports scientists (Beamish and Ritchie, 2006). In Australia, the focus on elite sport and winning through science was adopted by the Federal Government (Green and Houlihan, 2005). Sport was seen as an important part of Australian national culture and huge amounts of funding were given to universities, sports governing bodies and stand-alone agencies with labs and other facilities. In the United Kingdom, the growth in sports science closely followed growth in the United States and Eastern Europe. But the growth in the discipline was slower due to a failure to capture funding streams from the public and private sectors, and a problem with training sports scientists with sufficient knowledge and skills themselves (sports science degrees were slow to be introduced, and even where they existed they were often multi-disciplinary and applied, rather than theoretical and research-driven). As historically successive British governments did not think professional or elite sport (or any sports) worthy of their funding or attention, sports policies aimed at winning medals and promoting participation were un-coordinated or non-existent (Green and Houlihan, 2005).

Sports science, then, has had to fight to legitimize itself in academic institutions (other scientists not treating it seriously), in governments (science funding should be reserved for things deemed important to national security or economic success) and sports themselves (coaches being reluctant to change their tacit knowledge). More recently, sports science has had to recognize the growth of academic interest in health and exercise, and physical activity more generally, and the discipline is often referred to as 'sport and exercise science'. The 'and exercise' in the new name reflects an argument among scientists in the discipline that too much attention has been focused on solving problems in elite sport, and not enough has been done to understand the role of physical activity in wellbeing. Other threats to the boundaries of the discipline include the splintering of sports science into the sub-disciplines inside it, such as sport and exercise psychology (which has its own courses, its own journals and its own textbooks). In this century, sports science develops in tandem with the development of modern, professional sport and/or the establishment of sport as a central policy concern for governments. Sports science initially developed in response to a need to have evidence-based strategies for improving elite performance but now politicians and policy-makers expect sports and physical activity – and sports scientists – to solve a range of political problems, sometimes problems that seem to have little connection to the aims and objectives of sports science. The balance between politics, sport and sports science suggests a pattern of power similar to that identified by Fuller (1993, 2000) in the governance of science: sports scientists are persuaded through funding competitions, the accounting of research outputs and the pressure of their own performance-management regimes to do what the funders want them to do, rather than pursue scientific problems in the idealized advancement of knowledge.

THE LIMITS OF SCIENCE, NATURAL SCIENCE AND SOCIAL SCIENCE

In thinking about sports science in this way, we are doing sociology of science. This is a relatively new academic discipline drawing on the history and philosophy of science (Collins, 1992; Latour, 1987; Merton, 1973; Woolgar, 1981). It is concerned with exploring science as a social activity, the relationship between science as practice, scientific method and the nature of theories, claims and consensus. Sociologists of science provide a strong critique of the scientific method, of truth and of science as understood by scientists, but this does not necessarily lead to extreme relativism. Being sceptical about some of the claims made by science and by scientists does not mean we throw out all claims about truth. But it does mean we have to think harder to establish why we trust science, and its claims, and what the limits of that trust might mean for sports science. Sociology of science is inseparable from the philosophy of science. How is sports science justified? How do sports scientists come to their conclusions? These are valid questions to ask and stem from those raised when questioning epistemological and ontological claims in science: what is this thing called science (as Chalmers,

1999, puts it in the title of his book)? What is the scientific method? Why do we trust scientific arguments? Can science tell us something true about the world? Is there a world we can be 'true' about?

Sports science is said to be a natural science or a hard science, in comparison with sociology, which is said to be a social science. Social sciences are stereotypically viewed by natural scientists as being concerned with narratives and particulars and descriptions of things, without having anything important to say by way of explanation or prediction. Social science is often qualitative in its methods, and its subjects are often impossible to test or manipulate under laboratory conditions. Natural science represents the best way to find things out about the world, and natural scientists are often identified as being concerned with using a particular method that is the best way of finding out the truth. In textbooks and popular accounts of science, the 'scientific method' is described and defined as being rational, objective, normative, valid and reliable (Chalmers, 1999). Scientists use statistical models to test the veracity of their findings and claims. They use controlled experimental conditions to test hypotheses, or they use experiments to gather facts that they develop into general theories about the world. The Baconian account of science is that scientific knowledge progresses through a process of induction. We observe, gather data, then we find out the truth. An alternative account of science is to say we start with a theory, and test its truthfulness against the data. This is the hypothetico-deductive account of the scientific method (Bird, 1992).

Let us consider a hypothetical example. Let us say we are having a conversation and I tell you I think carrot juice makes you run faster (before we continue, let me point out this is not something I actually think, I am just pretending for the argument that I am making in this book). Now in what ways might I try to justify that truth-claim to you? I might say I believe it because I eat carrots and I run fast, or I might say I believe it because all the good runners I know drink carrot juice. I would be appealing to my experience, but you would find such truth-claims weak, because my experience should not count for anything in trying to persuade you. I might say I believe carrot juice makes you run faster because my friend told me and I believe her. That would again be a weak claim. But I might say something more sophisticated. I might say I believe it to be true because Aristotle says so in one of his books and he is always right. How do we know it to be true? We could rely on experience and authority, but these are often wrong, and always lack any objective reason to believe in them. Or we could point to some proof that has been gathered that is valid and reliable, and meets the criteria by which we assess proper scientific truth-claims.

Let us say I tell you I believe the claim because Stephen Hawking did an experiment that showed people who drank carrot juice ran faster than those who did not drink it. Why do we trust Hawking's experiment? What method has he chosen to convince us? What philosophical argument has he put together to prove the original hypothesis? There are different ways to be convincing. We could say our belief in the claim is because of our socio-cultural bias. We trust Hawking because we know he is really clever (if you really don't know who he is look on the internet, or watch *The Big Bang Theory*). He is a scientist with a good track record. In practice, most of the general public will only ever get this far when they think why they believe things – people believe things because teachers and the media tell them the beliefs are reasonable and in line with scientific norms. Proper scientists have to read the original research to find out what other scientists have done and why they are making claims about things. Scientific knowledge is tested in the philosophical analysis of the published research. So I might tell you I trust Hawking's claim about carrot juice because he has used a scientific method, inductive reasoning, to come to his conclusion. Hawking has made repeated observations of carrot-juice fuelled runners. He has compared their performance to runners not on the juice, and he has compared the same runners 'before and after' carrot-juice drinking. He might even have used 'double-blind testing', so that the runners and the researchers do not know who is on the carrot juice. But whichever way he has done the research, ultimately the foundation of his method is inductive logic. He has seen the carrots work for a hundred people in his study, and the inference is that this effect will work on anyone, that carrot juice really does work.

The problem with inductive logic has already been discussed briefly in the chapter on performance enhancement (Chapter 8), but it is important enough to discuss it again in more detail. It is associated by philosophers today with David Hume (1978), who first clearly articulated the problem with inductive methods. The problem is this: no matter how many times you observe something, you cannot make a valid logical leap from the observations to any certainty about the truth of a hypothesis. But we do this all the time, both in everyday life, and in science and natural philosophy. And that is the problem. We think we know things about the world based on observation and the gathering of facts. But our confidence in the truth of our knowledge is wrong-headed of us. Hume asks us to think about the rising of the sun, and asks us: where does the sun rise? In the east, of course, is what our answer would be. But how do we know that? We might say we have seen it rise in the east a million times, and we might show Hume all the old records from the Chinese and the Babylonians. Hume might then say: okay, some people in the past saw it rise in the east, and you might have seen it rise there yourself, but where will the sun rise tomorrow? In the east, you might say, because it always has done. But past form is no guide to future truth, and specific observations cannot simply be general truths about all things at all times. So we cannot say carrot juice makes you run faster, even if we have the experimental data that seems to show it to be true.

One way to solve this problem is to resort to Popperian falsificationism. Karl Popper was an influential twentieth-century philosopher of science, who argued that for science to work and for knowledge to progress, science had to work not by proving things were true (impossible because of the induction problem), but by showing things were false. For Popper (2005), a proper science operated by testing and disproving hypotheses, which is possible to do with as few as one observation that contradicts a hypothesis. What does that mean? Consider the statement 'all football fans are hooligans'. How can we show this to be true? How can we prove it? It is impossible to prove, no matter how many hooligan fans we observe; but it is easily disproved and shown to be false by the simple observation of one fan who is clearly not a hooligan. Falsificationism is a great idea and an excellent solution to the problem of induction. It saves the progress of scientific knowledge. We could easily see how we might do an experiment to disprove the hypothesis that carrot juice makes you run faster. But most scientists do seem to want to prove their hypotheses and theories to be true.

Another twentieth-century philosopher of science, Thomas Kuhn (1962), took a different approach to Popper. Instead of saying 'this is how science should work if we're going to do anything about truth', Kuhn looked at how science actually works. He argued that most science operates within a social network and community and framework of knowledge (what he called a paradigm) as 'normal science'. Most scientists agree that normal science operates and succeeds because of its rule-following within a paradigm of assumptions and hypotheses. In the paradigm of science today, the problem of induction is solved by adopting statistical tests of probabilities and causal effects. So everybody in science might agree that having a one in ten million chance of being wrong about a hypothesis is good enough to work with, and secure enough to build scientific knowledge (Psillos, 1999). Certain knowledge is replaced by probable knowledge. For Kuhn, normal science dominates scientific practice, but eventually it is challenged by one or more findings that undermine its foundations. When normal science breaks down it goes through a revolutionary phase before a new paradigm emerges. That paradigm, crucially, is incommensurable with the previous one: it cannot be compared, and we cannot say one is 'more true' than another. The question is – in what sense are sciences said to be different paradigms? And are there different paradigms of sport and exercise science?

From Popper, we see that rather than trying to prove carrot juice makes us run faster, it is our job to try to disprove the hypothesis 'all people drinking carrot juice will run faster'. From Kuhn, we can see that there is a paradigm within sports science that sets the limits of normal investigations, using probabilities. Our carrot-juice hypothesis then becomes a puzzle to be solved using agreed tools and methods. And crucially, it is sports scientists who pass judgement on what is an epistemological problem for sports science – in this way, the problem of induction is sidestepped. For sports scientists to generate knowledge they need access to technologies in the lab that reduce uncertainties, but also access to scientific journals and academic libraries. To help sports science succeed, scientists need to be fully trained in statistics and complicated laboratory procedures. The success of sports science depends in part, then, on its socio-cultural context, and the socio-economic strength of the country in which the scientists work.

One other problem faces sports scientists: the problem of realism. Consider another hypothetical example. We want to help England win the next soccer World Cup, and historically the team has failed at penalty shoot-outs, so we are trying to see if we can give the team psychological training to help them kick penalties under pressure. What is the theoretical basis of this problem? What assumptions are we making about reality? Let's say we will make each player change his socks before taking any penalties in training. Every player will then be told to change their socks before taking penalties in the World Cup. There is evidence that a ritual like this can help to associate particular practices with particular states of mind (Damisch, Stoberock and Mussweiler, 2010). What we are doing is seeing if the players can stay as focused under pressure as they are on the training ground. In fact, we are not concerned with being 'focused', we are concerned with concentration. And we know from psychology that concentrating on something is to do with attention, which is a cognitive process. Attention is 'selective concentration' – the way in which we seem to filter out some of the noise around us to listen to the conversations that matter to us, for example. William James (1890) began work on attention in the late nineteenth century, working from introspection (thinking about himself).

But what is it that is behind this attention state, this selective concentration? What is really going on? It is a mental process, but that does not make it much clearer. Some people might say it is something to do with your soul. Some will say it is shorthand for a physical state, specified in terms of neurons firing and not firing in the brain. Some will say it is something more than the chemistry of the brain, but not quite something like a traditional soul. Some people will just say it is a description of the player's ability to perform a task in a busy environment, and that's all we can say about it. Some people might just tell us attention is just attention, get over it. The latter sentence is a version of what philosophers call common-sense realism (Chalmers, 1999). We know what it is. We know explanations of behaviour which use attention work. We also know it describes people's behaviour pretty much as we see it. We can all experience it in action. Our experience tells us that people have mental states, psychological theory describes reality, and reality is really there.

Unfortunately, all the evidence for common-sense realism can be used to describe a world where we are brains in jars, subject to aliens who make us believe in reality. It is possible to imagine a situation where we are fooled by our senses, or deliberately manipulated to think the world is the way we see it. In Plato's famous Cave Allegory in *The Republic*, reality is the Ideal of the Forms (Plato, 2007). We can only ever have partial knowledge of the Forms since we cannot experience them. What we think of as 'truth' is like a shadow on a wall in a cave. In his First Meditation (in his *Meditations on First Philosophy*) Descartes (2003) outlines three 'skeptical' arguments about reality: our perceptions deceive us; dreams are as real as reality; and God could be tricking us. This is why his entire philosophy, as spelled out in his Second Meditation, starts from the one axiom he takes to be the only truth: I think therefore I am. Berkeley (2009) argued against the Cartesians by admitting that matter did not exist, but that did not matter. Science could find out the truth because God made the non-material ideas in our mind behave in a way that was rational and ordered. These ideas are ordered in a way that makes sense to us. Only through accepting idealism can natural philosophy (science) be defended from outright scepticism, since idealism is predicated on certainty and regularity.

This is a huge philosophical problem for science. Some people might just choose to give up and drop out of science at this point, if everything is like the Matrix. But scientists are confident about the reality of the work they do. Why? One possible solution is to look at the way language works, and say that when we talk about truth, we really do mean the truth. So if there is a truth-claim in a scientific paper, the truth really is the truth, based on something really real. Popper believed we can have a sense of approximation to truth, and theories can provide us with something close to reality through the idea of verisimilitude. Popper said verisimilitude is the measure of truth content minus the measure of falsity content in a theory. We can compare two theories and say one corresponds more closely with the facts. He said through this calculating machine of 'truthness' we can reach an approximate truth about 'reality'. Is this how scientists actually work? Critics of verisimilitude claim it introduces an element of instrumentalism (Psillos, 2009). Instrumentalism is ontological scepticism: it says we don't know (can't know) about the truth of our concepts of reality. All we know is 'what works'. This has happened in science in history, and we can see it happening in science now. Van Fraassen (1980) says all science is based on real knowledge of what can be observed, but instrumentalist knowledge about what cannot be observed. But it is difficult to make a sharp distinction between what can be seen and what cannot be seen: what is the nature of the 'seen' in something like a BMI measure? Even though some scientists do seem to be instrumentalists, ultimately the aim of science is to understand reality. Instrumentalism seems to be too cautious in its commitment to theories and it seems to lead us into ontological and epistemological relativism (where we have no way of being certain about anything).

The physical limits of sports science

In the last fifty years, there has been a huge surge of record-breaking in most elite sports. People are running faster, people are scoring more goals, people are lifting heavier weights, and people are throwing things farther than before. Sports science and elite sports coaching is partly responsible for this development: athletes are being made, and new technologies are being introduced to improve performances. However, some academics have raised the question about the physical limits of human biology and human-constructed technologies (Nevill and Whyte, 2005). In the 100 metre sprint, as an obvious example, the world record has been continually improved upon, but there seems to be an upper limit to human performance. No human seems to be born or made to be able to do anything but take the record a tiny fraction of a second closer to nine seconds. The nine-second barrier might one day be broken by some freak of nature but the history of the record and our knowledge of physiology and biomechanics mean we will probably never see the world record drop to seven seconds. What this might mean for sports science is a physical limit to its usefulness. If there are limits to record-breaking due to the limits of human evolutionary design, at some stage sports science will lose its claim to provide a winning edge, and will perhaps become obsolete as a science. Of course, there is nothing except ethics to stop sports scientists producing genetically-modified athletes.

QUESTIONS TO CONSIDER

What physical limits might be at work on technologies? What sports might be unlimited by biology?

REFERENCE AND FURTHER READING

Nevill, A.M. and Whyte, G. (2005) 'Are There Limits to Running World Records?', *Medicine and Science in Sports and Exercise*, 37, pp. 1785–88.

The solution in modern science seems to be in accepting the way in which models, and the mathematical structures behind them, operate as approximations of reality. Cartwright (1983) has argued that all scientific laws lie about reality. Scientific laws are laws that hold only under *ceteris paribus* conditions, situations that are idealized and abstracted from actual messy real-world conditions. Look at examples in sports science like using proxy scores on VO_2 as a marker of fitness. (VO_2 is a commonly-used measure for assessing the maximum rate of oxygen consumption during physical exercise.) For some people the measure will be a good approximation, for others they will be fitter or less fit than the scores. But overall, the modelling works and is more 'real' than the everyday reality of individual scores. Hence the reality of science is somehow expressed through models. French and Saatsi (2006) have suggested that realism in science is best understood through appealing to mathematical structures – to models. Any attempt to extend realism beyond these structures leads us into ontological and epistemological dangers, as we saw. But progress and understanding is 'saved' by taking this structural view of realism.

What does this mean for sports science? Consider attention and our work with England's men's soccer team. We could take an instrumentalist approach and not worry about the nature of the mental state that underpins a footballer's 'focus'. In practice, this is what many sports scientists do: apply theories and gather data without worrying too much about reality – only what works. But we would like to know what is 'actually' going on, wouldn't we? We do want science to be based on realism. So maybe what we need to do is understand the idea of a cognitive process as a *ceteris paribus* law, that models an underlying structural reality ... so if a footballer is on the spot again, we can have confidence about something. Again, if sports science is to be able to build proper models, sports scientists need to have the mathematical competence and the access to equipment and research papers that comes only with wider socio-economic controls of power and wealth.

Sports medicine, winning and ethics

Modern scientific medicine has become an essential part of elite sports science and elite sport's practices. Medical sciences have introduced a wide range of technologies that can help elite athletes, from oxygen tents that aid recovery and physiological checks on general health, through to pain-killing injections and first aid in the middle of a competitive event. Doctors and other medical practitioners abide by a professional ethical code that says they must not breach their duty of care for a patient. Their meaning and purpose is to heal the injured and sick, to provide advice and guidance to those who are ill, and to make sure the profession's ethics are not brought into disrepute. As

Anderson and Jackson (2012) show, the ethics of modern medicine and the business of elite, professional sport do not fit easily alongside each other. Doctors feel uncomfortable giving injured athletes injections to keep them playing, and often feel they are under pressure from coaches and managers to keep athletes in the competition rather than looking after their health and wellbeing. Sports medicine has become a lucrative part of sports science, and even though sports governing bodies create policies that protect their athletes from being harmed, medical practitioners and scientists can always be found who will give the coaches the justification and the material needed to keep an athlete going.

QUESTIONS TO CONSIDER

What epistemological problems face sport medicine? What is the legal and policy framework for sports medicine today?

REFERENCE AND FURTHER READING

Anderson, J. and Jackson, S. (2012) 'Competing Loyalties in Sports Medicine: Threats to Medical Professionalism in Elite, Commercial Sport', *International Review for the Sociology of Sport*, 48, pp. 238–56.

CONCLUSION

Elite sports success has been found through the application of rigorous sports science research in physiology, nutrition, biomechanics and psychology. It is now commonplace for sports governing bodies, national sports committees and professional sports clubs to have professional sports scientists working full-time as advisers. Sport coaching as a practice has become more professional and scientific in its approach, through the adoption of scientific training and education, and the proliferation of science-based sports degrees. This has all led to some results, especially in sports such as cycling and running, though the extent to which sports science interventions have directly caused sports success is debatable. The scientific training needed to understand sports science research papers had proved a limiting factor in knowledge being passed on to coaches and athletes, and like other scientific research, sports science is often the subject of simplistic claims or misrepresentations in the media. But sports science has undoubtedly been successful in elite sport. The success of sports science is ultimately connected with socio-economic factors such as the wealth of nations, the budgets given to the governing bodies of sports, and the economic interests of corporations that own brands, patents and technologies. Sports science has proven its potential in the domain of elite sports, but this only proves the economic power of rich nations to buy sports success – and it is not clear that this will continue indefinitely. It is still to be demonstrated that sports sciences, with the exception of psychology, have provided any sustained way of improving other aspects of physical culture, though such benefits may well be possible. In the next chapter, we will focus the critique on biological essentialism – how does sport construct myths about 'race' and 'sex'?

EXERCISES

1 How has sports science developed as a science and a subject in this century?
2 Is sports psychology reducible to brain chemistry? Discuss.
3 In what ways does tacit knowledge and folk science continue to inform sports coaching and sports science today?

Chapter 11

Biology and Essentialism

SUMMARY OF TOPICS

▨ *Definitions: 'race', ethnicity, 'sex', gender*
▨ *The role of modern sport in constructing false ideas about 'race'*
▨ *The relationship between modern sport and contested ideas about gender and 'sex'*
▨ *The social and cultural values associated with modern sport*

In the last chapter I discussed the limits of sports science. In this chapter, the science of biological essentialism will be discussed in relation to modern sport. People involved in sport (including some academics) still say women are 'weaker' than men, or black athletes are faster than white athletes. When pressed, these people refer to various popular scientific accounts of genetics, biomechanics, physiology or psychology. Most people think in stereotypes about the sporting physicality of men, and the sporting physicality of black people – and these stereotypes are based on a limited understanding of biology and sociology. This chapter will examine the ways in which differences in rates of participation and differences in elite performances are explained away by essentializing problematic categories such as 'race' and 'sex' as biological truths. On 'race', it will be argued that the dominance of 'black' athletes in some elite sports is a measure of racism, social exclusion, belief in stereotypes and limited opportunities for socially disadvantaged young people. On 'sex' differences, it will be argued that sports have always been used to give men room to develop and express dominant forms of masculinity – the history of modern sport is of men playing sport and being given the opportunity to play sport, while women have been discouraged from participating.

Testing for sex, testing for gender: the Olympic problem

Historically, the Olympic Games were revived in the nineteenth century by men for men, and the question about the sexual organs or sexual markers of the participants was never really considered in 1896. Men were men and the athletes were men, competing against one another to prove who would be the best man at that particular sports contest. Women were not allowed to compete against men, and their involvement in sport was discouraged and generally side-lined. By 1900 women were grudgingly admitted into the Olympics, but in segregated events and in very restricted circumstances. Over the course of the century women struggled to increase their presence in elite sports events, and although the trajectory was progressive women's sports and women athletes were still mainly segregated, and still given less prominence than their male equivalents. In the late twentieth century, stories started to circulate about men secretly competing as women for certain countries in certain sports. This rumour was based on the assumption that men were naturally stronger and faster than women, and any woman who beat her rivals in a convincing fashion was 'suspect' – especially if her body shape was not stereotypically feminine. This led to the creation of sex testing regimes at the Olympics and other elite events, crude physical examinations of genitalia, and latterly gender tests that used body samples to find a range of contested sexual markers (Wiesemann, 2011). These tests have humiliated women athletes and subjected them to tests that male athletes have never had to suffer. They also impose a narrow definition of what it means to be female, and normalize the stereotype that women are weaker than men.

QUESTIONS TO CONSIDER

What is the recent history of the scare story? What else is at stake in the testing?

REFERENCE AND FURTHER READING

Wiesemann, C. (2011) 'Is There a Right Not to Know One's Sex? The Ethics of "Gender Verification" in Women's Sports Competition', *Journal of Medical Ethics*, 37, pp. 216–20.

DEFINITIONS: 'RACE', ETHNICITY, 'SEX', GENDER

This entire chapter is a strong critique of 'race' and 'sex' as essential differences that make one group of people better than another at sport. But some preliminary definitions are needed here, even if we reject them later on. 'Race' is a term still used today to identify groups of humans who supposedly share common ancestry that is exclusive to them. This definition is incredibly problematic as it is based on an assumption that there are discrete biological differences between the races, and that races actually exist – that is why I used the term in inverted commas. Ethnicity is a term used to describe the culture and language that a group of people might hold in common with each other, which is distinctive from the culture and language of another group. We are all supposed to have an ethnicity – mine might be associated with whiteness or Englishness, perhaps. 'Sex' is the biological sorting of humans into two categories – male and female – based on sexual organs and chromosomes (which give rise to some secondary sexual characteristics). The sorting is not always so clear cut, and many humans actually have a range of biological characteristics associated with both sexes (Fausto-Sterling, 2012). Gender is often used as a term to describe the social construction of male and female, the labels created by humans for each other and for themselves – though it is now common to see the term used in place of 'sex'.

ON 'RACE' AND SPORT

Many people in sport – and some sports scientists – still believe that black people as a 'race' are better than white people as a 'race' at certain sports events, most notoriously sprinting. The argument seems to go that black people have different physiologies than white people, that they have denser fast-twitch muscle fibres. Many people in sport will also believe that white people as a 'race' are better than black people as a 'race' at swimming, which is said to be because black people physiologically are heavier boned. This is nonsense, bad science and egregious logic at work. But why do people believe it? You do not have to read far in the library to see such beliefs appearing in textbooks and even in some research papers published in sports science journals (for example, see Tucker, Santos-Concejero and Collins, 2013). Racial difference is normalized in the teaching of sports science to explain differences in elite performance. Many examples can be found. For example, the well-known exercise physiology textbook by McArdle, Katch and Katch (2001, pp. 801–2), in its fifth edition, has this to say:

> Racial differences in physique may significantly affect athletic performance ... compared with whites and blacks, Asian athletes have short legs relative to upper torso components, a dimensional characteristic beneficial in short and longer distance races and in weight lifting

This sounds very definitive. But at this point in the book the only evidence provided is a reference to a book about Olympic winners written in the 1960s. Philosophers of science say that remarkable claims need remarkable evidence (Papineau, 1996; Psillos, 1999). If you told me that drinking a certain fluid would improve my recovery rate after training by five per cent, and you showed me the research paper that made that claim, I would accept your claim because it was unremarkable. There is no controversy about such claims. There are no miracles involved, no egregious leaps of logic. If you told me that praying to the Goddess Athena would improve my recovery rate (beyond what might occur due to the placebo effect) I would be right to reject your claim, even if you had a research paper that claimed it to be true. I would need far stronger evidence before I accepted your claim, because to accept the claim would mean I would need you to prove to me that Athena existed, that she listened to prayers, and that she had the ability to work miracles on my behalf. So why is it that people in sport and in sports science still believe that races exist, and that they determine sporting success?

Racial sports science is the kind of sports science that promotes such claims. It has a long history in sport, and is bound up with the origins of modern sport. But it has become a matter of common opinion in bars and pubs where sports are discussed, mainly because of the growing visibility and presence of black athletes at elite, professional levels of sports. It is believed that the dominance of black athletes in basketball is because 'white men can't jump' (Hall, 2001). It is believed that the dominance of black people in the medals tables in sprinting and other athletic events is because black people are naturally physical, strong, and fast. Some sports scientists themselves have argued that the reason why so many black athletes have dominated sprint events at an elite level since the 1980s is just because 'black people are faster than white people', and they have claimed to provide scientific evidence that demonstrates this (see Tucker, Santos-Concejero and Collins, 2013).

The physiological difference, the edge for black athletes as a 'race', is often explained by claiming that black people as a biological, genetically distinct 'race' have more dense fast-twitch muscle fibres than white people, as John Entine (2000) argues. Entine also claims that sports science shows that black people have a higher bone density than white people, which accounts for the lack of black swimmers at elite level. Although Entine is a journalist, his arguments are based on the work of actual sports scientists. The belief that 'race' affects performance is a controversial one, but it is one that still appears in the work of scientists and sports scientists (see Van Damme and Wilson, 2002). This belief has to be viewed sceptically, but it is tied up with folk notions of 'race' and sport. Assumptions about the abilities of people because of their 'race' are still widely prevalent in sport. Coaches still believe that black people make better sprinters, for example, and young athletes are pushed into sprinting or out of sprinting depending on the colour of their skin (Eitzen, 2012). In rugby league, in the 1990s black people were shown to be in positions where speed, not skill, was important (Long, Carrington and Spracklen, 1997).

So where does this come from? These folk notions of 'race' seem to come from an over-confidence in genetics and heredity as arbiters of biological attributes, and weakly considered attempts to account for observed facts (the dominance of black athletes at sprint events since the 1980s being the most obvious example). What is being reified in this egregious argument is the spurious notion that there is a pure, authentic blood-line and kinship inside a community, and an impure blood-line among the evil, unknown Others who do not belong inside the community. In my home country, we do not elect our Head of State – that Queen or King is worshipped for its ability to be born from the same blood-line as its predecessor. We still try to find our ancestors, drawing genealogical maps that prove we are descended from some mythologized father figure, proving to ourselves that we belong to some far-away village or town, even though the simple maths of genetics proves only that everybody is related to everybody else, and we are all far removed from our distant ancestors (Gould, 1997; Hoberman, 1997). 'Holy Blood' is an old folk belief, and one that is observed by anthropologists across different cultures and societies (Douglas, 1991). The folk myth of blood and race/nation is easily observed in the work of JRR Tolkien, who was deliberately evoking these notions at a time when England was in the middle of a debate about Englishness – his hero, Aragorn, is a hero and King-in-exile because he has the blood of the higher men, the Numenoreans, running through his veins. His views on taxation, war and peace, governance, diplomacy and so on are irrelevant.

'Blood' attained pseudo-scientific legitimacy in the nineteenth century, when scientists started to make claims about struggles and competition between the 'races', which were identified as being bound by blood and ancestry. Charles Darwin's 1859 *The Origin of the Species* (Darwin, 2009) showed the importance of heredity, of breeding, in the emergence of species with a better fit to their environment. Although Darwin was wary of making the leap from his evolutionary theories about animals to a discussion about human society, others were not so shy. The ruling and middle classes of the Western nation-states took Darwin's theory of evolution through natural selection to account for the decline of the urban working classes in their own countries. They used Social Darwinism to prove that the European or white or Aryan race was the superior one, so empires and massacres and economic subjugation were just the 'natural' order of things (Daynes and Lee, 2008; Spracklen, 2013b). 'Race', then, justified Western hegemony but also justified elite public opinion about the degeneracy of the lower classes and other 'races'. Before Darwin had published his work, Malthus (2008) had suggested that human society would eventually outstrip the supply of food and resources. A Malthusian fear of the growth of the urban working class and the foreigners in colonies and on the doorstep (in New York, in London and all over the Western world) gripped the middle classes (Daynes and Lee, 2008).

Social Darwinists such as Galton developed accounts of change in human societies that suggested a disaster was on the way, because some people were degenerate but those were the ones breeding (Galton, 1883). This led to the legitimation of scientific racism, the claim that races were physiologically distinct and in competition with one another, but also that the white 'race' could be improved through eugenic policies of selective breeding and removal of undesirables (Gillette, 2007). Conveniently, Social Darwinism seemed to prove the superiority of the ruling classes, and their 'blood'. Social Darwinism also gave folk notions of race a scientific 'sheen' at a time when science was seen to be the only way to progress (Gould, 1997; Kohn, 1995). The fallacy of scientific racism is easily seen when it comes to the problem of how many races existed. Scientists agreed there was a white or Aryan 'race', but even with this 'race' there were debates about who was in it and which country represented the purist stock. Other 'races' were less easily defined and delineated, because of course these races were only figments of the imagination (Daynes and Lee, 2008). Scientific racism suggested that black people and other assorted foreigners were 'naturally' inferior, so no amount of civilizing could bring them up to the standard of the white/Aryan races (of course, that gave the white Europeans an excuse not to bother trying to improve the lives of their imperial subjects).

Scientific racism dominated physical anthropology and genetics as it developed in the early twentieth century, especially in the United States (Gould, 1997; Kohn, 1995). Scientific racism and Social Darwinism led to normative projects such as eugenics. Many mainstream politicians in the West in the early twentieth century supported steps to encourage selective breeding and to sterilize supposed 'undesirables'. This in turn led quite logically and inexorably to the atrocities of Nazi Germany and the end-point of Auschwitz (Gillette, 2007). In the aftermath of the Holocaust, scientists started to undertake research that undermined the foundations of 'race'. Firstly, there is far more genetic diversity in communities and countries than the racial scientists claimed (Gould, 1997). People have been travelling around the world for many years, hundreds and thousands, and have been starting families with people who are not closely related to them. Secondly, we are one species. We share far more with one another than we do not share (Daynes and Lee, 2008).

Following the Second World War, the United Nations systematically discredited scientific racism and the notion of 'race' (Brattain, 2007; Gould, 1997). But a remnant of such thinking remains in society, in sport, and in science. People still use the word and concept of 'race' uncritically, naïvely accepting that such a concept exists in the same biological and essentialist way as a species. Hence, when sports scientists refer to essential qualities of black people, they are starting out with an assertion that a black 'race' exists to which those qualities can be assigned. 'Race' is a term used to denote a group of people that supposedly share characteristics based on a shared biological heritage. It is not a concept to be comfortable with, and we should be wary about using it in everyday discourse, because to do so seems to imply we think there are these discrete biological entities. The United Nations adopted the concept of ethnicity. Ethnicity is an attempt to capture the cultural, national, linguistic, religious and historical background of a particular person or group of people and pigeon-hole them in a meaningful way. It is a concept that has come into favour to replace the more difficult and uncomfortable terminology of 'race'. So, ethnicity is a term used to denote a group of people who supposedly share characteristics based on a shared cultural heritage. But this potentially creates the same problem of essentialism – stereotyping and assumptions. Should I drink tea and eat fish and chips because I am English? Is ethnicity about self-determination? Can it account for multiple identities? Can it account for identities changing over time? Ethnicity can become essentialized stereotyping in the same way as 'race' (Berry and Bell, 2012).

'Race' and racism are normalized in modern sport. There is a wide body of research that suggests that there is, or was, a significant amount of racism in sport (Long and Spracklen, 2010; Spracklen, 2013b). In a study in 1995, thirteen per cent of English rugby league fans said it was acceptable to racially abuse a player (Long, Carrington and Spracklen, 1997). There are countless examples of high-profile sports stars, commentators and coaches being racist and using racial stereotypes. There are many stereotypes that exist in sport about 'racial groups'. We have seen the claims about black people being faster than white people, but others exist: Asians are too weak for tough contact sports, or, historically, Jews make good basketball players (which has now been replaced by the stereotype that Jews can't play basketball – see Spracklen, 2013b). This is, of course, absolute nonsense. Why? Because according to the Human Genome Project the genetic differences within 'racial groups' are often greater than those between groups (McCann-Mortimer, Augoustinos and LeCouteur, 2004). It is generally recognized that specific needs of minority ethnic groups have been ignored or marginalized by sports providers. There are problems of under-representation in some sports, such as canoeing or golf. There are problems of 'stacking' or over-representation in some sports. There are problems of racism across sport and leisure. And there is the problem of the lack of progression into administration and coaching in some sports. All these are social, cultural and political problems. They are not determined by biological fitness. But the hard determinism is still rolled out in sport and sports science.

As we have seen, one of the key sources for arguments in favour of 'hard determinism' is Entine (2000). Entine is an advocate of Nature over Nurture. Entine believes he has a good argument to prove black people are faster than white people, and says this is due to the nature of black people (their genes). This has a false premise. Entine and supporters of hard determinism are actually weak scientists, and their logic is not only false but egregious. Their assumptions are based on false premises about the existence of races. The egregious argument goes like this. Entine and the others start with the following observations: some black people can run really fast (this is a true observation); and those black people who run really fast have tended to beat white people who run fast but not quite as fast as them over the last few years (also a true observation). But then they take these specific observations and turn them into premises. So we get: there are two races called 'black' and 'white' (a completely false premise); black people in general run really fast (a false generalization of particular observations); and those black people have always beaten and always will beat white people (the most egregious premise of them all). Therefore, say Entine and the others, black people are faster than white people, and 'it's all in the genes'. The logical leaps are unjustified, and the premises are false. Let me explain more carefully. First of all, there are no such things as races – there is no scientific evidence for them, as we have just seen. Secondly, black people do not run really fast – most black people run as slowly as most people in general. Thirdly, black people have only dominated certain sports at certain periods in history (for instance, Jews dominated basketball in 1930s America and boxing in 1930s England). Entine and others like him are taking a particular case of Westernized professional athletics and a few other professional sports, and making a logically false inductive leap to generalizations.

The two rugbies and the 'Big Polynesian' myth

In Australia and New Zealand (and to an extent in North America) the two versions of rugby have become sports where non-white players of Polynesian and other Pacific Island descent have been successful. This success has been mediatized through the reporting and analysis of professional rugby leagues, professional clubs and big games such as international tests and the National Rugby League's State of Origin series. Huge Polynesian rugby players, often with tribal tattoos, are presented to television viewers as dangerous, tough men with the 'natural' build to be the best rugby players. There is an assumption in rugby union and rugby league that Polynesians are suited to rugby because of their 'racial' distinctiveness, and in New Zealand, this has led to white parents discouraging their children from taking part in rugby alongside Polynesians, who are stereotypically defined as being naturally bigger and stronger than white boys (as it is mainly boys) of the same age (Grainger, Falcous and Jackson, 2012). Discussions about the growing dominance of Polynesian players in Australian and New Zealand rugby league are always associated with their status as biological Others: the normalized, racialized physicality of Polynesians accounts for the growing numbers of Polynesians and other Islanders in the game in Australia, at both junior and senior levels. This is of course based on a myth of racial difference: a myth that Polynesians are genetically stronger and genetically different to the white race. The rise in the number of Polynesian professional rugby players in league and union is a fact, but one that has more to do with the way both rugbies have developed in Australasia, and the way in which professional sport has become a way for poor non-white New Zealanders to become successful.

QUESTIONS TO CONSIDER

Where else does this stereotyping happen in sports? What is the role of professionalism and commercialization in all this?

REFERENCE AND FURTHER READING

Grainger, A., Falcous M. and Jackson, J. (2012) 'Postcolonial Anxieties and the Browning of New Zealand Rugby', *The Contemporary Pacific*, 24, pp. 267–95.

As Marks (2003) and St Louis (2004) argue, the prevalence of scientists asking these sorts of questions in sports science is evidence that sports scientists are asking the wrong sorts of questions. St Louis believes this is because of the whiteness of scientists and their underlying folk prejudices about the Other. Marks is more circumspect, but believes sports scientists have allowed themselves to be swayed by folk genetics. Both believe that the fact of black dominance in sprint events is entirely due to social and cultural reasons: racism, assumptions about ability, role models, opportunities, and the poverty that makes professional sport one of the few ways in which poor African Americans (and others) can achieve a measure of success and respect (Hall, 2001).

The real problem with all this kind of sports science is this: there is no such thing as a black race, or a white race. There are no discernible genetic differences between 'black' people and 'white' people: in fact, the latter are a sub-set (genetically speaking) of the former (Daynes and Lee, 2008; Marks, 2003). The Human Genome Project has definitively stated that differences within so-called racial groups are in fact greater than those between those groups. Phenomes (such as the ability to throw a hoop) cannot be mapped on a one-on-one basis onto genomes (genetics), so there can't be a causal link associated with heredity. What is happening is that sports scientists are making a category error: they are starting with an assumption that races exist, and designing experiments on that basis. Hence the gobbledygook of claiming, as in the fast-twitch fibre experiments, that African Americans (a diverse group) are defined as West Africans (Entine, 2000). In fact, what the scientists are showing is that most successful sprinters are American, and the best sprinters have more fast-twitch fibre. Of course there could be differences ascribed to Nature, but how can we identify them through the background noise of environment, social background, nutrition, development and migration? What matters is this: humans belong to one species; and evolutionary pressures and competition operate at the level of the species. So we could say *Homo sapiens* make better long-distance runners than *Homo erectus* – but in the absence of the latter, what's the point?

Why, then, is this myth still around? Social Darwinism was a powerful force in the creation of modern society, and shapes the way we think today. Racism is still a huge problem. Entine is not a scientist, he is a right-wing journalist associated with far-right think tanks in the States. Finally, there is the pursuit of success in sports science combined with cultural obsessions with heredity and background. We know the tensions exist between the need to produce results for external bodies (faster, higher) and the demands of professionalism and scientism. So it is no surprise that sports scientists, in their pursuit of success, allow themselves to be swayed by the social construction of Holy Blood.

ON GENDER, 'SEX' AND SPORT

We have seen how 'race' has been constructed within sport. In this section, I am going to give a similar critique about sport's role in constructing gender. Feminist scholars have argued that there is a 'gender logic' at work in all cultures and all societies, but particularly so in modern society. Gender is the outcome of a number of choices, negotiations and contestations within the structure of the gender order and wider social structures (Butler, 2006; Connell, 1987). In our modern, Westernized society, gender is based on a two-category classification system, which is supposedly mapped neatly onto underlying biological characteristics: one's 'sex'. In most government systems, new-born babies are assigned the sex of male and female. In census surveys and other research one's sex is assumed to be either male or female. Even where surveys use the term gender rather than 'sex', you are one or the other, and the sexuality associated with gender is taken to be unproblematically heterosexual. The gender logic assumes there are two mutually exclusive categories: heterosexual male and heterosexual female. These categories are perceived in terms of difference, and as 'opposites'. This system leaves no space for those who do not fit into either of the two categories (Butler, 2006). The two categories, however, are not equal when it comes to access to power. Historically, heterosexual men have had access to more power than heterosexual women, as we have seen.

'Sex', then, remains biologically determined, even though there aren't many differences between men's and women's bodies. There are many similarities, and we share a great deal of the same design, order and substance. While there are some obvious differences between men and women because of their sexual characteristics and chromosomes, the question for sports science and others involved in sport is how much difference there is. There is an assumption made by people in sport that men and women cannot compete against one another in many sports competitions, because men have an unfair physical advantage over women (see McArdle, Katch and Katch, 2001). This is one of the reasons why women's sport has developed its own competitions and events and governing bodies, so that women can compete fairly against one another (Hargreaves, 1994). Men, it is argued, are just better at certain sports than women – men are given the status of being physiologically or psychologically superior to women in sports where strength and speed matter. People who make this kind of argument recognize that men and women come in all sorts of shapes and sizes, but they claim the best man will always be better than the best woman. I want to show that this claim is untested and unproven.

Another reason for the development of women's sport, of course, is the activism of liberal and radical feminists who made opportunities for women available because of years of indifference from the men who run sport (Hargreaves, 1994). Sports were created for the construction of the heterosexual male gender. As already mentioned, gender is culturally produced and has rigid boundaries. Gender logic is about the oppression of women and men who do not fit the elite version of masculinity through prejudice. Gender logic and the gender order maintain the power of men and what some feminists call the patriarchy of men (Connell, 1987, 1995). In this struggle to make men powerful and to put women in their place, modern sports and physical culture play key roles. Judith Butler (2006), an important gender theorist, with a theory of gender drawing on symbolic interactionism and 'queer studies', argues that gender is performed. Men and women become men and women by conforming through rule-learning and rule-following. They learn the 'heteronormativity' of modern society, the ways in which our cultural practices such as sports reify and reaffirm heterosexual masculinity. Butler's ideas do allow the gender logic to be challenged by human agency. She discusses the notion of transgressive performativity, for example, when hegemonic notions of gender are challenged. In a sports context, this might be seen when men and women take part in sports that are typically seen as 'masculine' or 'feminine' (Caudwell, 2007). However, the possibilities for transgression of heteronormativity in sport are limited.

Modern sports were constructed to protect the interests of men, and since their construction they have been the most conservative heteronormative cultural spaces. Consider the Olympics again. The Olympics had a moral function in Western European society in their initial years, and right into the second half of the last century. Sport was seen as a moral good, promoting fair play, manliness and civilized behaviour amongst the upper classes. It also had a utilitarian function in its promotion to the lower classes: it was seen as a way of promoting the greatest good for the greatest number of people. And it is this moral dimension to the history of sport that leads us into one of the key debates within the sociology of sport: in what way does sport create and maintain stereotypes of maleness and femaleness, and un-equal distributions of power between men and women?

There are hundreds of research studies that show sport does create and maintain unequal power relationships between men and women. Men's sport is valued more than women's sport. Men in sport are in their 'natural' phys-ical culture, whereas women in sport are seen as transgressors or somehow abnormal. Male athletes are represented as being strong and powerful, women athletes are represented as objects of heterosexual male desire.

Ruth Jeanes (2005) undertook a small study of young women aged be-tween ten and eleven playing football. We can look at this study more closely to discuss wider themes about sport and gender. Jeanes cites research that suggests football plays an important role in establishing masculine identity.

She also cites research about the way gender identities are shaped in childhood. Her theoretical framework draws on the idea of hegemonic masculinity: the dominant, heterosexual norm of maleness. Jeanes also situates her work in the fact of the male-dominated nature of football participation in Europe. Her research has four main areas: the young women's understanding of gender and femininity (what they think gender is and what it means to be female); their perceptions of football and how gender affects those beliefs (if they believe football is for boys, or for girls, or for either…); how the young women construct their own gender identity (how they create a sense of who they are, how they use things to define their 'girlness'); and the impact of football on girls' gender identity construction. One of the respondents, Mary, says (cited in Jeanes, 2005, p. 90):

> Football is a good sport I think because everyone thinks it is a sport not for girls and they say oh no girls are rubbish at football but I like showing them it is not.

What do the other young women say? They see masculinity and femininity as opposites (they understand the social construction as distinction). But they recognize that different masculinities and femininities exist. They understand the link between football and masculinity. And they feel the need to conform to acceptable feminine behaviour. Sociologists argue that sports construct our ideas of gender: by playing some sports and not others, boys are taught how to be boys, and girls are taught how to be girls. Connell (1987) describes the gender order as the historical pattern of dominance of men over women. Connell argues that games and sport are key sites for the replication and maintenance of the gender order: men are taught how to be men and women are kept in their place. Sports become celebrations of masculinity. Gender is not fixed in nature – therefore, people must work to maintain definitions.

Technological enhancement: bigger, higher than what?

The very notion that men are 'naturally' better at sport than women is undermined by the artificial nature of all sports, and the artificial nature of modern society. At an evolutionary level, humans have not changed for hundreds of thousands of years. But we have changed enormously as a result of our capacity to change our surroundings. Through language we have shared ideas, developed culture and built our communities. An alien scientist observing our planet would find all our obsessions and cultural habits very strange. Everything that we have around us is a product of human endeavour and human invention. We are technological animals that continually adapt and innovate new ways of being. Sports are just one of those crazy ways we have made our lives filled with things that are utterly meaningless, but at the same time utterly meaningful. All sports contests are derived under artificial conditions. They are not natural contests. We only think the 100 metres is important because we have made it so. In our natural, pre-culture state, such a contest would have been a waste of valuable energy and thought. Sports are a technological enhancement of our biological natures, and as such they reflect the prejudices of those who constructed them (Jonsson, 2010). Just as we live in a world of right-handed pens and scissors, which make everyday tasks hard to achieve for left-handed people, so sports designed by men for men exclude women. Technologies like sports construct narrow, artificial versions of gender.

QUESTIONS TO CONSIDER

How else is gender created through technologies? What is our natural state?

REFERENCE AND FURTHER READING

Jonsson, K. (2010) 'Sport beyond Gender and the Emergence of Cyborg Athletes', *Sport in Society*, 13, pp. 249–59.

Leisure and sport are sites for preserving forms of gender logic that privilege men and marginalize women. Dominant leisure and sport forms highlight and reward virility, power and toughness. Sport images and discourse glorify a heroic manhood based on being a warrior. Girls and women are then treated as invaders. Girls and women in sports often threaten the preservation of traditional gender logic. Through history, myths have been used to discourage participation by girls and women. Encouragement varies by sport, and whether the sport emphasizes grace or power. Being a 'tomboy' is okay as long as traditional 'femininity cues' are presented (Jones and Greer, 2011). Elite women athletes often fear being tagged as ungrateful, man-haters, or 'lesbians'. Corporate-driven 'celebrity-feminism' focuses on individualism and consumption, not the everyday struggles related to gender. Empowerment discourses in sports are tied to fitness and heterosexual attractiveness, so women athletes have little control or political voice in sports or society at large. Women are allowed to become elite athletes only when they do not challenge the power of men. So they compete against each other, but are strongly discouraged and legislated against competing against men. This means women do not get far enough into elite sports to test the upper limits of their performance abilities. A woman who has been through a highly professional soccer development scheme should be able to be as good as any other professional, but very few women have been allowed the opportunity to play alongside men. A woman might one day run faster than the fastest man at the 100 metres, but men have a longer history in the sport, and their vested interest, so it is unlikely it will happen soon. But it is possible.

CONCLUSION

On 'race', I have shown that the dominance of 'black' athletes in some elite sports is a measure of racism, social exclusion, belief in stereotypes and limited opportunities for socially disadvantaged young people. It is not a fact to be used to support the existence of essentialized 'races' that have different biological attributes. Sport has an ignoble role in perpetuating these racist ideologies, which is partly due to modern sport's development in the age of Social Darwinism and scientific racism, and partly due to the naïve nature of the rush to find short-cuts to success. On 'sex' differences, I have shown that sports have always been used to give men room to develop and express dominant forms of masculinity – the history of modern sport is of men playing sport and being given the opportunity to play sport, while women have been discouraged from participating. These debates around biological essentialism show that modern sports and physical culture are sites of instrumentalization and hegemonic imposition of white, Western, masculine interests. Sports and physical culture cannot be removed from the cultural web around them. They are products of our social and cultural imagination, and subject to the political contestations that shape and limit that imagination. In the next three chapters, the social and cultural contexts of modern sport will be examined in more detail. The next chapter will focus on sports fandom and how sports fans have created communities of belonging that are both welcoming and exclusionary.

EXERCISES

1 How is sexuality essentialized in sports?
2 Is it ever right to say a certain group of people prefer a certain sport or physical culture? Discuss.
3 What is the role of the media in perpetuating stereotypes?

Chapter 12

Watching Sport

SUMMARY OF TOPICS

▪ Definitions: fandom and sports fans
▪ Understanding the difference between watching and playing sport, and answering the moral question about which is better for us
▪ The development of sports fandom and its relationship with commercialized sport
▪ Sociological theories and research about sports fandom

Sports fans often judge each other's authenticity on the strength of how long they have been fans, and how much they know about sports (Jones, 2000). I believe I have enough history and knowledge to count as a proper, authentic sports fan. I was taken by my father to watch soccer and rugby league throughout my childhood (the men's versions of these sports, as women's sports were not then seen as being of a 'professional' standard). Every winter Saturday I was out at a lower league or non-league soccer match, watching one of the local semi-professional clubs or indulging in my father's obsession to try to visit every non-league soccer ground in the north of England (for those not in the know, non-league soccer in England was all the amateur and semi-professional football that went on below the level of the professional Football League – to confuse you even more, non-league soccer has a myriad of separate leagues, and it is now possible for a club to go from park football on a Sunday morning through the amateur leagues into the top tiers of non-league soccer, then through to the Football League and the Premier League). Sometimes on a Saturday we would get to watch Leeds United, our nearest big soccer club, at their Elland Road ground. I was a Leeds United fan, but I also liked Bolton Wanderers, who were a bigger club at the time. Later, in my teenage years, I switched my soccer loyalties to the non-league club Bradford Park Avenue, a club that has once been in the Football League and which has been re-created by diehard fans.

On a winter Sunday we watched rugby league. We were lucky that we had plenty of professional rugby league clubs close to home. I supported Hunslet because they were my father's club when he was a child, but I also supported Bramley because that was where we lived. I liked Bradford Northern, too, because they were a bus ride away and they were the closest rivals of Leeds – who I hated with all the passion a true rugby league fan from south of the River Aire could find. Rugby league was and is the most important sport in my life. I associate with the sport and watch it on television when I can. I read about it every day on-line. I will feel pleased with the world when I hear about rugby league being played in new territories, down south in England where league struggles against rugby union and soccer, or in some strange far-away country such as Canada or Russia. I have given up on soccer. I became disillusioned with the sport in the 1990s, when the Premier League was set up and the English game became so big everybody seemed to become a soccer fan. So, although I am sceptical about soccer and biased towards rugby league, I still see myself as an authentic sports fan. I still turn to the back pages of my newspaper, where the sports section is, and glance through the stories. I am interested in what is happening in all sports, though perhaps I am more of a sports critic than a sports enthusiast. When the Olympics were on the last time they came around, I did not stay in watching all the action. In fact, as a runner, I made a point of going out doing my physical activity during the key events, and when people tried to engage me in conversation about Usain Bolt I would shake my head and tell them the last thing I wanted to do was to sit by a television watching someone else do sport.

In the last chapter I critiqued the claims made in sport about biological essentialism. Many of these claims are believed by fans, and cultivated by fans. This chapter begins by asking the question – is watching sport as good as playing sport? Fandom will be defined and explored as a wide sociological and cultural concept. Academic research from history and sociology of sport will explore the development of sports fandom, and its ubiquity in modernity. We will explore the debates in sociology and cultural studies about fandom, social identity, belonging, embodiment and commercialization. We will explore the notion of serious leisure as a way of understanding sports fandom. I will then argue that in modern physical culture there is no causal relationship between watching sport and playing it, but some people who start as fans become participants, and some participants become fans.

IS WATCHING SPORT AS GOOD AS PLAYING SPORT?

To answer that question we have to consider the different meanings of the word 'good'. Like the debate earlier in this book about the meaning and purpose of playing sport – the value of sports and physical activity – what is meant by 'good' is some sort of biological, psychological, moral or social benefit. Now we saw in those earlier chapters that playing sports and taking part in physical activity is almost certainly good for our bodies (with a few conditions), and does seem to give us some psychological benefits, providing it is something that we freely choose to engage in as a form of communicative leisure (Habermas, 1984, 1987; Spracklen, 2009). The moral and social benefits of sports and physical activity are less clear, and the claims made that they are morally and socially superior than any other form of human activity have to be looked upon with healthy scepticism. However, that said, there is evidence that some people do get some moral and social value from participating in some kinds of physical culture.

So there is a question mark over what sort of value sports have, and what benefits they might bring to individuals, communities and societies. But let us assume for the moment that we agree that there are some benefits that can be claimed for playing sports and engaging in physical activity. When we ask the question about watching sport, we want to know if it has similar biological, psychological, moral and social benefits as we might think playing sport accrues. Our first response would be to say that watching sports, especially if we are watching them on television or on a computer screen, is no match for playing sports in terms of physical health benefits. We do not need scientists to be confident in claiming that running around and working our bodies is better physiologically than remaining in our seats, motionless except for the moment we move for a drink. Worse, there is evidence that being a sports fan watching sport on television is bad for stress levels (Woo and Kim, 2003). However, in terms of psychology, there is evidence that feeling one is part of a team, supporting one's team through the trials of sports events and contests, is good for one's mental state – we all feel we need to belong somewhere (Whannel, 2013). Watching sports with other sports fans is an important way in which we define who we are. We can build bonds, find common causes and fit in, making new friends and important connections. Watching sport has the potential to be culturally rich and satisfying, bringing communities and nation-states together. However, watching sport also brings out the worst kind of irrational behaviour in many people. All too often, sports fans create exclusionary symbolic communities, welcoming only those who wear the same team's colours, and turning on rival sports fans with symbolic and real violence. The answer to the question, then, is this: watching sport can provide a number of psychological, social and cultural benefits in the same way that playing sport provides some of those benefits, but these are contingent on the activity and the individual and the social and cultural networks that shape the watching activity.

DEFINITIONS: FANDOM AND SPORTS FANS

Watching sports is a form of fandom. Historically, as we have seen, sports fandom became part of the development of modern sports when professionalism changed the culture of sports clubs. Formal competitions, and derby matches between rival towns, brought thousands of spectators to sports events. These spectators were consumers of popular newspapers and magazines, and saw sports contests as legitimate things to support in their leisure time. Clubs and governing bodies of sport responded to this mass interest in their sports by pursuing professionalism and commercialization even further (Collins, 2013a; Crawford, 2004). This led to the development of professional leagues, professional players, and formal separations between spectators and athletes that even now shape the construction of sports stadia. In the early years of professional sport and sports spectatorship, people paid to watch their local teams because those teams somehow represented their locality. Going along to the match was an opportunity to socialize, drink, gamble and find vicarious satisfaction in the activities of the athletes. For lots of sports fans today, this connection with live spectatorship remains central to their definition of their fandom and their identity (Crawford, 2004; Giulianotti, 2002). They might also watch sport on television, and discuss sport with their friends, and read about it – but this is only one part of what being a sports fan is meant to signify. However, most people who define themselves as sports fans today will not watch the events and matches in a live setting, because they are too far from the stadium, or the prices are too high, or they do not feel the need to validate their fandom by being at the live events (Giulianotti, 2002; Ludwig and Schierl, 2013; Roberts, 2004; Whannel, 2013). For some sports fans who identify with the notion that 'true' fandom is attendance at live events, people who follow sports at one step removed from the live experience (watching it on television, reading about it in the media) are not 'true' fans.

Fandom is the subject of many socio-cultural analyses of popular culture. Sports fandom is no different from the kinds of fandom associated with watching soap operas, or popular music genres, or science-fiction franchises such as Star Wars and Star Trek, or any other kind of fandom you can name (Jenkins, 2012; Murray, 2004). The problem with much of the research literature on sports fandom is that this connection has been down-played, marginalized, or ignored altogether. Watching sport is exactly the same as watching any other thing on television, or reading a book, or going to some kind of live event. These are all things we do in our leisure time to find pleasure, satisfaction, belonging and identity. These are all things that are the products of the commodification of leisure. We are encouraged to pay money to consume products created by the popular culture industries instead of creating things ourselves or taking part in things of our own volition. Modern spectator sports might best be described as one part of the wider entertainment industry, as I will argue in more detail in the final two chapters of this book. Being part of a fan community means surrendering to the rules of taste – and the forms of social and cultural capital – in a Bourdieusian habitus (Bourdieu, 1986). Some of the ways in which fandom is constructed are truly communicative. People do feel they can find a sense of community and belonging through sharing jokes about Captain Kirk, or wearing a Moroccan rugby league jersey in a bar in the south of France, or arguing over which album is the band Enslaved's best (the answer is *Eld*, obviously, with *Frost* a close second). One might be free to critique elements of the product one is consuming, and one might be free to develop communicative spaces where commercialization is contested, but if one remains in the habitus it becomes impossible to avoid making a pact with instrumentality. Fans can argue with each other over the increase in commercialization, or the ways in which individual players or actors or musicians might 'sell out', but in identifying with and buying the thing that shapes the habitus (soccer, rock music, Star Trek) they limit their ability to be truly free from the grip of modern capitalism.

One other idea from fandom studies is the notion that there are different levels of belonging in the imaginary communities of fandom (Anderson, 1983; Dittmer and Dodds, 2008; Elias and Scotson, 1994). These imaginary communities have a number of symbolic boundaries, through which individual fans have to pass to gain entry to the deeper levels of belonging (Jenkins, 2012; Jindra, 1994). The symbolic boundaries are constructed from knowledge about the things the fans follow (the history of the sport, for example, or the history of the soccer club, or the rules of the sport), from symbols and images and icons (understanding the significance of home and away jerseys), from language (knowing that calling soccer by that name in England is a gross error), from practices (attending matches), and from physical artefacts (wearing the correct clothing). At any time those symbolic boundaries will be protected by gatekeepers and those who seek to reject the 'false' or un-authentic fan from finding belonging and community there. So despite the instrumentality of popular culture, and the products and services consumed by fans, it is possible to find a communicative leisure space in fandom, where fans themselves police the boundaries of belonging and exclusion (Murray, 2004).

A HISTORY AND SOCIOLOGY OF SPORTS FANDOM

Historians and sociologists of sport have been keen to track the continuities between modern sports fandom and spectatorship in pre-modern times. This has been done usually so that particular sociological explanations of modern problems with sports fandom can be theorized and supposedly explained away. The violence of some sports fans, especially soccer fans, is a well-known problem in modern sport. Why do some soccer fans feel the need to be violent to each other? Why do they cause so much havoc? Why fans in soccer, and not fans in other spectator sports such as rugby or cricket? Why at this point in time? Sociology of sport has been dominated by theories that use the civilizing process and figurational theory of Norbert Elias (1978, 1982) to explain hooliganism. For these theorists, modern sport has become increasingly less violent and more codified, and hooliganism is explained as a 'de-civilizing' spurt, a regressive trend against the tide of civilizing norms and values (Dunning, 1986, 1994; Dunning and Rojek, 1992; Dunning and Sheard, 2005; Elias and Dunning, 1986). For the figurationalists and other functionalists, modern sports need to be contrasted with earlier forms of sport that were violent.

As I discussed earlier, in my book *Constructing Leisure*, I begin with a brief account of the riots of the circus factions in Byzantium at the time of Emperor Justinian (Spracklen, 2011). The circus factions had dominated Roman culture for hundreds of years, and were associated with chariot-racing teams as well as criminality, factionalism and political struggle. They were examples of mass spectatorship, of fans following teams, of fan violence. Too many histories of sports fandom and sports violence, however, have referred back to the circus factions, or the gladiatorial games, as if there is a smooth continuity between our culture and the culture of these people who lived thousands of years ago (Coakley, 2003; Elias and Dunning, 1986; Guttmann, 1986). Yes, of course there are some continuities such as the Western inheritance of Classical philosophy and literature, and the religions of Christianity and Islam. But these Roman and Byzantine leisure activities, while being clear examples of a proto-instrumental leisure form, are not the same as modern spectator sports. The gladiatorial games have more in common with television than they have with sports, and the circus factions were more like mafia gangs than hooligans (Spracklen, 2011). Huge crowds have gathered throughout history to watch things such as popular preaching, the delivery of justice, the return of armies and the coronation of rulers. Such spectacles play similar functions to sports spectatorship, but there are important differences. Modern spectator sports are founded on commercial transactions, whether that is an entry fee at the stadium, or a subscription to a sports channel, or intrusive sponsorships deals. Crowds in pre-modern spaces tended to come together freely, and dispersed just as quickly once the spectacle was over. Sports fans enter into social contracts with their clubs and their sports and become fans for long periods, paying money and promoting the sport through their own evangelical commitment to it.

Soccer hooligans and sports violence

The soccer hooligan has become a folk devil of our times. In the United States, one of the things most people 'know' about England is it is the home of soccer hooligans, crazed fans with skin-heads who smash things and each other and the police at regular intervals. For many British sociologists of sport, soccer hooliganism was the product of a particular stage in Britain's late twentieth-century decline. Hooligans are seen as atavistic remnants of a residual, working-class male culture subsumed by post-industrialization, and by soccer's gentrification. Soccer's hooligan culture of the 1970s and 1980s is even the source of a nostalgic subculture of books and films, which all portray the violence and far-right-wing politics of the hooligan gangs in lascivious detail. Sports policy-makers and politicians are keen to propagate the notion that hooliganism was a strange aberration, something that happened but which is now something that no longer happens. Violence, however, has not gone away from modern sports fandom. There is still an under-current of soccer hooliganism, and many hooligan gangs still have links with far-right groups such as the English Defence League. Soccer hooliganism is not just something that happens in England. There are organized gangs of soccer supporters involved in fights and criminal activity in countries across the world (Duke and Crolley, 1996). And there is violence associated with sports that are not soccer. Even in Canada and the United States, sports fans can run amok. The connection between violence and fandom is more complex than it first appears.

QUESTIONS TO CONSIDER

Why do some sports have reputations for violence? How is this violence related to wider problems in society?

REFERENCE AND FURTHER READING

Duke, V. and Crolley, L. (1996) 'Football Spectator Behaviour in Argentina: A Case of Separate Evolution', *The Sociological Review*, 44, pp. 272–93.

Modern sports led to the construction of modern sports fandom. The emergence of paying spectators at sports events came with the appearance of an urban working class with leisure time and spare money. The leisure time of the urban working classes in modern nation-states was legislated for by reformist politicians and campaigners against the evils of industrialization (Spracklen, 2011). This happened first in Europe, but it spread with modernity. It was argued that working men and women needed time away from work at the end of the week beyond the traditional day of rest on Sunday. Saturday afternoons became free for leisure time, and spectator sports filled that gap. For the relatively well-paid working-class man working in the towns, watching the local sports team rapidly became the normal leisure activity after finishing work on Saturday lunchtime. Married or single, a working-class man could pay to get into the ground, have a drink and a bet, go to the pub after the match, and still have some money in his wage packet to cover the rest of the week's expenses. Despite concerns about the morality of sports from some religious commentators concerned with gambling and drinking, watching sport became the mark of urban working-class men as professional sports spread around the world in the twentieth century.

The other interesting aspect of fandom in the first years of modern sport is its local character and local evolution. The local character of sports fandom has already been discussed, but it is worth elaborating in more detail. The fans of clubs and sports attached themselves to the spectacles close to home. Following a sport or sports club meant supporting one's local community, the town or village or city district, or one's region or nation. For many sports fans, the whole point of being a sports fan is to cheer on the team who represent the local community. Local loyalty was initially fostered through the athletes being from the same locality as the fans: teams really did represent the community (Nash, 2001). As professional sport shattered this link between places and players, most sports fans still found identity and belonging through the local sports club, but some fans transferred their loyalty to one of the elite clubs of professional sport (Giulianotti, 2002; Roberts, 2004). National identity and community were nurtured by the swift development of international sporting competitions, so it became possible for a sports fan to support their local club, their chosen sport and their home country against all rivals. This made sports fandom deeply problematic, and there are countless examples of sports fandom being a source of racism, sexism, xenophobia and fascism (King, 1997).

If the elite classes decided what sports were first introduced into a particular town or city, working-class fans could demand changes to the way those sports were played, or even transfer their loyalties to newer sports as they were introduced. The evolution of soccer in England is an excellent example of this. By chance, soccer was introduced in the south and east of the country, while rugby was the version of football introduced across much of the north of England. However, soccer started to compete with rugby very early in its history, especially when it became professional and working-class men started to have professional soccer careers (Russell, 1988). In places in the north such as Leeds and the Yorkshire Pennine towns, rugby managed to keep its spectator base and its paying customers. But in other places such as Liverpool, Manchester and Preston (all now with world-famous soccer clubs), rugby clubs converted to soccer, or lost ground completely to soccer clubs. All professional sports have needed paying spectators to balance the books and stay afloat. As sports became more commercialized, the number of paying spectators also became a way to convince potential sponsors and buyers that the club was sustainable (Collins, 2013a; Roberts, 2004). So clubs started to invest in players and facilities to guarantee sports fans came to see their club and not a rival club nearby. Through the twentieth century, as the media transformed from the press to radio and television, the matter of sports fandom became a national industry, with sponsors targeting particular sports and clubs and the less-rich sports and clubs struggling to keep their spectators from changing their allegiance.

In many countries, local sports clubs continue to be a source of pride for local, working-class fans (Beissel, Giardina and Newman, 2013). Sports clubs might even represent different social classes and political allegiances, as is the case in Egypt, where being a fan of a particular club marks you as being a member of a political group (El-Zatmah, 2012). But most sports fandom comes from sports clubs and sports that have been transformed by the pressures of commercialization and commodification. This has led to the gradual gentrification of sports fandom in countries such as the United Kingdom and the United States. Traditionally, sports fans who attended live events were working-class men, and this remains the case in many countries around the world. In some countries, women are formally banned from attending sports matches, or informally constrained through the patriarchy of local cultures (Chehabi, 2006). In the gentrification of sports fandom, the spectator bases of professional sports clubs have become more middle class, as well as becoming more multicultural and more balanced in terms of gender (Pope, 2011). For residual working-class male fans, this is often seen as a betrayal of their space and their culture. They do not want their exclusive working-class male culture being opened up to others (Giulianotti, 2002; Nash, 2001). While the decline of working-class solidarity and community, and the loss of the connection between locality and local sports, is something that is to be regretted, the opening up of sports spaces to a wider range of people is a good thing. It is, however, a shame that the loyalty of working-class sports fans has been ignored in favour of maximizing profits – and the bourgeoisification of sports fandom may well mean the replacement of one exclusive male culture with another one.

Rugby league and northern English identity

In Chapter 5 of Spracklen (2009), the south Leeds districts of Hunslet and Bramley, a northern English locality steeped in rugby league, are described. Once a thriving, working-class area where people did live in back-to-back housing tucked between the pub and the factory and the rugby ground, by 1996 this locality had changed completely. In Hunslet, the local rugby league club had been moved from the area, the terraces were gone, and the factories were closed. In Bramley, the club survived into the next century. New people lived in new houses, built on the wasteland. The white men who watched Hunslet and Bramley dreamed of the glory days of the clubs, associated themselves with their past, their geography. They became northern men by being part of rugby league. For the people of Hunslet and Bramley who still supported the local rugby league clubs, rugby league and its northern-ness was natural – 'normal', unchallenged, essential – part of the fabric of everyday life for all the people in the past in their imagined communities. Its whiteness remained invisible, unchallenged. And just as it was in the past, so they imagined it in the 1990s and in this century. Today was the same as yesterday, the tight-knit community and family links remained the same as they had ever been; what the men did is what they had always done – the men went down the pub, watched the game, and came home to find their tea on the table. 'The Split' of 1895 was transformed symbolically into a heroic saga of working-class resistance to evil southern middle-class hegemony and control.

QUESTIONS TO CONSIDER

How have other sports captured this sense of locality? How has commercialization changed rugby league?

REFERENCE AND FURTHER READING

Spracklen, K. (2009) *The Meaning and Purpose of Leisure*, Basingstoke, Palgrave Macmillan.

With the increased globalization of elite sports as popular cultural products, sports clubs in Europe and the United States found fans in countries around the world (Roberts, 2004). The National Football League (NFL) clubs in the States have become hugely popular in parts of the world that have no history of American football, or no contemporary American football scene (Dyreson, Mangan and Park, 2013). The availability of NFL action on television, along with the careful marketing push of the NFL and the branding of the clubs, has led to supporters appearing all over the world. The same thing has happened to English Premier League soccer, so that Manchester United now has more official fan-club members outside the country than inside it (Roberts, 2004). Sports clubs and professional sports leagues are businesses that seek to maximize their supporter base, as fans remain loyal and spend money on branded products (Horne, 2006). Most clubs and leagues have embraced the internationalization of their fan base, even where local fans complain of being marginalized or priced-out of attending the home ground (Brown, 2008; Horne, 2006).

Sports fandom provides community, identity and belonging. It can also be a form of what Stebbins (1982, 2009) calls serious leisure. Many fans are driven by their commitment to their sport or their club to travel huge distances, to spend enormous amounts of money, and to spend enormous amounts of time and effort being a fan. It takes years of hard work to generate the knowledge and skills to be a serious fan (Giulianotti, 2002). To get into the inner levels of the symbolic communities of sports fandom one needs to prove one's commitment and authenticity in negotiating all the boundaries. Some of this is specific knowledge about matches and athletes and histories, some of it is about the rules of the game. But there are other things to understand and elucidate that are less obvious, the essential details that make one a true or proper fan compared to the 'fair-weather' fans who might talk about the sport but fail to grasp its true nature. Serious fans will argue that they are different from the sort of sports fans who appear whenever there is a mega-event, or whenever there is something on the television. Serious fans will say they have 'earned' the right to be treated differently to 'armchair' fans because they have spent twenty years on the terraces, following their team through the good times and the bad times. They will say they are different because they come from the home town, or their father is from that locality (Nash, 2001).

Sports fandom today has become driven by nationalism and globalized popular culture. In professional team sports and in the Olympics, nation-states compete against one another in televised mega-events. Thousands of people cheer on their nation's athletes at the huge sports grounds. They wear their nation's colours and wave their nation's flag (Porter and Smith, 2013). This nationalism is replicated in the homes of millions of armchair sports fans, and in bars that are showing the events live on their giant television screens. Sports fans and the protagonists of the sports media suggest that entire nations come to a halt when such mega-events are happening. While it is true to say there are millions of sports fans united in a sense of community and belonging when one nation-state takes on another in the sports arena, there are always more people in each nation-state who do not allow themselves to be beguiled by this banal form of nationalism (Billig, 1995). Many people carry on working, some have other passions to pursue, others positively loathe the obsession with victory and competition. Such patriotism all too often becomes exclusive in its construction of national identity. Sports fans learn to loathe their country's international rivals, and their attachment to the national side reflects narrow, racist forms of national identity and belonging (Smith, 2009). Governments indulge this patriotism as a means of identifying their political leaders with the athletes, a crude form of political manoeuvring that often fails when teams lose, or athletes and fans mock the presence of politicians at such events.

Sports fandom is a product of modernity, of popular culture, and the commodification of leisure. Historically, many sports fans in professional sports were members of sports clubs, with voting rights and representation on decision-making bodies (Collins, 1999, 2006). This democratic model of sports fandom is still found in some sports, and in some sports clubs. Sports fans in this relationship might still have been used by the management of the sports and clubs as sources of regular income, but the distribution of power allowed fans to have some control over the destiny of the club. In Germany, for example, professional soccer clubs still have this distribution of power to members and minor shareholders enshrined in their league rules. Many sports clubs look to the various fans groups to help them when they need to raise additional funds, and there are clubs that are established as fully supporter-run co-operatives (Brown, 2008). However, the model of modern sports clubs is essentially a capitalist one. Individuals or corporations can buy shares in clubs, sold privately or on the stock market, and in practice sports fans have no say in the running of the clubs unless enough of them can buy shares and combine in actions at the company Annual General Meeting. Sports clubs have become the playthings of the tiny proportion of the world's population who have millions of dollars of spare cash (Horne, 2006; Millward, 2013). They might present themselves to the fans as genuine fans of sport, or the club they have just bought, but they have a limited notion of fandom. Fans of elite, professional sports clubs are seen as stupidly loyal consumers, individuals who will continue to give clubs their money (as season-ticket holders, as buyers of merchandizing and food and drinks) even where the clubs give nothing back. Obviously, some fans do reject this passive consumer role. There are the fans who do not go to watch sports live anymore, those who have given up sport altogether, or those who transfer their support to lower-level sports clubs and events. But these are a tiny minority of sports fans. Most elite, professional sports clubs continue to have tens of thousands of supporters in their home grounds, hundreds of thousands of fans watching or following the club elsewhere, and continue to make huge amounts of profits in their commercial operations (Roberts, 2004).

Watching sport to playing sport?

One of the stated reasons governments and policy-makers invest in sports mega-events, such as the Olympics and Paralympics, or the men's soccer World Cup, is to increase sports participation (Rowe, 2012). It is now seen as politically unacceptable to plough public money into these events for self-grandeur or simply for profit-making. Instead, there is a well-worn belief that watching sport, either in the shiny new stadium, or on television, will transform fans into participants. This is the reasoning behind the idea of 'legacy': demonstrating that watching sport and making profit from sport can be used to increase sports participation (among lots of other things). For trans-national sports organizations, talking about legacy makes their mega-events and their pursuit of corporate sponsorship more ethical. The events turn into community development projects, nurturing people into sports participation, and providing moments of daring and sports success that make the fans jump off their seats and onto running tracks. The politicians and policy-makers buy the sports organizations' claims about legacy because they think it will win them votes and show they are doing something morally correct. In practice, the concept of legacy is dodgy ontologically and epistemologically. It is difficult to know what it actually is, and almost impossible to measure. Watching sports events might make someone want to do more sport, but for most people who watch these events, the end-point is switching off the television until the next event comes on.

QUESTIONS TO CONSIDER

What is the history of the idea of legacy? How else might legacy be measured?

REFERENCE AND FURTHER READING

Rowe, D. (2012) 'The Bid, the Lead-up, the Event and the Legacy: Global Cultural Politics and Hosting the Olympics', *The British Journal of Sociology*, 63, pp. 285–305.

CONCLUSION

Being a sports fan is in the end no different to being any other kind of fan. Being a sports fan can be a healthy source of belonging and identity, a way to have fun, affirm choices and make friends. Watching Star Wars is no more likely to make someone become a Jedi Knight than watching sports will make someone play sport. In modern physical culture there is no causal relationship between watching sport and playing it, but some people who start as fans become participants, and some participants become fans. Sports fandom is an essential part of the culture of sport. The history of modern sports shows that watching sports was just as important to the sustainability and development of sports as playing them. The notion of the sports spectator was a new one, but soon became indivisible from being involved in running a club or playing sport. As elite sports professionalized and commercialized, the role of the fan changed from that of a member with rights to a consumer, who was expected to keep on spending to keep the sports in business. The sports industry and its connection to instrumentality is the focus of the next chapter.

EXERCISES

1 'Sports violence is the product of broken society'. Discuss.
2 What is the role of gender, intersectionality and power in sports fandom?
3 What is the relationship between watching sport and watching horror movies?

Chapter 13

The Sports Industry

SUMMARY OF TOPICS

▓ *Definitions: popular culture and commodification*
▓ *The historical construction of the sports industry*
▓ *The rise of professionalization and commercialization in modern sports*
▓ *Sports and popular culture today as products of instrumental rationality*

Sports fandom and its unhealthy relationship to the instrumentality of modern sport was the focus of the previous chapter. In this chapter the focus is on the industry itself. Is the money paid to professional athletes a fair reward for the work they do? They would answer yes, of course. First of all, most professional athletes only get paid relatively modest amounts of money (Scully, 1995). Second, those that do get paid large amounts of money have sacrificed so much time and effort to become elite athletes, and their careers are high-risk and short in duration. If we asked members of the public about the money paid to professional athletes the answers would be more sceptical. Some people, sports fans especially, might say that the professional athletes deserve everything they receive in terms of salaries, bonuses and sponsorship deals. Some people might compare the amount of money elite athletes get to the money made by movie stars and globally renowned singers and musicians, and argue that athletes deserve the same rewards as those in the entertainment industry. Some might say elite athletes should get the same kind of rewards as bankers and global entrepreneurs. All these answers are framed by the utilitarian logic of the market. The athletes get what the market thinks they deserve: a combination of what clubs and sports organizations might be willing or able to pay, the going rate among rivals, and an amount that sports managers think is not grossly offensive to sports fans. Another way of answering this question is to focus on the huge amounts paid to a select few and claim this is immoral and unfair (Rahman and Lockwood, 2011). A regulated salary system would give more money to those athletes on small wages but would limit the amount of money the high-earners could make. This would redistribute wealth to clubs and athletes, and would also mean that elite athletes are not paid the vast sums of money most people will never come close to earning. While this might be the most ethical solution to the problem of professionalism without a retreat to full-blown amateurism, it is not realistic given the recent history of modern sports. In the second half of the previous century, modern sports became fully professionalized, fully commercialized – and sports and athletes became commodities, bought and sold under strict, neo-liberal market conditions.

In this chapter we will explore the professionalization and commercialization of sport through wider debates about the commodification of popular culture. The chapter will explore historical and philosophical debates about the values of sport – and will go on to look at the professionalization of sport seen in the second half of the twentieth century and through to this day. I will discuss the impact of commercialization on physical culture; on the experience of sports, and the sense of community found in sports. I will argue that the rise of the sports industry reflects the commodification of other aspects of popular culture, and like that commodification there are profound problems for individuals and agency.

DEFINITIONS: POPULAR CULTURE AND COMMODIFICATION

Commodification is the trend in modern society that reduces culture and identity to commodities with market prices. Popular culture might be a form of culture that is already completely commodified, or it may be a form of culture that resists such commodifying pressures. Commodification is linked to the spread of commercialization, Westernization and Americanization. The cultural theorist Stuart Hall sees popular culture as a place of potential resistance to capitalist power, through the agency afforded to identity-making in subcultural scenes, but popular culture is also something that is constantly co-opted by capitalists and governments in their efforts to keep control of the masses (Hall, 1993). In *Between Camps*, Paul Gilroy (2000, pp. 30–1) discusses the role of commodification, Americanization and the creation of a globalized popular culture (of American films, Americanized media and brands, and Americanized markets typified by the spread of Disney, Fox, Nike, and so on) in the translation of particular ideologies of whiteness:

> Problems of compatibility and translation have been multiplied by the globalization of culture...Certain common features, like the odd prestige attached to the metaphysical value of whiteness, do recur and continue to travel well, but they too will be vulnerable to the long-term effects of this crisis.

For Gilroy, then, whiteness is something that serves as an absolute metaphor for Western political and economic power over the construction and direction of modern culture – which is the direction of commodification. Social and cultural theories of commodification draw on Marxist accounts of capitalism and the loss of individual power and agency. Commodification is an extension of the effects of modern capitalism on society, and the establishment of unequal power relationships in rigid social structures. However, one does not necessarily have to be Marxist to recognize the fact of commodification. Sociologists influenced by Max Weber's concept of rationality in modernity will see that such marketization and bureaucratization of social relationships is a consequence of the loss of the traditional and the rise of the rational. Others influenced by Talcott Parsons (1964) would also recognize the increasing commodification of the world, especially the commodification of the social and cultural values we might place on some function or other in an ordered, modern society (such as the replacement of Christian charity in the West by a culture dominated by a model of individual gain). For Weberians and Parsonians, the process of commodification driven by modernity is just as real, though the ability to resist its effects is still given prominence.

On the Marxist, structuralist side of sociology and social theory, the Frankfurt School has had the biggest influence on theories of commodification. Adorno (1947, 1991) was deeply pessimistic about the impact of modernity and modern capitalism on culture. He believed that the creative spirit of art, the genius of the beautiful and the humanity of high, elite culture were all in danger of being lost by the commodification of modern society. For Adorno, the invention of the radio, spectator sports and the creation of the popular music industry removed human expression and appreciation from music and movement, replacing them with passive consumption of ersatz (fake, but made to look real) sports, pop and jazz. What was happening to sport, music and high culture was happening in every part of human society, argued Adorno. Humans were becoming passive consumers of material goods, living in a world where everything could be bought and sold, including humanity itself. This fear of the tide of materialism, economic rationality and modern capitalism is also present in the work of Jurgen Habermas (1984, 1987). Habermas's (1990) theory of the state of modernity relies on the fight to stop a tidal wave of what he calls instrumentality – commodification and materialism – sweeping human agency away in areas of our life such as leisure and sports. Unlike Adorno, Habermas does not believe that complete commodification is inevitable, but he does believe it is happening and it is difficult to stop.

Foucault argued that the capitalist phase that emerged out of the Enlightenment, and in which we still live, objectifies and commodifies the human body. His concept of embodiment came from his reading of what he called the genealogy of madness and hygiene in his key early works *The History of Madness* (re-published 2006) and *The Birth of the Clinic* (1973). In the former, he demonstrated that the status of madness as a physical problem or disorder was a function of the increasing power of regulation, capitalist economy and science. In the latter, he showed how the role of the expert medical professionals (and their appearance at the end of the nineteenth century) turned traditional relationships between the doctor and the patient into routinized, rationalized, commodified systems of control and coercion. What matters for the modern state, for Foucault (1991), is the control of its citizens, the removal of those who are not productive workers, and the policing of civilized behaviour. Through the process of embodiment in popular culture of things such as 'race' and gender, individuals learn how to read the wishes of the state, of modern capitalism, into the control of their own bodies through policing illness, body size, appearance, depression and wellbeing; this embodiment makes us into good citizens and makes us relatively powerless against the manipulations of our rulers.

What all these social and cultural theories of commodification have in common is an acceptance of the historical fact of commercialization. This is the simple trend of turning our everyday lives and lived culture – our sports, preferences, tastes and networks – into commercial, profit-driven, profit-making enterprises. Such a turn to commercialization is dependent on its sustained impact on the tools, machinery and management practices of modernity, but it is present in all periods of history where market economies have existed. In the Roman Republic, for example, private wealth dictated whether a free man was a senator, a member of the equestrian order, or one of the lowly plebians. Private wealth could be inherited as well as earned in economic exchange, so men who wanted to move up the social ranks chased patronage as well as becoming speculators. Commercialization – the turning of everything into a market – seems to be a particularly human process: it is the nature, extent and pace of commercialization that is troubling in the modern world. The logic of the market has spread from the public sphere to our leisure lives.

Commodification of the athlete

Modern sports have one primary aim: the need to win competitive events. Modern, professional sports have an additional aim of making profit from the event. Winning in a competition does not necessarily equal making profit, and the history of modern sport is filled with tales of clubs and sports spending beyond their means and going bankrupt. However, modern sports administrators and owners believe that winning does help them turn a profit, and there is some truth to the notion that winning teams and athletes attract sponsorship, spectators and merchandizing spend. The myth that winning leads to economic success and profit drives global entrepreneurs to invest heavily in professional, elite sports that generate huge turnovers. In these global sports, athletes are ultimately powerless. They join development programmes at early ages that mean they sacrifice training for other careers and opportunities for higher education. Only a tiny proportion of the athletes who are on talent development schemes make it as full-time, professional athletes. Most of them end up rejected from sport, demoralized and lacking in training for anything else in life. They, however, might be the lucky ones. As Walsh and Giulianotti (2001) suggest, athletes who do become full-time professionals have short working careers, subject to termination through injury, or being sold off cheaply at short notice to other clubs. Athletes have little control in what happens to their career – and when it ends, often at short notice, they have little clue what to do next.

QUESTIONS TO CONSIDER

How is this played out globally? How is sport different from other careers?

REFERENCE AND FURTHER READING

Walsh, A.J. and Giulianotti, R. (2001) 'This Sporting Mammon: A Normative Critique of the Commodification of Sport', *Journal of the Philosophy of Sport*, 28, pp. 53–77.

PROFESSIONALIZATION AND THE VALUE OF MODERN SPORTS IN HISTORY

Modern sport's origins are a curiosity. But it can be seen, as I have discussed earlier in the book, that it was a product of the late nineteenth-century tension between different urban classes, and a product of wider pressures on leisure and Western society. It could not have appeared at another time, or in other place in the world: it needed technological change, an urban working class given some freedom and wealth, and the freedom of industrial capitalism. Attempting to understand the history of modern sport without an exploration of similar modern, instrumental trends of commodification and professionalization in other leisure and culture forms is simplistic: too many histories of sport become Kiplingesque 'just-so' stories taken out of the context of instrumental pressures on Western nineteenth-century leisure at the height of modernity. Modern sport was just another leisure site – like modern tourism, like the alcohol industry – where Habermasian instrumentality (Spracklen, 2009) met a decreasing but still significant amount of communicative action. So, in their evolution and development, modern sports had communicative value for their participants and their spectators. For the participants, there was the sense of being part of a symbolic community, learning new skills and improving one's health doing something freely. For the spectators, there was the same sense of community and belonging, alongside pride in the successes of one's local team.

Where athletes were truly amateur, sports participation could be truly communicative, even if the very notion of amateur, as we have seen, was a social and cultural construct. If one had the right cultural capital and class status, and the right access to power and wealth, one could choose to play sports for the sake of playing them, to join in the webs of significance surrounding the acts of playing and participating (Bourdieu, 1986). Being truly amateur meant not taking too seriously the demand to win. Amateurs were never ideal amateurs, and the ethical code of amateurism was never really followed literally, but amateurism did inspire other ways of playing sport other than aiming to win at all costs. The myth of amateurism continued to inspire communicative sports participation, as Morgan (2005) has argued. Some sports governing bodies upheld strict rules of amateurism throughout the twentieth century, and others established separate competitions for professionals and amateurs. The International Olympic Committee and the International Rugby Football Union resisted professionalism for many years, even when it became obvious most amateur athletes were being paid, and the money from sponsors and television companies had changed the sports from celebrations of humanism to marketplaces for profit-making. In the Communist East, professional sport was banned because it was recognized that such sports were a product of capitalism and instrumentalization, not the product of co-operation and participation (Riordan, 1991).

The Communists were arguably right to defend amateurism, though their solution did not stop professionalization happening in sport, even before the fall of the Iron Curtain and the spread of a form of democracy to Russia and its satellite states. Sports became instrumental, professional and commercialized, almost as soon as they were invented. The communicative choices made by fans to support their local teams only enabled capitalist rationality to take over the systems of sports clubs. In the second half of the twentieth century, the pursuit of victory led to the maximization of the capitalist model of sports. Rules governing amateurism were forgotten or overturned. Restraints on salaries and the movement of athletes were dropped. Clubs became private or listed companies, free to be bought and sold by incredibly rich business tycoons. The sense of community and belonging among fans was utilized to increase profit margins, shareholder bonuses and the bank accounts of sports agents and athletes (Zimbalist, 2003). Sports governing bodies had to pursue professionalization of coaching and management, which led to strategies to maximise funding and sponsorship. Gibson (1993) uses the work of Nietzsche to explore the purpose of sport. Nietzsche claimed the Enlightenment was over, and rationality was to be replaced by emotion and struggle. In the new world, free will would be replaced by the will to power – a Darwinist struggle of might that would see the emergence of a new race of *übermensch*. In modern, professionalized sport, argues Gibson, the purpose of sport has become to test and support struggles between such 'supermen' – the Olympics then becomes a realization of Nietzsche's nightmares of the modern.

Although Veblen (1970) was the first sociologist to notice changing patterns and significations of leisure consumption associated with the increasing affluence of Western elites in the first half of the twentieth century, it was only in the period following the Second World War that leisure, sports and physical culture (in the modern West) started to be associated with the construction of cultural identities. Some scholars observed that young people used their leisure lives and spaces to create alternative, counter-cultural identities (Hebdige, 1979). Stanley Parker (1972, 1976) noted the emergence of leisure consumers, and leisure choices made within the flux of rapid societal change; Ken Roberts argued that increasing concern with leisure in a post-industrializing West was leading to the establishment of leisure policies and managers in the public sector, and leisure industries in the private sector (Roberts, 1978). Other sociologists and philosophers started to argue that changes to working practices brought about by automation, computerization and globalization would result in more free time for individuals, and hence more need for leisure activities (Smigel, 1963). In the context of modern sports, fans were identified as interested consumers, and distinctions between fans of different sports were manipulated to sell exclusive belonging and identity. Working-class fans were consumers of a sort of mass culture delineated by the soccer terraces and the bars (or their North American equivalents), but other spectator sports such as tennis were priced out of the mass market (Bennett, Cunningham and Dees, 2006). The consumption of these sports was live, unmediated. At the same time, sports on television could be used as false markers of class identity. Some sports were sold to viewers as 'aspirational', events they had to watch to become a member of a higher class, such as rugby union and golf (Pope, 2011). The link between sports and the supposed class-nature of their spectators and participants allowed corporations, marketers and sports organizations to move through the shifting networks of conspicuous consumption. In all these networks, watching sports became linked to buying things associated with that sport, either directly-linked merchandizing or indirectly-linked products from sponsors.

Global television and gambling

Sports have proven to be an essential part of the television portfolio, attracting large sections of local television viewers, and often those in market segments deemed to be desirable by corporations and advertising agencies. Sports broadcasting deals have led to huge markets for Western professional sports in other countries. The English men's soccer Premier League, for example, is popular in many Asian countries such as Malaysia, Indonesia and Thailand. This has led to a confluence of leisure activities: watching sports on television while simultaneously gambling on outcomes. The global gambling industry is partly legitimate and regulated, and partly run by illegitimate and illegal syndicates. Billions of dollars are gambled on the outcomes of top-level soccer, cricket and other televised sports. This has led to a widespread culture of fixing matches and scores – to assist the gangs running the illegal gambling syndicates, but also to make money for those seeking to exploit gambling systems (McNamee, 2013). Professional athletes have been found guilty of match-fixing, and allegations continue to emerge that certain sports or certain events have been fixed. It is easy to see how athletes and match officials might be tempted to fix matches. There are many events that might be one-off tournaments with no relation to the business of the main league, so it is easy to persuade oneself that cheating does not matter. There is also the fundamental human weakness to corruption to consider, and the huge amounts of money offered.

QUESTIONS TO CONSIDER

How prevalent is this? How deep does the match-fixing go below the elite levels?

REFERENCE AND FURTHER READING

McNamee, M. (2013) 'The Integrity of Sport: Unregulated Gambling, Match Fixing and Corruption', *Sport, Ethics and Philosophy*, 7, pp. 173–4.

In the twentieth century, sports became fully modern, as they became indistinguishable from the entertainment industry. Modern sport became fully professional, with increasing funds invested by private corporations and nation-states in the business of sports. Being a professional athlete or a professional coach became a lucrative career option for young people, who were increasingly trained at a young age in the elite performance development programmes. Sports participation became marginalized in the policies of governments and sports organizations. Professional sports management brought with it sports marketing strategies, business plans and expansion of sports franchises into new markets. The local feel of sports evidenced in the first half of the twentieth century was replaced by the globalization of modern, elite professional sport. The growth of radio and television saw professional sports become a normal part of everyday life. Professional sport was regulated and transformed into a factory system, with professional clubs churning out new stars for the popular press, and athletes becoming professionals earlier and earlier in their childhoods (Collins, 2013a). This was still men's sport, and only a handful of sports were secure in the modern sports industry – those that had sufficiently large spectator bases, or had sufficient influential supporters in the industry or in politics. Soccer spread around the world as a harbinger of Westernization and professionalization, proving itself to be a perfect product of the entertainment industry as successive deals were made to make the World Cup and other international competitions visible to a global television audience (Harvey, Rail and Thibault, 1996). Other sports such as American football concentrated on their core support in home countries, developing franchise systems and new rules that made them fit for television.

This evolution of modern sport in modernity was mirrored by similar developments in the wider entertainment industry. Popular music, for instance, was also something that became marketized and commodified in the commercialization of popular culture in the twentieth century. Radio stations found pop music to be an excellent way of attracting listeners and thus companies looking to market to those listeners. To be played on radio, music had to fit a certain template musically and structurally. Pop music became something empty of rebellion and meaning, but with strong emotional resonances (Bennett, 2001). Pop musicians became pop stars, their lives public property in the media, but at the same time protected from the public by agents, label managers and compliant journalists. The most successful pop stars earned huge amounts of money and achieved celebrity status, and like elite athletes these pop stars found their celebrity made more money for them and for their sponsors. Sports stars were pushed in the same way as pop stars, but their supposed 'clean-cut' public images made them more attractive to sponsors and advertisers than disreputable musicians or actors (Rojek, 2006). As the twentieth century came to a close, it was becoming possible for sports professionals to be celebrities in popular culture even if their sports prowess had faded. Sports stars became a part of the world of tabloids and reality television, selling products such as computers, cars, razors, phones and shoes (Rojek, 2001). Sports stars married other celebrities in public, and the seemingly ironic coupling of footballer and model became part of mundane reality (Cashmore and Parker, 2003; Couldry and Markham, 2007).

Sportization of popular culture

If modern sport has become shaped by popular culture and the cult of celebrity, popular culture in turn has been shaped by modern sport (McDonald, Mihara and Hong, 2001). Reality television programmes are proof of this sportization. Once upon a time, television programmes carried subtle messages about love and loss, hope and despair, and were shaped by the Classical distinctions between tragedy and comedy. In this century in particular, reality television has become the dominant paradigm in the entertainment industry. In reality television shows, especially those that follow the formula 'perfected' by *The X Factor* and *Pop Idol*, members of the public are whittled down to a handful of 'players' who fight it out each week to survive through to the final. The 'players' are surrounded by coaches and mentors and others who give them help to sing or dance. We are shown the lows and highs of the training programme, and told the same story about each 'player': the unhealthy relative, the emotional problems with their parents, their own struggle with poverty. We identify with the singers as we identify with our athletes. But each week there is an objective test of each player, a supposedly 'live' competition against the others, in front of the judges, just as in gymnastics and many other sports events. Our votes are counted and the winners of the finals are given professional contracts and sponsorship endorsements. And, like professional athletes, some of them become celebrities with a level of fame unrelated to their talents.

QUESTIONS TO CONSIDER

How long has this been happening? How else is sportization at work?

REFERENCE AND FURTHER READING

McDonald, M., Mihara, T. and Hong, J. (2001) 'Japanese Spectator Sport Industry: Cultural Changes Creating New Opportunities', *European Sport Management Quarterly*, 1, pp. 39–60.

SPORTS AND POPULAR CULTURE TODAY

Modern sports are part of modern popular culture, and part of modern leisure lifestyles. It has been suggested that we now live in a postmodern society, or an age of postmodernity (Featherstone, 2007). This has some truth in it. The world today is different from the world of the middle of the last century. There is a global class of travellers in today's society, and industrial jobs in mills have been replaced by post-industrial jobs in the service sector. The internet has brought people closer together, and popular culture has become globalized, so that it is possible to be a fan of American baseball while living in the middle of India. Leisure has, it is argued, become postmodern, or has been changed due to the shift towards postmodernity evidenced in Western societies (Blackshaw, 2010; Rojek, 2010). Leisure has become, as Blackshaw (2010) argues, following Bauman (2000), liquid. That is, the nature of the subject of leisure, sports and physical culture has changed as society has become postmodern.

In my own research on rugby league, for example, the pessimism and nostalgic yearning of Hunslet and Bramley supporters contrast with the excitement and optimism initially associated with the commodified spectacle of Rupert Murdoch's new world order of rugby league (Spracklen, 2009; Spracklen, Timmins and Long, 2010). Rugby league is a successful industry in Australia, with big crowds, wealthy sponsors and battles to screen matches of the professional elite. In the United Kingdom, rugby league has always been professional in name (allowing payments to players), but very unprofessional in its business (struggling to attract crowds, struggling to make a profit). When News Corporation first offered millions of pounds of funding in exchange for exclusive rights to televise rugby league in 'Europe' (in practice, England) and Australia, the game of rugby league was split between loyalists (traditionalists) and those who took the cash or bought the global (expansionist) vision. In the north of England, some rugby league fans opted to defend the game against any change or expansion (Denham, 2000). But ultimately, in England and in Australia, the game's clubs, sponsors and administrators all accepted and welcomed the involvement of Murdoch's global media empire (Andrews and Ritzer, 2007; Denham, 2000; Rowe, 1997).

The growth of television coverage, via News Corporation (which owns the *Sky* satellite channel), of the European (English) Super League and the (Australian) National Rugby League has led to the game expanding into new regions and territories around the world (Spracklen, 2007; Spracklen and Spracklen, 2008). In many of the developing areas, the involvement of students, attracted by television coverage, has been a catalyst to drive expansion (Collins, 2006). In one of my projects looking at the globalization of rugby league, all the respondents from the international rugby league on-line forum, by their very involvement in the game, were believers in the globalization of rugby league: they all saw the benefits of television exposure and commercial sponsorship, and all welcomed the professionalization of the game (Spracklen, 2009). However, despite their enthusiasm for expansion and globalization, they were reticent about abandoning rugby league's working-class history. Most of the respondents had some connection to the game's working-class heartlands of Brisbane, Sydney or the north of England: either they themselves were born there, or they had family there, or they had lived there for some period. As such, they saw in their expansionist work the project of spreading the idea of rugby league as a working-class masculine game – even when they admitted that they themselves were not working class or they explained that rugby league in their particular developing country was played by middle-class students.

Clearly, rugby league is globalizing and, in doing so, demonstrates all the material, demographic, technological, social and cultural flows of globalization (Appadurai, 1996) – as well as the dominant flow of Westernization (commodification, professionalization, Americanization via Australia) identified by Hall (1993), Giddens (1991) and Bauman (2000). Leeds Rhinos exemplify this globalizing rugby league phenomenon, and Headingley Stadium is an outpost of the conspicuous commodification and consumption of professional sport (Horne, 2006). Watching the World Club Challenge between the Rhinos and the Storm on television, with the sound of the commentators muted, one could be forgiven for mistaking the match for any other global team sport spectacle: the prominence of sponsor logos, the huge crowd in the dazzling lights of the stadium, the multicultural nature of the hypermasculine professional athletes, the designs of the jerseys and the tricks of the TV studio, all part of the Americanization of global sport (Denham, 2000). Turn the commentary up, however, and despite the Americanized style of delivery, the rough tones and flattened vowels remind the listener of rugby league's connection to the imaginary, and the imagined, working-class world of the north of England.

There is, then, one contradiction. Rugby league is, like its union counterpart, a commodified product, its elite competitions part of the global calendar of passive consumption (Horne, 2006), its international profile fuelling participative and commercial expansion into new markets. In this expansion and development, the postmodern nature of commodified sport becomes apparent. News Corporation and other multinational sponsors create supranational leagues; rugby league clubs change, lose their local identity and become businesses in the same way as elite football clubs have done. As Denham (2000) has argued, rugby league's embrace of Americanization and commodification, a postmodern turn itself, is evidence for the dissolution of identity and liquidity of structure (Bauman, 2000) associated with postmodernity. The existence of Leeds Rhinos and the World Club Challenge provides evidence for some post-modern shift away from high modernity (Giddens, 1991), from the traditional, fixed working-class communities and identities typified by the Hunslet of the mid-twentieth century (Spracklen, 2009). Leeds itself is a microcosm of the move towards postmodernity and the decline of the traditional, industrial base of the working-class economy. The globalization of rugby league demonstrates some embrace of the rationality of instrumental capitalism at the end of mod-ernity (Habermas, 1990), perhaps the beginning of postmodernity. There are emerging rugby league competitions in dozens of countries around the world, encouraged by the showing of the game on local television networks and the availability of information on the internet. But in Hunslet and Bramley, indi-viduals still choose to identify with working-class communities of modernity, expressing communicative action (Habermas, 1986, 1987) in resisting the con-formity of the Super League. What rugby league in Leeds demonstrates is the complex nature of globalization, the relationship between the local, national and global that Featherstone (2007) argues is the crucial tension in global, glo-balizing culture. Rugby league in Leeds appears to be an example of glocaliza-tion, the local adaptation and response to a globalizing trend (Giulianotti and Robertson, 2007).

Rugby league is just one example of the way in which sports have devel-oped and expanded their markets and business globally, through the sale of rights and sponsorship deals. Sports programming has played a crucial role in the spread and normalization of satellite or digital television. Media corporations pay billions of dollars for the right to broadcast modern, pro-fessional sports events. When television first became part of popular cul-ture, the bidding wars for exclusive rights to broadcast sport were either inconsequential or non-existent, as the number of channels was restricted. The development of cable, satellite and digital broadcasting technology has multiplied the number of corporations fighting for subscriptions and shares of audiences and advertising. As with radio, digital television has cre-ated a 'gold rush' for popular sports such as soccer, and events such as the Olympics, with broadcasters scrambling to outbid each other to get the lu-crative deals. The huge sums involved mean that sports governing bodies are willing to compromise their rules and regulations to make the sports more suitable for television, either through changing the timing of competitions or making the sports more 'viewer friendly' – so rugby union, following its professionalization in the 1990s, has scrapped some of its more arcane rules to make it easy to follow on television; and rugby league in Australia has considered allowing more stoppages for ad breaks.

National and international governing bodies of sport, such as the NFL, IOC and FIFA, still control on paper the governance and direction of their sports: they still elect members of committees, debate rule changes at their councils and engage in competitions to select successful bidders for big events. But the power within all professional sports organizations has become centralized – *de juro* and *de facto* – in the hands of powerful paid executive officers or chairs (Booth, 2011). Important decisions might still be rubber-stamped by the democratically elected delegates at a national or international council, but agendas and recommendations come from elite power-brokers who receive regular briefings from corporate lobbyists. It is a matter of record that some international governing bodies of sport – the IOC and FIFA – have been the centre of bribery allegations and scandals over under-the-radar lobbying and persuasion (Jennings, 2011). But although the influence of sponsors is less obviously illegal and corrupt than the bribes paid to smooth the success of bids for big events, it is still an important source of power in modern sport. Commercialized, commodified, professional sport needs sponsorship to ensure the profitability of the leagues, the sports and the events. Some individual executive officers might benefit illegally from kick-backs, but the public face of modern sports is the power that sponsors (broadcasters and others) gain from putting their money into the system. In the London Olympics sponsors such as Visa and McDonald's found themselves able to dictate exclusive rights to usage and services in the Olympic Park. Sponsors gained the best seats for their clients and staff, and had access to the fast lanes reserved for the use of the IOC throughout the capital. For all the supposed multicultural diversity of the London Olympics (the spectacle of the opening ceremony with its 'new' Britain, and the feel-good factor reported in the press), the fact is that the actual local, working-class residents of East London, a truly multicultural demographic, found themselves unable to access the park because of the costs of the events, and unable to drive through their streets because of the corporate sponsors and IOC bureaucrats cruising through the reserved lanes. The only regeneration of the area has come in the form of the Westfield Centre, a huge shopping mall privately owned by a trans-national corporation, filled with retail outlets owned by big corporations.

With globalized cycles of bidding and hosting, the impacts and continuing legacies of sporting mega-events like the Olympics are of obvious interest to academics and policy-makers. The Olympic Games have become a symbol of the globalization of sport, replacing the amateurs of Baron de Coubertin with the globalized, professional travellers of today. Countries compete for medals, but the main competitions are those between the mega-star celebrity athletes, trained at high-altitude camps, supported by millions of dollars of coaching and science. The Olympics have become the subject of billions-worth of advertising and marketing deals, construction projects, television rights and political lobbying – the global audience for the Games attracts the attention of huge corporations looking to increase market share or break into emerging territories. To accept the Olympic Games into a city is to demonstrate that city's global importance, its modern society within a global community of modern cities. For host countries, the same urge to be seen to be part of the globalized society of modernity is evident: for Spain, Barcelona 1992 followed the emergence of democracy after the death of Franco; for China, Beijing 2008 symbolized the arrival of China as a geo-political world power. As well as supposedly beneficial policy connections between these mega-events and tourism and leisure, such as increased profits in host-city hotels and legacies of facilities available to promote participation in sport, there are local and global policy consequences on tourism and leisure that challenge the notion of benefit (Hiller and Wanner, 2011).

CONCLUSION

Modern sports are now effectively controlled by a small number of transnational corporations, who have been allowed by national and international political institutions to develop a neo-liberal global capitalism that benefits their shareholders beyond anything and anyone else (Horne, 2006). The sports–media complex is part of a wider entertainment industry that has commodified global, Western popular culture. That is, the rise of the sports industry reflects the commodification of other aspects of popular culture, and like that commodification there are profound problems for individuals and agency. When most people think about sports and physical activity, they no longer immediately think of the sports they might play in their leisure time. Instead, they think of the latest international tests between nation-states, or the gold medal winners at the Olympics. And when they think of those things, they think of the sports stars and the products they endorse. Corporations would not invest so much of their own money in advertising if they thought it was useless. We are all tricked by the hegemony of global capitalism's sports industry. We are also easily fooled by the nation-states and hegemons that prefer us to be consumers of sports and popular culture than free-thinking rebels. In the next chapter, sports fandom and the sports industry combine in a critical analysis of sports fashions.

EXERCISES

1　Discuss professionalization of sport in your own country.
2　How will celebrity culture shape sport in the future?
3　How can modern sports break free from the global industry?

Chapter 14

Sports Fashions

SUMMARY OF TOPICS

- Definitions: trends and fashions
- Understanding trends in sports participation and sports fandom
- Sporting fashions and sports in fashion: changing tastes and the politics of distinction
- The rise of instrumental rationality in sports

In the last two chapters sports fandom and the sports industry were discussed and critiqued. If you play or watch a sport that does not have a global reach or global audience, you will probably feel exasperated that your sport is not as successful as others at attracting potential fans, athletes and sponsors. You will know that your sport is great to play and/or watch, and you might have spent some time trying to convince your friends and classmates your sport is as worthy as the fashionable, trendy sports they like. Why does everybody want to watch soccer or basketball, for example, and not canoeing or dressage? Why do people take part in certain forms of physical activity such as running or exercise in a gym, but not other things like long-distance or competitive running?

This chapter will look at trends in sport and physical culture – participation rates, local fashions for local sports against the globalization of sport, and the blurring of the boundaries between physical culture and popular culture in films, tattooing and clothing. It will discuss the history of sports and sociological theories of rationalization, control and the postmodern. I will argue that sports fashions, especially the crossover between physical culture and popular culture, are not an expression of a postmodern turn, but are a reflection of the globalization of physical culture and modernity – which has consequences for those who might want to resist that trend. Before we discuss any of that, let us look at the concept of fashion in more detail.

DEFINITIONS: TRENDS AND FASHIONS

In a descriptive sense, trends are just the way things might increase or decrease over time, or across space. In our everyday usage, trends are evident in the way things come and go in and out of our own personal lives. Trends are objects or words or some other form of human symbol or activity that become widespread, or which remain marginal, but which are subject to the whims of popular culture. There might be a trend for a certain kind of footwear, say the sports trainer or sneaker, which has increased over the last thirty years. That trend might also have spread into different countries from the ones where it first started. Managers and others in the capitalist system are keen to have knowledge of trends ahead of their competitors, so they can make the right investments.

Trends, then, are fashions in tastes in culture (Bikhchandani, Hirshleifer and Welch, 1992; Lieberson, 2000). In anthropological research among pre-modern cultures, and in historical and archaeological research, there is a consensus that humans go through these fashions for the things in their lives even where there is no capitalist system (Hanley, 1999). What people like to do, or to collect, or to wear, changes over time as they find out what others are doing. Even pre-modern cultures quite remote from the impact of colonialism and capitalism adopt novel fashions from their neighbours, adapting them and taking them as their own (Mead, 1929). In Classical Rome, fashions in hair styles, clothing, literature and food and drink can be traced in the evidence of coins and paintings, as well as the critical comments about such trends in the work of politicians and writers. Earlier in this book Ammianus Marcellinus was mentioned. He was a fourth-century critic of the Roman culture of his day. In Book 14.6 of his history (in Ammianus Marcellinus, 2004, p. 48), he digresses on the ruling classes of Rome:

> In this state of things, the few houses which once had the reputation of being centres of serious culture are now given over to the trivial pursuits of passive idleness, and echo with the sound of singing accompanied by wind instruments or the twanging of strings. Men put themselves to school to the singer rather than the philosopher, to the theatrical producer rather than the teacher of oratory. The libraries are like tombs, permanently shut; men manufacture water-organs and lutes the size of carriages and flutes and heavy properties for theatrical performances.

On the lower classes, again in Book 14.6, he is equally scornful of what they do with their time (ibid., pp. 49–50):

> ...some spend the night in bars, others shelter under the awnings of theatres... They hold quarrelsome gambling sessions, at which they make ugly noises by breathing loudly through their nose; or else – and this is their prime passion – they wear themselves out from dawn to dusk, wet or fine, in detailed discussion of the merits and demerits of horses and their drivers. It is most extraordinary to see a horde of people hanging in burning excitement on the outcome of a chariot race.

But where do these tastes and fashions come from? And why is it that some fashions are judged to have aesthetic, cultural or moral value, whereas others are scorned by critics like Ammianus Marcellinus for being without any worth? Philosophers of fashion and cultural theorists interested in fashions have not solved the problem of what fashions are and where they come from, but they can give us some suggestions that will help us make sense of sports fashions (Bourdieu, 1986; Featherstone, 1987; Gans, 2008; Lieberson, 2000). None of these suggestions implies one form of fashion is better than another. There is no objective way of saying sneakers are better or worse than walking boots. But there is a way of exploring why people might prefer to wear sneakers rather than walking boots. First of all, people start doing something that is interesting to other people, and copy it because they think it has aesthetic value. That is, people like the thing that the other person is doing and want to do it themselves for their own pleasure and gratification. Secondly, people copy other people because they think the thing the original person does has some moral value. Wearing sneakers might be a way of 'fitting in' to the norms and values of a particular subculture, and might be a way of demonstrating moral competencies, whereas wearing walking boots might be associated with deviance or rebelliousness. Thirdly, people copy other things that people do because they believe such things have cultural value; that is, that acquiring them gives them cultural capital, or demonstrates coolness (Frank, 1997; McRobbie, 2004), or taste (Bourdieu, 1986; Featherstone, 1987).

What is considered fashionable – what sports we like, what sports clothes we wear – is the site of a contestation of meaning and power between individuals, subcultural groups and the superstructures of capitalism and the media (Bourdieu, 1986). For some people, these decisions are made deliberately and as conscious acts of rebellion or resistance (Hebdige, 1979): for example, young people might deliberately wear sneakers to school, even though the school may have a uniform policy that bans them. Sneakers have a symbolic resonance of coolness (Danesi, 1994), but they are also socially and aesthetically acceptable in most situations (notwithstanding any specific policy that bans them). Individuals who rebel only go so far in their rebellion (Hebdige, 1979). They will choose to wear something that marks them out as a rebel, but that rebellion conforms to the norms and values both of society and of the subculture that shapes the fashions. Most people, then, choose things from a small range of acceptable cultural or subcultural items. In practice, people look to other people and make their choices so that they fit in with the group, or a sub-group within the wider group (Bourdieu, 1986). So we wear sneakers because everyone we know wears sneakers, and we wear jeans because everyone else wears jeans. If we are male we do not wear skirts or dresses because these items are designated as being 'correct' for females, but 'incorrect' for males. These rules might seem arbitrary and unfair but we abide by them and normalize them in our everyday choices. In normalizing them, we are also engaged in accepting wider cultural and societal norms. We accept that men and women are coded differently through the things which the media and wider society assign to them (Gans, 2008; McRobbie, 2004). We buy into cultural capital, taste and status distinctions through our understanding of the subtle forces of *habitus* and power that impose on us what we think are normal things and free choices (Bourdieu, 1986).

So we ultimately wear sneakers because a number of trans-national corporations have colluded with each other and the entertainment industry to sell sneakers as something 'cool' for us to consume (Featherstone, 2007). We see celebrities endorsing sneakers in adverts and in the media (Rojek, 2001, 2006). Advertising tells us we will be part of the 'in crowd' if we but sneakers. Let me be clear about this. This is not a conspiracy theory that says everything is secretly controlled by some faceless others. There is not a secret room in which governments and corporations come together to agree to make sneakers and soccer fashionable to keep us all docile and un-free. But decisions are made by governments that increase the freedoms of corporations to act against our communal interests. And decisions are made by corporations to manipulate our wishes and desires through the use of advertising and marketing. Fashions, then, are constructed by us, but are also used by superstructures and hegemonic powers to construct us.

Sports as games on-line

On-line gaming became a trend in leisure even before the construction of the World Wide Web at the end of the twentieth century. People were using the first version of the internet to play text-based role-playing games. With the arrival of the World Wide Web, the reduction in costs to get on-line and the widespread dissemination of technologies, the 1990s saw the internet become a daily reality in many Western workplaces and homes. The first generation of dial-up modems ensured that on-line gaming was slow and limited in its scope and size, but the next generation of broadband connections allowed gamers to interact on-line in games that played out as if in real life – one could be truly immersed in an interactive game playing alongside people from different countries around the world. Sports games developed for off-line stand-alone games platforms were adapted for on-line use, and sports gaming became a key part of the games industry. On-line sports games allow gamers to become managers of their own sports clubs, competing in leagues and cup tournaments and other sports events. The complexity of these on-line games means that there are now millions of virtual teams and athletes competing against one another in competitions that shadow the real world. The virtual sports clubs and competitions are, however, branded with the same sponsorship logos as their real-world equivalents (Besharat, Kumar, Lax and Rydzik, 2013), and the clubs and sports are themselves officially licensed.

QUESTIONS TO CONSIDER

How else is the internet used to promote sports? How is it used to promote fashions?

REFERENCE AND FURTHER READING

Besharat, A., Kumar, A., Lax, J.R. and Rydzik, E.J. (2013) 'Leveraging Virtual Attribute Experience in Video Games to Improve Brand Recall and Learning', *Journal of Advertising*, 42, pp. 170–82.

TRENDS IN SPORTS

Modern sports themselves are a recent fashion, compared to other human activities. They have only been around since the nineteenth century, and the spread of these sports around the globe only really happened in the twentieth century. This period is the age of modernity, which is the age of rationalization and capitalism. In Spracklen (2013a, p. 34) I write about the theories of Weber in relation to the age of modernity, the rise of consumption in leisure, and the development of what Weber (1992, 2001) identifies as the age of rationality. For Weber, the age of rationality is the outcome of the rise of capitalism. Workplaces become industrialized, and popular culture and society become defined by consumerism and fashions. Modernity becomes something defined by conspicuous consumption of leisure goods. This is something identified by Veblen, whose *The Theory of the Leisure Class* (1970 [1899]) critiques the emergence of an elite class obsessed with fashions and material goods. This leisure class is the forerunner of the leisure class that existed in America and Europe in the late nineteenth century. For Veblen, the modern fashion of sports, both playing and watching, is an example of the increasing rationality in modernity, and an example of the way in which society becomes tricked into consumption and display.

We can witness the increase in rationality in modernity in the increasing codification of sports (Malcolm, 2005). This trend has seen the rules and systems that govern sports become more bureaucratic over the years. From rule-books agreed by men in blazers over an agreeable glass of wine, modern sports have become machines of instrumentality, driven by complex procedures controlled by professional executive officers. If part of the cause of this instrumentalization is the control and elimination of violence, as suggested by the figurationalists (Elias and Dunning, 1986), another part of the cause is the Habermasian systems that have become part of modern management cultures (Habermas, 1984, 1987). Sports have become, as we have seen, important industries with billions of dollars at stake. This leads to legal challenges against decisions made in sports, such as the transfer of players or the awarding of events to particular cities. The use – or threat of use – of the law makes sports governing bodies and professional sports clubs invest in robust systems of decision-making. The initial aim is to make systems clear and simple, but the instrumentality at the heart of modern management systems takes over. This robustness creates bureaucracies that end up making decision-making more opaque. In modern sports, this means governing bodies, governmental sports bodies and international organizations that employ thousands of managers and officers, responsible for every aspect of sport from child protection to corporate sponsorship. Monitoring and evaluation of performance becomes routinized in every aspect of modern sports management, just as it has become normalized in other areas of employment. What is unique about sport is the way in which this instrumentality impinges on the ways sports are coached and played, as well as managed. The rules of sports become carefully monitored and assessed, and officials become professional arbiters of rule-following. Athletes become driven by the instrumental needs of the system, winning or losing according to the strategies of the coach and the profit-making strategies of the system.

In this instrumentalization of sport, participation rates become measures of the success or failure of individual sports (Coalter, 2013). In the expansion and development of sport in the twentieth century, sports became globalized, becoming leisure activities that provided elite arenas for nationalism and Cold War politics (Houlihan, 1991). Governments across the world encouraged sports participation and supported the formation of local Olympic Committees and national sports governing bodies. In the postcolonial era, the number of new nation-states increased each decade, and each tried to use sports as a way of defining their national identity and improving the wellbeing of their citizens. But sports were allowed to develop independently of government targets, and in some countries sports governing bodies were suspicious of government interference in their development. This *laissez-faire* approach to sports development and participation saw many inequalities entrenched in sports: men's sports were privileged over women's sports; middle-class and elite sports were funded over working-class sports; and white, Western sports were normalized at the expense of other sports and physical activities. The first form of inequality was a product of the gender order and this participation trend has been evident wherever sports have spread. Even now men's sport has more privilege and power than women's sport, and the whole notion of having separate sports for men and women remains normal in sport. The second and third forms of inequality were and are more contested, as we have seen elsewhere in this book. Some sports have continued to be constrained by class and ethnicity, while others have provided opportunities for individual agency and subaltern resistance (Carrington and McDonald, 2008).

What matters for the argument about instrumentality is the way in which participation rates became a matter of assessment in annual monitoring and evaluation systems (Coalter, 2013). Sports started to be judged by their supporters and the media by their ability to attract new participants. Sports became measured by their sponsorship and their income and their profits, which were said to be indicators of support (Horne, 2006; Kerr and Gladden, 2008). And governments started to demand that sports receiving public funding had to account for that money through targets on increasing participation rates – not only overall, but amongst targeted groups that were under-represented in sports. This was a laudable aim with a pure motive. Sports governing bodies should not be expected to receive government funds without making some effort to be accountable for that spending. And targeting development work at under-represented groups such as ethnic minorities or women and girls is morally just, righting the wrongs of previous years, when many sports remained exclusive clubs for elite, white men. But the consequence of this performance management is the development of a Foucauldian regime of self-regulation and governmental surveillance (Foucault, 1991, 2006) whose primary aim is to complete and approve various whole sports plans, strategies and action plans (Spracklen, Long and Hylton, 2006). Participation rates become manipulated and obscured so that official data reported up the system makes each individual sport look good (Breedveld and Hoekman, 2011). Where sports fail to achieve their participation targets, or fail to provide data that looks like they are meeting the targets, they are castigated in the media and lose out on funding, as if it is their fault entirely that people are not playing their sport (Coalter, 2013). There could be all sorts of reasons why people might choose not to take up a sport that is offered to them – it might not be trendy or fashionable, it might be associated with a particular class, or they might just be scared about taking part, or there might just be gradual decline in participation across all sports (which is probably the case in most instances). But these performance systems make the sport itself entirely responsible for declining numbers (and a similar instrumentalization is at work at elite levels of sport, where sports with gold medals get the money for more gold medals, and those that do not get gold medals get their funding cut). So the logic of the system funds the development and performance work of sports that are historically successful, and generally well-supported by corporate sponsors and private trusts, while punishing sports that are not established.

This logic can also be seen at work in the trend of turning sports into entertainment (Rowe, 2004). Here the logic is that of capitalism, preferences of the market and the quest to fill television channels with output that has strong viewing figures. It is simply wrong to assume there is a causal link between aesthetics, value and popularity (Edgar, 2012). Sometimes there are things that are hugely popular in popular culture that have a lasting, aesthetic appeal: we might think of the popular novels of the nineteenth century such as those by Charlotte (*Jane Eyre*) and Emily Brontë (*Wuthering Heights*), which had great appeal when first published, which still have appeal now, and which are considered artistically and universally as great pieces of work. These things might be said to have some intrinsic merit to them, as well as being products of popular culture and mass tastes. But all too often things that are popular have little or no intrinsic value, aesthetically, morally or culturally. So sports that become popular on television become crude sites of emotional manipulation and aggression, where the tricks of television turn viewers into irrational beings easily swayed by slow-motion replays, 'expert' commentary, rock music and fancy adverts (Morris and Nydahl, 1985).

The final trend in this section is the tension between local diversity (local cultures and local sports) and global conformity. If modern sports are prime examples of globalization and commodification, they are not simply imposed globally on pre-existing local sports and pastimes. If modern sports are symbolic of the trends in popular culture towards Westernization, homogeneity and Americanization, then the fact remains that this trend has not been complete. The sports that have become globalized such as soccer and the Olympic sports became popular world-wide before America became secure in its global hegemony. These sports, as we have seen, represent older imperial and capitalist hegemonies of Western European culture. When these sports were spreading across the world in the shadow of colonialism, American popular culture created its own sports that stood as symbols of American independence from Europe: baseball, basketball and (American) football (Gorn and Goldstein, 1993). While each of these sports had European precedents, they became unique popular sports for the new nation-state of the United States of America. While some people in America tried to challenge the uniqueness of American sports through trying to import sports such as soccer and cricket, the isolationist period of American popular culture in the early twentieth century ensured that these three sports were sufficiently established and normalized in the eyes of the average American to be 'popular'.

When American cultural hegemony started to take hold in the second half of the century modern sports such as soccer, cricket, (ice) hockey and rugby had already become established in other nation-states as the sports of the 'people'. These people were young, working-class and bourgeois men. Soccer and these other team sports were easy to follow, and provided spectators with a visceral, entertaining experience. They became symbols of modernity in the new nation-states of the postcolonial era, as well as the already modern nation-states of Central and South America and the British Dominions (Lechner, 2009). Where the United States had colonial interests and direct rule of countries, in places such as the Philippines, Cuba and Japan (after the Second World War), American sports found cultures where they could be adopted as symbols of modernity (Dyreson, Mangan and Park, 2013). But with the Cold War struggle with Communism, American cultural hegemony was held back from becoming a global phenomenon. Ironically, the Cold War allowed Olympic sports to develop across the world in each political bloc and among non-aligned states, as vehicles of political ideology (Beamish and Ritchie, 2006). The struggle with Communism led American popular culture to become less innovative and more conservative. This meant the existing American sports became deep-rooted symbols of American identity, and they became part of the 'all-American way of life' that was perceived to be under attack by foreign ideas. Soccer became associated with Spanish-speaking foreigners from beyond America's borders (Delgado, 1999). With the fall of the Iron Curtain, America pushed out its cultural hegemony into most of the world, and its sports have travelled out, too. Basketball is now truly global, with professional competitions and televised tournaments in any country where there is urbanization and industrialization. American football and baseball have travelled less, but there are professional teams and leagues in many countries.

The globalization of martial arts

Martial arts are the various fighting sports that originated in the Far East in countries such as China and Japan. There are a number of these sports, but the ones that are perhaps best known in the West are judo and karate. These sports were products of specific cultural and political circumstances, re-inventions and constructions of authentic traditions at a time when these countries were under the threat of colonization or political and economic control by Western countries (Velija, Mierzwinski and Fortune, 2013). In Japan, for example, these martial arts became cultural activities linked strongly to cultural conservatism at a time when America was imposing its cultural hegemony, in the second half of the twentieth century. However, these martial arts also spread out from Japan and other Eastern countries to become global sports with strong international organizations and representation in the Olympics. This happened because martial arts benefited from a surge of Orientalist fashion in the twentieth century in the Western world. In the years following the Second World War in particular, Chinese and Japanese culture became widely appreciated by the Western elites. This led to a wider popularization of these cultures and their traditions in popular culture more broadly. For martial arts, this meant the development of films based on the feats of martial artists-turned-actors such as Bruce Lee, and the airing in Britain of television programmes made in Japan on the famous story of Monkey. This trend in popular culture brought with it thousands of new adherents to karate, judo and other martial arts, and sustains them to this day.

QUESTIONS TO CONSIDER

Is Orientalism at work today? Are there other examples of sports that have followed a similar route to globalization?

REFERENCE AND FURTHER READING

Velija, P., Mierzwinski, M. and Fortune, L. (2013) 'It made me feel Powerful: Women's Gendered Embodiment and Physical Empowerment in the Martial Arts', *Leisure Studies*, 32, pp. 524–41.

In this century, despite the on-rush of American sports through American cultural hegemony, and despite the earlier globalization of certain European sports, there are still plenty of locations where unfashionable sports survive – and plenty of sports and pastimes that remain fashionable in their specific localities. There are sports such as Gaelic football and hurling that are popular among certain communities because they provide a sense of parochial, regional or national pride (Rowe, 2003). These sports might have become globalized in the distribution of participants and supporters in the migrations of the last one hundred and fifty years, but they remain marginal. There are sports that have tried to become global sports but have so far failed in their attempts to be truly global, such as rugby league. There are sports and pastimes that have been shaped by earlier traditions in local cultures, which retain pre-modern ideas in modern shapes, such as the many forms of wrestling and fighting that exist around the world (Saeki, 1994). Then there are the global sports that have been shaped by local concerns and re-made in ways that suit local audiences and participants. Soccer, for all its globalizing tendencies, has become very different across its many markets, becoming a sport for the new elites in Japan and China, but one marginalized for its association with migrant communities in Australia.

SPORTING FASHIONS AND SPORTS IN FASHION

In the twentieth century, sports clothing fashions were initially unconnected to popular culture. People wore certain kinds of gear to play competitive sports, such as baseball shirts with team logos, or cricket whites with the team colours marked out on the V of the jumper (Collins, 2013a). When people participated in more informal forms of sport and physical culture, they resorted to wearing simple clothes unadorned by labels or advertising, often clothes that served as everyday wear. The sports clothing industry emerged as participants demanded special forms of clothing, and as developments in organic and industrial chemistry led to the invention and utilization of plastics and new fabrics. At first special clothing for sports participation was the preserve of the elite classes, who had the money to buy clothes that marked them out as golfers, or horse-riders, even if they rarely did either. In the second half of the twentieth century, special clothes for mass sports participation became a normal part of physical culture. Companies appeared with international advertising campaigns, targeting people to buy swimming costumes, tracksuits, sneakers or running shorts (Boden, 2006). The growth of the market for sports and physical culture fashions followed the growth of the 'leisure society', that period in the 1950s and 1960s when commentators and politicians believed that – as a consequence of the rise in wealth and a rise in technological automization – more people would have more time to take part in leisure activities (Smigel, 1963). Men and women were encouraged to play sports and do physical activities such as walking and swimming, and the new technologies of fashion production allowed cheap products to be consumed by the rising middle classes.

By the final years of the twentieth century, sports goods were ubiquitous on the high streets and in the shopping malls. Sports fashion has become a global industry of questionable ethics, where cheap shoes and shirts are put together in the sweat shops of the developing world and sold at enormous profit to Westerners (Roberts, 2004). Labels on sports goods have become designer brands, adding irrational value to such goods on account of the cultural capital the names accrue (Featherstone, 2007). Taking part in sports as a participant has become an expensive business when it comes to the pressure from adverts and the media, and one's peers, to buy the latest piece of kit, or the latest shorts. One has to buy the right food and drink supplements, the right pedometer or heart-rate monitor, let alone the running shoes and the all-weather luminous jacket. To be a fan of a sport is even more demanding. If one follows a particular team, one has to buy the team colours, which change every year. Team colours are brashy, shiny and often covered in the brands of corporate sponsors. Wearing these colours makes you a walking legitimation of global capitalism. Some sports clubs do not treat their fans with such contempt, and there are those honourable clubs that keep the same colours every year, or who limit or forego the crude branding. But most clubs and sports organizations have a complete range of clothing and branded merchandizing that they encourage their fans to buy. One could choose not to buy the latest colours, of course, but there is sufficient social and cultural pressure to ensure that the new colours sell well (Boden, 2006; Roberts, 2004; Rojek, 2010).

In recent years, there has been a blurring of the boundaries between (sports and) physical culture and popular culture in films, tattooing and clothing. Sportswear has become part of everyday fashion. Tracksuits and sneakers were initially adopted by youth subcultures as markers of resistance and rebellion (Gans, 2008; Hebdige, 1979). In the last decade of the twentieth century they became part of mass, popular culture, when people in modern societies around the world all seemed for a moment to be dressed in 'shell-suits' and branded sneakers. The fashion did not remain so completely absolute in its global reach as we entered this century, but sportswear remains significant in modern popular culture and modern fashion in a number of important ways. First, tracksuits, sports-branded clothing and sneakers remain popular among young, working-class people in many Western or Westernized countries. For these people it is still a marker of their resistance to mainstream society, though they are stigmatized by commentators in the mainstream and the bourgeoisie, who call them derogatory names (Jones, 2012). Secondly, sportswear is still worn by the bourgeoisie and the elite, but it is encoded and branded differently than that worn by the despised working classes. Sportswear for the elites is branded kit designed for outdoor leisure, or unbranded but expensive 'classic' clothing that draws on an elite sport such as rugby or tennis (Buckley, 2003). Thirdly, sneakers and sportswear, especially team colours, are used by middle-class hipsters to get the look of some previous decade, in a playful, postmodern pastiche of nostalgia (Featherstone, 2007; Taylor, 2009).

Sports stars, fashion shoots and sexuality

Sports stars have become celebrities who are recruited to sell products to consumers in the global marketplace. At first, sports stars were recruited to advertise products that were associated with sports. But often, sports stars sell products only loosely related to their sports participation, if at all. Sports stars become celebrity bodies that link the desire of the product to sexual desire. This sexual desire is not simply heterosexual lust for the semi-naked body of the sports star. While there are many examples of women athletes used to sell products to men who are attracted to the sexual objectification of the women, the adverts tap deeper sexual desires. Male athletes, for instance, appear semi-naked in adverts for after-shave or underwear. Some of the target audience for these adverts are gay men, who respond on a superficial level to the eroticism of the images. But heterosexual men also seemingly react positively to the images. This is due to a combination of homoerotic desires latent in heterosexual men, but also the desire to be a successful, masculine, heterosexual man just like the sports star in the advert (Yeates, 2013). So the men who respond to the adverts want to be just like the sports star. They want to have the model wife he has. They want his well-toned, muscular body with its six-pack of stomach muscles. They want to be a successful athlete. They desire this so much they think buying the after-shave will make them more like the sports star.

QUESTIONS TO CONSIDER

How else do these adverts work? How do women respond to adverts with female athletes in them?

REFERENCE AND FURTHER READING

Yeates, A. (2013) 'Queer Visual Pleasures and the Policing of Male Sexuality in Responses to Images of David Beckham', *Visual Studies*, 28, pp. 110–21.

The re-invention of the past through sports clothing is seen in the films and television programmes that are consciously set in some period between the invention of modern sports and the present day. Hollywood has always been interested in re-inventing the past for the sake of making profits. Sports have become a key site for the heightened drama of the moving screen, places and activities that define a generation or merely act as a site for the personal challenges of the protagonist. Sports and movies are simplified versions of reality, so it is natural that they have influenced each other in popular culture. Movies about baseball cannot help tackling the meaning of the American dream, and movies about baseball tell baseball fans how to consume baseball. Sports stars become actors, playing extensions of their sporting personalities, and actors make a show of attending sports matches, to show they have the common touch (Rojek, 2006). In this postmodern popular culture space, sports fashions and cultural fashions collide to make new forms. Tattoos, traditionally the permanent mark of alternative subcultures and the criminal classes, became a normal part of everyday popular culture in the first decade of this century (Kosut, 2006). Sports stars and athletes have been torch-bearers for the inkification of popular culture, revealing their new tattoos to the media and revelling in the coolness they think the tattoos give them. The fashion has spread between athletes from out of the margins of popular culture. Having a tattoo became normal for rock musicians first; then it spread to actors and models before coming to the world of sport.

CONCLUSION

People do get pleasure from sports fashions and the consumption of sport, and for many people such fashions can be affirmative lifestyle choices. It has been suggested that the sportization of fashion, and the crossover between physical culture and popular culture, is indicative of a postmodern turn (Lewis and Gray, 2013). It is true that we live in a different world to the one of the last century, and sports and leisure are activities that give people the chance to make meaning in their lives. People now are more likely to use sports and physical culture to define their social identity, their networks of belonging and their place in society. Some of the playfulness of this identity-making might be described as aesthetically postmodern, or belonging to societies that exist in an age of postmodernity. But that does not make our society and our sports postmodern in an ontological or epistemological sense. Sports fashions, especially the crossover between physical culture and popular culture, are not an expression of a postmodern turn, but are a reflection of the globalization of physical culture and modernity – which has consequences for those who might want to resist that trend. Our ability to limit the impact of instrumentality, the powers of American cultural hegemony, or the powers of global capitalism, is constrained by those powers. Sports fashions and trends in sport limit our ability to make free choices about what kind of sports and physical culture we want to take part in, and how we want to represent our sports participation in popular cultural forms. The overall argument of this book is re-capped and expanded in the final conclusion chapter, which follows.

EXERCISES

1 What will be the trends in sports in the next fifty years?
2 How does sports fashion spread between cultures and classes?
3 What is the difference between popular culture and physical culture?

Conclusions: The Future of Sport

In this final, concluding chapter, a brief summary of the main arguments throughout the book is made. The chapter then looks at what the immediate future of sport might look like, if the trends identified at the beginning of the chapter continue. The book will question the potential of sports and physical culture as redeeming features of modernity if the trends remain the same, but will make a number of suggestions about how both might be re-shaped to make them fulfil that potential.

THE MAIN ARGUMENTS FROM THIS TEXTBOOK

Why do we play sports, why do we watch sports? Why do we take part in some physical activities and not others, and why do we think these things are good for us? This book tries to answer all of those questions. First of all, we enjoy them, of course, and we get profound satisfaction from doing sports, watching sports, talking about sports, being sports fans and consuming sports fashions. They provide belonging, friendship, identity and succour from the travails of modern life. Physical culture is something that gives us meaning and purpose. But it also shapes us in ways that we might not wish for.

I started by looking at the history of sports and physical activity, and specifically the creation and development of what I called modern sports. These sports were a product of a period of high modernity, which started in Europe and North America in the second half of the nineteenth century, and continued into the twentieth. Modern sports are defined by what Jurgen Habermas identifies as the tension in modernity between different ways of thinking, different rationalities: the communicative reason associated with free interaction, free choices and open discourse; and the instrumentality that reduces debates about value to economics or some other simplified rationality (Habermas, 1984, 1987; Spracklen, 2009). Sports had a number of contradictory purposes in the nineteenth and twentieth centuries, when sports and physical education as we know them became part of a shared physical culture of modernity. They were activities that allowed individuals to come together to make meaning in their lives, in that free, communicative sense – giving enjoyment and a sense of belonging to their participants and to spectators. But sports, physical education and physical culture were tools of instrumentality right from their invention in the nineteenth century – and this use of sports as tools of instrumental power has continued to this day. The values of sports in their original form were those that had a communicative nature. As we have seen in social psychological models of motivation, when sports are more like leisure than work, they have real value for their participants. This is what I have called communicative leisure (Spracklen, 2009, 2011, 2013a, 2013b). Physical activities become communicative leisure when they are entered into freely, where they shape the democratic space of the Habermasian lifeworld, and where they are not spaces for the domination of humans.

Sports are one sub-set of leisure, or one sub-set of physical culture. Sports are difficult to define, but they are connected to the notion of fair play and moral behaviour. They are forms of physical culture that have fixed rules, organizing structures and competitions. Physical culture can be useful in supporting individuals in their desire and need to make free choices about their bodies in modernity – but the meaning and purpose of sports is morally ambiguous. Some of the supposed moral, psychological and spiritual benefit argued for sports will come from feeling physiologically fitter and mentally sharper, but some of that benefit will come from being trained to be a hard worker, a follower of orders; and some will come from physical activity diverting us away from supposed unsavoury leisure activities. The moral good argument for sport fails because it is not clear what divides the correct ethos of sport and the amoral or immoral practices and behaviours supposedly condemned: athletes and others taking part in sports and other physical activity cheat, drink, steal, attack others and destroy things just like anyone else; some of their bad behaviour is actually as a result of their sports activities. In other words, the arguments that sports and physical culture are inherently morally good are incoherent. There are a multitude of ethical and moral imperatives within sport and between sport and other parts of society. Furthermore, all kinds of non-physical activities could be viewed as just as morally good for individuals such as reading a book or admiring a painting. Sports, then, do not have anything special about them. Some forms of physical activity are good for us because we freely choose them and we like them – because they are communicative. As we have seen in this book, modern sport, throughout its short history, has been bad for people when it has been forced upon us as a means of fostering nationalism or masculinity, or a way of becoming something someone else, the person in power, wants us to be. This is one of the causes of the decline in participation: the rise of sport as a part of the entertainment industry, and the commodification of athletes that leads to the egregious pursuit of victory at all costs at the elite levels.

Sports and physical culture do give clear benefits to individuals and to society. There is a psychological benefit from participating in sports, both from the perspective of individual character/personality and from the interaction between individuals in social settings. The latter interaction further benefits society through encouraging strong social bonds and shared belonging. Again, using the theoretical framework of Habermas we can say that sports, like other forms of leisure, can be communicative: they can be activities or spaces where people come together to interact freely and to develop the lifeworld of the public sphere. It is important to note that other forms of leisure have that same social and cultural quality – the ability to be used freely by humans to build belonging and further human development – and sports and physical culture are arguably not the best forms of leisure to be communicative, given their role in perpetuating hegemony and social inequalities. However, it is clear that it is the physicality of physical activities such as sports that make them important in tackling psychological problems and improving psychological wellbeing. Going for a run or dancing works the body and mind in a positive way that reading a book does not, even if reading a book might be something more communicatively free. But if physical activity is potentially so beneficial, the question becomes: who gets to benefit? The confidence and the ability and the power to do sport are limited to those who have cultural hegemony over the practice. I feel I have the right kind of capital and power and autonomy to make choices about my leisure lifestyles. I can afford to work flexibly to give me time to run, and I am paid well enough to be able to buy a house in a town with no air pollution and access to open hills. This has ethical and sociological consequences. The benefits of sports and physical culture, then, are tempered by the problems that follow the distribution and allocation of both moral and social benefits. We need to understand the inequalities that historically existed in our society, and the inequalities that still exist, giving power to some at the expense of others.

Some say sports and physical culture encourages a sense of wellbeing. Wellbeing is a problematic term in itself, and it is impossible to say that sports improve it. It could be that the people who already feel they live 'well' lives are the ones who are likely to take part in sports and other forms of physical culture: the measurements then become a way of confirming that those with most power, wealth and freedom are the ones who are taking part in sports. If you feel secure in life, you will feel happy, you will do more constructive leisure activities, such as sports, the arts and communicative leisure; if you are insecure in life, you will feel stressed and possibly unhappy, and you will not engage in meaningful leisure activities, nor will you use your leisure time productively. I have shown that some people do get some sort of satisfaction from some sports and physical cultural activities – and physical activity is something that can improve people's biological, physical health. So perhaps the people who benefit right now from physical culture, the ones who get the improvement of their wellbeing, are the elites of our nation-states, the people with power – and the overall wellbeing of humanity is left unaltered as those with limited power (or no power at all) derive no benefit from physical culture. Of course, sports can also lead to all kinds of harm, biologically, psychologically and socially, for those who participate (and those who are forced to participate). The pursuit of excellence pushes athletes into all kinds of unhealthy and abnormal practices. Failing to become full-time professionals leads to enormous levels of dissatisfaction and unhappiness among young athletes. Children miss the fun and joy of unstructured play and creative, active recreation, the communicative leisure forms of physical activity, so they do not take part in physical activities as adults.

In modern physical culture there is no causal relationship between watching sport and playing it, but some people who start as fans become participants, and some participants become fans. Sports fandom is an essential part of the culture of sport. The history of modern sports shows that watching sports was just as important to the sustainability and development of sports as playing them. The notion of the sports spectator was a new one, but soon became indivisible from being involved in running a club or playing sport. As elite sports professionalized and commercialized, the role of the fan changed from that of a member with rights to a consumer, who was expected to keep on spending to keep the sports in business. The sports fan has become a thrall to the power of the modern sports industry, which is a part of the wider global entertainment industry. Some fans might choose to resist the commercialization of sport, but that resistance is inevitably limited. Modern sports are now effectively controlled by a small number of trans-national corporations, who have been allowed by national and international political institutions to develop a neo-liberal global capitalism that benefits their shareholders beyond anything and anyone else. The sports–media complex is part of a wider entertainment industry that has commodified global, Western popular culture. That is, the rise of the sports industry reflects the commodification of other aspects of popular culture, and like that commodification there are profound problems for individuals and agency. When most people think about sports and physical activity, they no longer immediately think of the sports they might play in their leisure time. Instead, they think of the latest international tests between nation-states, or the gold medal winners at the Olympics. And when they think of those things, they think of the sports stars and the products they endorse. Corporations would not invest so much of their own money in advertising if they thought it was useless. We are all tricked by the hegemony of global capitalism's sports industry. We are also easily fooled by the nation-states and hegemons that prefer us to be consumers of sports and popular culture than free-thinking rebels.

What does this mean, then, for the idea of physical culture? Should we abandon talking about sports and leisure, and active recreation, and embrace physical culture? The two problems that seem to emerge with using physical culture to describe the activities we are interested in is the limited applicability of the term, and its loaded ideology. The limited applicability stems from the loaded ideology. Basically, physical culture seems to be used to only describe those kinds of activities that involve ordered physical activity. Physical culture seems to be sport plus activities that promote health and fitness plus maybe physical education. Physical culture does not include other forms of activity, and other cultural spaces, that might be counter cultural or counter hegemonic. This stems from the loaded ideology of the phrase 'physical culture'. It presupposes that the forms of culture and the capital we have, and the power we have to move between forms of physical culture, are unbounded. Physical culture becomes its own moral cause and effect, and people who participate in the limited forms of physical culture prove their superiority over the rest who do not participate. In fact, they are only able to participate because they have economic and cultural capital, and have enough autonomy given to them in return for their compliance with their own subjugation and place in the new bourgeois classes. By calling these things physical culture we hide the hegemonic trick of modern sport, and the instrumentalization of everyday leisure. That is, we give people the agency they do not have, and hide the constraints made in our everyday lives.

THE FUTURE OF SPORT

If you play sport and watch sport, if you're a sports fan, you will have often wondered where it will all end. Can we keep on assuming that there will be a winner of the Super Bowl? Will some sports disappear? When we think about these questions we are trying to predict the future. This is an impossible task, and anything you say might be held up to ridicule, because it is notoriously difficult to make predictions that turn out to be true. But academics do think about these things, and we should look at ways academics might answer the question about sport, given the trends that I have identified.

Ask a philosopher about the future of sport, and they would be concerned with the ways in which professional sports are becoming driven more by the pursuit of success. From an ethical perspective, sports are likely to become more and more spaces where anything goes in the pursuit of the ultimate goal. One might envisage a future where all performance-enhancing technologies are permissible because it becomes impossible to catch up with the makers and users. The next step in performance-enhancing technologies is genetically-modified athletes (Miah, 2007). It is not too difficult to imagine a future where manipulation of genetic material occurs that makes someone more likely to be a winning athlete. The next step might be cyborg athletes, enhanced with robotic technologies. Given the lust for physical combat, the thirst for blood that exists in sports spectators, one might also imagine a world of professional sport where killing becomes permissible and encouraged, in the confines of the sports arena. While we have seen that sports have become less viscerally violent, there is a commodification and commercialization of modern sports that already allows people to watch professional athletes get maimed in endless internet repeats. At the moment there is a strong moral antipathy towards killing other humans, but this might change if the humans competing in sports were seen as some un-human other, beyond the pale of human respectability. This might be a Faustian pact between the elite athlete and the sports industry, with individuals choosing to take the risk of death for the chance of a huge reward (which is not so far away from what happens in many sports today). Or athletes might be dehumanized so much that they lose their status as fellow humans and become no better than slaves.

Ask a sociologist of sport about the future of sport, and they will probably say that modern sports will continue to become more like global businesses, and sports will still be used to maintain the power and status of the world's ruling elites. Professional sport will continue to dominate the media, and the amount of money paid out to the top performers will continue to rise.

Modern sports will colonize developing countries and the lower classes, and will slowly squeeze out other forms of leisure and local forms of popular culture. Inevitably, some sports will become unfashionable and these will disappear. In the future, there will be fewer sports, but the survivors will have higher stakes. Domestic competitions will be replaced by global competitions. Participation rates will drop but sports will be a vital way for new urban middle classes to demonstrate they belong to the right kind of society. Sports will be used by new authoritarian movements to extol discipline, order, obedience and subservience.

At the same time, there may well be a limit to modern sport's expansion and commercial development. For one thing, the resources of the planet are finite, and unless we solve the problem of our impending environmental catastrophe we will end up with a reversal of growth and a collapse of the technologies that allow sport to be globalized and commercialized. We might also end up in a world that is controlled by new elites that do not value sport at all. Another future might be that the existing ruling elites might suddenly focus their attention on other forms of leisure and culture as ways of defining their own contemporary nature and values. Changes in norms, values and fashions led to the arrival of sports. They can lead to their departure, too. The middle classes might then emulate the ruling classes, and sports might become unfashionable. If this happens, the amount of money in sports will fade away, and there will be a residue of sports played and watched by marginal groups and the lower classes. The sports might be professional but the rewards will be small. The spectators will be few in number, and many sports will become folk traditions preserved in the archives of museums. The remaining sports might be targeted by campaigns of moral outrage and ultimately (and ironically) outlawed by the elites because they are perceived to be unhealthy and immoral.

FINAL THOUGHTS

Despite all that I have written in this Conclusion, I love running, and I like to think I am still a rugby league fan. I still think sports can have some redeeming values, so long as the impulse is communicative leisure. If we do not want a world where sports become even more a product of hegemonic instrumentality, we have to try to change sports now. That means making individual choices about what we do and do not do. For example, subscribing to dedicated sports channels only gives money to the sports–media complex. We should not only unsubscribe, we should do what we can to inform others about the harmful effects on sports and on society that such industries cause. We should join others in campaigning against the most harmful, visible examples of the instrumentality of sport. That is, we should join groups that oppose the destruction of entire blocks in cities for mega sports events. We should support activists working to expose the instrumentality of modern sport, and we should stop buying things. We should complain to editors and producers about the extent of sports coverage in the media, and we should try to find other things to talk about. That is, we should take more of an interest in politics, history and other parts of the human experience. If we want to remain sports fans, we should find sports clubs that are run as co-operatives, or which have taken a strong stance against racism or sexism. As sports practitioners (coaches and teachers and others), we should ensure that we develop programmes based on play and creativity and autonomy, not on control and discipline. We should lobby our politicians and governments to make sure they provide inclusive policies in schools and communities that promote active recreation and communicative leisure, instead of spending millions bolstering the sports–media complex. Our ability to make change happen is small, compared to the vested interests against us, but it is our moral duty to try to make the future better, so that all people can enjoy the free practice of physical activity. To paraphrase Karl Marx: sports fans of the world unite, you have nothing to lose but your cable subscriptions.

Glossary

This glossary gives you a brief definition of the key terms used throughout the textbook. You may be familiar with some or all of these from your own education and further reading, but if you aren't familiar with any of the terms then this glossary should help you. Be aware that all these terms are associated with academic debates about their meaning and relevance – this glossary by necessity is based on my understanding of the terms, and my use of them in this book. If there are other terms in the book that you do not understand you should search for them in an academic dictionary.

Agency – the freedom to act as an individual in the social world.

Amateur – historically used in sport to define participants who took part on a 'part-time' or unpaid basis, though the term was loaded with ambiguity and complexity. Used in popular culture to denote people who take part in things for fun, though again this definition is fraught with contested meaning.

Americanization – the spread of American ideas and culture to the rest of the world.

Authenticity – the idea that there is something that can be identified as being truer than another thing to ourselves, our culture, or our community.

Behaviourism – a field of psychology that does not create untestable models of structures inside the mind, but which uses experiments to test and predict animal and human behaviours.

Bourgeois – someone from the urban middle classes, or the form of culture associated with those social classes, which is caught between the high culture of the elites and the popular culture of the working classes. The word 'bourgeoisie' is used to refer to the entire class.

Capitalism – the economic system in which money is used to pay for people's labour and for purchasing goods, which are traded freely between companies and individuals. The 'free market' is a metaphor for the way in which capitalism works to find fair prices for buyers and sellers.

Class – sub-divisions of the social structure based on wealth, family, up-bringing and splits over what constitutes 'culture'. Sociologists usually identify three kinds of class: the upper classes (the rulers, the elites); the middle classes (the bourgeoisie); and the working classes who have least access to political, social and economic power.

Commodification – the way in which things become commodities; a process through which objects, ideas, people and groups in society are reduced to the status of goods bought and sold.

Communicative – a way of thinking and a way of acting with free will, without any constraint; a type of rationality used in discourse and exchange with others on a free and equal basis.

Culture – the processes, artefacts, ideas, rituals, narratives, myths, words and practices that bind a particular group of people together; also used, confusingly, to refer to a small set of elite aesthetic practices in the modern West, so make sure you understand the context where it is used.

Embodiment – ways in which bodies are used to construct identity, belong-ing, conformity and resistance.

Epistemology – the part of philosophy concerned with ways of knowing and coming to knowledge about the world.

Essentialism – a form of thinking that reduces complex issues to the simpler things that supposedly underpin the complex issues.

Ethics – the part of philosophy concerned with morality and the idea of goodness.

Ethnicity – a sub-division of the social structure and a social identity that comes from belonging to a certain group with a shared culture, heritage and religion.

Gender – a sub-division of the social structure based on the constructed 'gender order', the historical patterns of men's domination over women.

Globalization – the process in which the world's different cultures and coun-tries are becoming closer; the process in which those different cultures and countries are becoming similar through modernization, homogenization and Westernization.

Governmentality – the way in which governments control the public, and the way in which individuals control themselves on behalf of the state.

Gratification – the state in humans when we take visceral pleasure and sat-isfaction in something.

Habitus – a term used by Pierre Bourdieu to describe one's upbringing and the habits associated with it; also used by Bourdieu and in this book to identify places in which cultural capital can be accrued.

Hegemony – the way in which the elites use their power to keep people without power in that powerless state, through the use of persuasion and deception; the complete subjugation of the powerless by the powerful.

Identity – what we think we are and what we think others are; and what they think we are.

Ideology – frameworks of false (or untested) assumptions that are taken to be true by those who believe in them and act upon them.

Instrumentality – the way in which our ability to think is constrained by the logic of capitalism or the logic of the instrument/machine; the process by which our actions become constrained by structures and rules beyond our control.

Leisure – used sometimes in this book to denote an informal, loose, everyday kind of activity undertaken in free time; also used to describe everything that is described as leisure by leisure scholars (leisure is the sum of sport, tourism, popular culture, entertainment and informal, everyday leisure things).

Marxism – a theoretical framework that builds on the work of Karl Marx; Marxism provides sociologists with a way of critiquing modern capitalism.

Modernity – the period of time that began when the West started to move from feudalism and towards cities, science and capitalism; we are arguably still living at the end of this period of time.

Multiculturalism – the state of a nation or community where there are a number of cultural communities living in the same nation or community, and each cultural community has the same legal and moral status.

Ontology – the part of philosophy primarily concerned with what the world is, what the nature of reality is, and what things exist.

Physical activity – some kind of leisure form that involves the testing of one's body.

Physical culture – activities, the culture and ideas associated with physicality, that is, the playing of sports and the doing of physical activity and recreation.

Popular culture – a kind of culture that becomes common to all classes in society; a kind of culture associated with modernity and capitalism, such as pop music.

Post-Marxism – theoretical frameworks that have developed from Marxism, which share his concerns with capitalism and inequalities of power.

Postmodernism – a set of philosophical challenges to scholars who believe in science, reason and progress; a number of schools of thought that question truth.

Postmodernity – the period of time that follows modernity, in which social structures become less important; some scholars argue we are living in it now.

Professional – a historical category used in sports to define participants who were paid and identified as being 'full-time' athletes. Used in popular culture to define activities associated with work and payment.

Psychodynamics – a set of ideas and theories in psychology that assume there are underlying forces ('dynamics') in the mind of which individuals may not be consciously aware. The first and most prominent theorist of psychodynamics was Sigmund Freud.

'Race' – a sub-division of social structure based on false notions of race, used with inverted commas to denote the problematic nature of the term.

Rationalization – a process identified by Max Weber, in which modern society comes into maturity, through the construction by ruling elites of rational processes and systems.

Secular – used to describe things that are not part of the sacred domain. Also used to denote a culture, society or political entity (a public sphere or space) that is founded on the exclusion of faith and religion.

Society – the big community in which we live today, shaped by modernity and the West.

Sport – a sub-division of leisure associated with competition, formal rules and physical activity.

Structure – when used with 'social' refers to the frameworks that support and divide communities, cultures and modern society. A structuralist is a theorist who argues that social structures control and constrain humans.

Subculture – a sub-division of society or of popular culture in which individuals find identity and belonging, sometimes in opposition to society and popular culture but not necessarily so.

Theology – the academic study of religion and faith.

Utilitarianism – a theory of ethics that attempts to weigh up the consequences of actions. The theory is often reduced to the idea that the best action is that which causes the greatest good for the greatest number of people.

Whiteness – an identity associated with the majority ethnic group in the West.

West, The – a contested geographical community and culture associated with Western Europe, the United States of America, Canada, Australia and New Zealand.

Westernization – the spread of ideas and culture from the West to the rest of the world.

References

Adorno, T. (1947) *Composing for the Films*, New York, Oxford University Press.

Adorno, T. (1991) *The Culture Industry*, London, Routledge.

Alcoff, L.M. (2000) 'Phenomenology, Post-structuralism, and Feminist Theory on the Concept of Experience', in L. Fisher and L. Embree (eds) *Feminist Phenomenology: Contributions to Phenomenology Volume 40*, pp. 39–56, Dordrecht, Springer.

Allport, G.W. (1937) *Personality: A Psychological Interpretation*, Oxford, Holt.

Ammianus Marcellinus (2004) *The Later Roman Empire*, translated by A. Wallace-Hadrill, Harmondsworth, Penguin.

Anderson, B. (1983) *Imagined Communities*, London, Verso.

Anderson, J. and Jackson, S. (2012) 'Competing Loyalties in Sports Medicine: Threats to Medical Professionalism in Elite, Commercial Sport', *International Review for the Sociology of Sport*, 48, pp. 238–56.

Andrews, D.L. and Ritzer, G. (2007) 'The Grobal in the Sporting Glocal', *Global Networks*, 7, pp. 135–53.

Appadurai, A. (1996) *Modernity at Large: Cultural Dimensions of Globalization*, Minneapolis, University of Minnesota Press.

Archbold, V., Richardson, D. and Dugdill, L. (2009) 'Looking beyond Parametric Measures to Understand Children and Families Physical Activity Behaviours: An Ethnographic Approach', *Journal of Science and Medicine in Sport*, 12 (Supplement), S77.

Archetti, E. (1995) 'In Search of National Identity: Argentinian Football and Europe', *International Journal of the History of Sport*, 12, pp. 201–19.

Arditi, J. (1998) *A Genealogy of Manners: Transformations of Social Relations in France and England from the Fourteenth to the Eighteenth Century*, Chicago, University of Chicago Press.

Ashplant, T. and Wilson, A. (1988) 'Present-Centred History and the Problem of Historical Knowledge', *The Historical Journal*, 21, pp. 253–74.

Askwith, R. (2004) *Feet in the Clouds: The Tale of Fell Running and Obsession*, London, Aurum.

Atry, A., Hansson, M.G. and Kihlbom, U. (2012) 'Beyond the Individual: Sources of Attitudes towards Rule Violation in Sport', *Sport, Ethics and Philosophy*, 6, pp. 467–79.

Auerbach, S. (2010) 'A Right Sort of Man: Gender, Class Identity, and Social Reform in Late-Victorian Britain', *Journal of Policy History*, 22, pp. 64–94.

Backhouse, S.H., Ekkekakis, P., Biddle, S.J.H., Foskett, A. and Williams, C. (2007) 'Exercise Makes People Feel Better but People are Inactive: Paradox or Artifact?', *Journal of Sport and Exercise Psychology*, 29, pp. 498–517.

Bairner, A. (2001) *Sport, Nationalism, and Globalization: European and North American Perspectives*, Albany, State University of New York Press.

Balaguer, I., Duda, J. and Crespo, M. (1999) 'Motivational Climate and Goal Orientations as Predictors of Perceptions of Improvement, Satisfaction and Coach Ratings among Tennis Players', *Scandinavian Journal of Medicine and Science in Sports*, 9, pp. 381–8.

Baldwin, P. (1990) *The Politics of Social Solidarity: Class Bases of the European Welfare State, 1875–1975*, Cambridge, Cambridge University Press.

Balsdon, J. (2004) *Life and Leisure in Ancient Rome*, London, Phoenix.

Barthes, R. (1972) *Mythologies*, London, Cape.

Baudrillard, J. (1988) *Selected Writings*, Cambridge, Polity.

Baudrillard, J. (1998) *The Consumer Society: Myths and Structures*, London, Sage.

Bauman, Z. (2000) *Liquid Modernity*, Cambridge, Polity.

Beamish, R. and Ritchie, I. (2006) *Fastest, Highest, Strongest: A Critique of High Performance Sport*, London, Routledge.

Beck, U. (1998) *Democracy without Enemies*, Cambridge, Polity.

Beissel, A.S., Giardina, M. and Newman, J.I. (2013) 'Men of Steel: Social Class, Masculinity, and Cultural Citizenship in Post-industrial Pittsburgh', *Sport in Society*, published on-line at DOI: 10.1080/17430437.2013.806032.

Beiswenger, K.L. and Grolnick, W.S. (2010) 'Interpersonal and Intrapersonal Factors Associated with Autonomous Motivation in Adolescents' After-school Activities', *The Journal of Early Adolescence*, 30, pp. 369–94.

Bennett, A. (2001) *Cultures of Popular Music*, Buckingham, Open University Press.

Bennett, G., Cunningham, G. and Dees, W. (2006) 'Measuring the Marketing Communication Activations of a Professional Tennis Tournament', *Sport Marketing Quarterly*, 15, pp. 91–101.

Bentham, J. (2007) *Moral Realism and the Foundations of Ethics*, New York, Dover.

Bentley, M. (2006) 'Past and "Presence": Re-visiting Historical Ontology', *History and Theory*, 45, pp. 349–61.

Ben-Yehuda, N. (1989) *The Politics and Morality of Deviance: Moral Panics, Drug Abuse, Deviant Science, and Reversed Stigmatization*, Albany, State University of New York Press.

Berkeley, G. (2009) *Principles of Human Knowledge and Three Dialogues*, Oxford, Oxford University Press.

Berlin, J.A. and Colditz, G.A. (1990) 'A Meta-analysis of Physical Activity in the Prevention of Coronary Heart Disease', *American Journal of Epidemiology*, 132, pp. 612–28.

Berry, D. and Bell, M.P. (2012) 'Inequality in Organizations: Stereotyping, Discrimination, and Labor Law Exclusions', *Equality, Diversity and Inclusion: An International Journal*, 31, pp. 236–48.

Besharat, A., Kumar, A., Lax, J.R. and Rydzik, E.J. (2013) 'Leveraging Virtual Attribute Experience in Video Games to Improve Brand Recall and Learning', *Journal of Advertising*, 42, pp. 170–82.

Biddle, S.J.H., Fox, K.R. and Boutcher, S.H. (eds) (2000) *Physical Activity and Psychological Well-being*, London, Routledge.

Bikhchandani, S., Hirshleifer, D. and Welch, I. (1992) 'A Theory of Fads, Fashion, Custom, and Cultural Change as Informational Cascades', *Journal of Political Economy*, 100, pp. 992–1026.

Billig, M. (1995) *Banal Nationalism*, London, Sage.

Bird, A. (1992) *Philosophy of Science*, London, UCL Press.

Bishai, D. and Nalubola, R. (2002) 'The History of Food Fortification in the United States: Its Relevance for Current Fortification Efforts in Developing Countries', *Economic Development and Cultural Change*, 51, pp. 37–53.

Bishop, H. and Jaworski, A. (2003) 'We Beat 'em: Nationalism and the Hegemony of Homogeneity in the British Press Reportage of Germany versus England during Euro 2000', *Discourse and Society*, 14, pp. 243–71.

Blackshaw, T. (2010) *Leisure*, London, Routledge.

Blair, S.N., Cheng, Y. and Holder, J.S. (2001) 'Is Physical Activity or Physical Fitness More Important in Defining Health Benefits?', *Medicine and Science in Sports and Exercise*, 33 (Supplement), S379–S399.

Bloomer, W.M. (1997) 'Schooling in Persona: Imagination and Subordination in Roman Education', *Classical Antiquity*, 16, pp. 57–78.

Boden, S. (2006) 'Dedicated Followers of Fashion? The Influence of Popular Culture on Children's Social Identities', *Media, Culture and Society*, 28, pp. 289–98.

Bodnar, I. and Perenyi, S. (2012) 'A Socio-historical Approach to the Professionalisation of Sporting Occupations in Hungary during the First Decades of the Twentieth Century: The Coach', *The International Journal of the History of Sport*, 29, pp. 1097–124.

Bonde, H. (2009) 'The Struggle for Danish Youth: Fascism, Sport, Democracy', *The International Journal of the History of Sport*, 26, pp. 1436–57.

Booth, D. (2003) 'Hitting Apartheid for Six? The Politics of the South African Sports Boycott', *Journal of Contemporary History*, 38, pp. 477–93.

Booth, D. (2011) 'Olympic City Bidding: An Exegesis of Power', *International Review for the Sociology of Sport*, 46, pp. 367–86.

Borch-Jacobsen, M. and Shamdasani, S. (2012) *The Freud Files: An Inquiry into the History of Psychoanalysis*, Cambridge, Cambridge University Press.

Borsay, P. (2005) *A History of Leisure*, Basingstoke, Palgrave.

Bourdieu, P. (1986) *Distinction*, London, Routledge.

Brailsford, D. (1992) *British Sport: A Social History*, Cambridge, Lutterworth Press.

Brattain, M. (2007) 'Race, Racism, and Antiracism: UNESCO and the Politics of Presenting Science to the Postwar Public', *The American Historical Review*, 112, pp. 1386–413.

Braun, R. and Vliegenthart, R. (2008) 'The Contentious Fans: The Impact of Repression, Media Coverage, Grievances and Aggressive Play on Supporters' Violence', *International Sociology*, 23, pp. 796–818.

Breedveld, K. and Hoekman, R. (2011) 'Measuring Sports Participation in the Netherlands: The Need to go beyond Guidelines', *European Journal for Sport and Society*, 8, pp. 117–32.

Breivik, G. (2007) 'Skillful Coping in Everyday Life and in Sport: A Critical Examination of the Views of Heidegger and Dreyfus', *Journal of the Philosophy of Sport*, 34, pp. 116–34.

Briggs, A. and Burke, P. (2009) *A Social History of The Media*, Cambridge, Polity.

Brink, D. (1989) *Moral Realism and the Foundations of Ethics*, Cambridge, Cambridge University Press.

Brown, A. (2008) 'Our Club, our Rules: Fan Communities at FC United of Manchester', *Soccer and Society*, 9, pp. 346–58.

Bryson, A. (1998) *From Courtesy to Civility: Changing Codes of Conduct in Early Modern England*, Oxford, Oxford University Press.

Buckley, R. (2003) 'Adventure Tourism and the Clothing, Fashion and Entertainment Industries', *Journal of Ecotourism*, 2, pp. 126–34.

Burke, M. (2001) 'Obeying Until It Hurts: Coach–Athlete Relationships', *Journal of the Philosophy of Sport*, 28, pp. 227–40.

Butler, J. (2006) *Gender Trouble: Feminism and the Subversion of Identity*, London, Routledge.

Butler, R. (1987) 'Task-involving and Ego-involving Properties of Evaluation: Effects of Different Feedback Conditions on Motivational Perceptions, Interest, and Performance', *Journal of Educational Psychology*, 79, pp. 474–82.

Butterfield, H. (1968) *The Whig Interpretation of History*, London, Bell.

Cameron, J. and Pierce, W.D. (1994) 'Reinforcement, Reward, and Intrinsic Motivation: A Meta-analysis', *Review of Educational Research*, 64, pp. 363–423.

Carless, D. and Douglas, K. (2013) ' "In the Boat" but "Selling Myself Short": Stories, Narratives, and Identity Development in Elite Sport', *The Sport Psychologist*, 27, pp. 27–39.

Carless, D. and Sparkes, A. (2008) 'The Physical Activity Experiences of Men with Serious Mental Illness: Three Short Stories', *Psychology of Sport and Exercise*, 9, pp. 191–210.

Carr, A. (2011) *Positive Psychology: The Science of Happiness and Human Strengths*, London, Routledge.

Carrington, B. (2004) 'Cosmopolitan Olympism, Humanism and the Spectacle of "Race"', in J. Bale and M.K. Cristensen (eds) *Post-Olympism? Questioning Sport in the Twenty-First Century*, pp. 81–97, Oxford, Berg.

Carrington, B. and McDonald, I. (2008) *Marxism, Cultural Studies and Sport*, London, Routledge.

Cartwright, N. (1983) *How the Laws of Physics Lie*, Oxford, Oxford University Press.

Cashmore, E. and Parker, A. (2003) 'One David Beckham? Celebrity, Masculinity, and the Soccerati', *Sociology of Sport Journal*, 20, pp. 214–31.

Caudwell, J. (2007) 'Queering the Field? The Complexities of Sexuality within a Lesbian-Identified Football Team in England', *Gender, Place and Culture*, 14, pp. 183–96.

Chalmers, A.F. (1999) *What is this Thing called Science?*, Brisbane, University of Queensland Press.

Chehabi, H.E. (2006) 'The Politics of Football in Iran', *Soccer and Society*, 7, pp. 233–61.

Clayton, B. (2013) 'Initiate: Constructing the "Reality" of Male Team Sport Initiation Rituals', *International Review for the Sociology of Sport*, 48, pp. 204–19.

Coakley, J. (2003) *Sports in Society: Issues and Controversies*, New York, McGraw-Hill.

Coalter, F. (2007) 'Sports Clubs, Social Capital and Social Regeneration: "Ill-defined Interventions with Hard to Follow Outcomes"?', *Sport in Society*, 10, pp. 537–59.

Coalter, F. (2013) 'Game Plan and The Spirit Level: The Class Ceiling and the Limits of Sports Policy?', *International Journal of Sport Policy and Politics*, 5, pp. 3–19.

Cohen, A.P. (1985) *The Symbolic Construction of Community*, London, Tavistock.

Cohen, S. (1972) *Folk Devils and Moral Panics*, London, Routledge.

Collins, H. (1992) *Changing Order: Replication and Induction in Scientific Practice*, Chicago, University of Chicago Press.

Collins, M. (2010) 'From Sport for Good to Sport for Sport's Sake: Not a Good Move for Sports Development in England?', *International Journal of Sport Policy*, 2, pp. 367–79.

Collins, T. (1999) *Rugby's Greatest Split*, London, Frank Cass.

Collins, T. (2006) *Rugby League in Twentieth Century Britain*, London, Routledge.

Collins, T. (2009) *A Social History of English Rugby Union*, London, Routledge.

Collins, T. (2013a) *Sport in Capitalist Society: A Short History*, Abingdon, Routledge.

Collins, T. (2013b) 'Unexceptional Exceptionalism: The Origins of American Football in a Transnational Context', *Journal of Global History*, 8, pp. 209–30.

Collins, T. and Vamplew, W. (2002) *Mud, Sweat and Beers: A Cultural History of Sport and Alcohol*, Oxford, Berg.

Connell, R. (1987) *Gender and Power*, Stanford, Stanford University Press.

Connell, R. (1995) *Masculinities*, Cambridge, Polity.

Connell, R.W. and Messerschmidt, J.W. (2005) 'Hegemonic Masculinity: Rethinking the Concept', *Gender and Society*, 19, pp. 829–59.

Cooper, C. (2012) 'Drug Cheating at the Olympics: Who, What, and Why?', *The Lancet*, 380, pp. 21–2.

Couldry, N. and Markham, T. (2007) 'Celebrity Culture and Public Connection: Bridge or Chasm?', *International Journal of Cultural Studies*, 10, pp. 403–21.

Crawford, G. (2004) *Consuming Sport: Fans, Sport and Culture*, London, Routledge.

Cross, D.W. and Carton, R.J. (2003) 'Fluoridation: A Violation of Medical Ethics and Human Rights', *International Journal of Occupational and Environmental Health*, 1, pp. 24–29.

Csikszentmihalyi, M. and LeFevre, J. (1989) 'Optimal Experience in Work and Leisure', *Journal of Personality and Social Psychology*, 56, pp. 815–22.

Csordas, T.J. (1990) 'Embodiment as a Paradigm for Anthropology', *Ethos*, 18, pp. 5–47.

Damisch, L., Stoberock, B. and Mussweiler, T. (2010) 'Keep your Fingers Crossed! How Superstition improves Performance', *Psychological Science*, 21, pp. 1014–20.

Danesi, M. (1994) *The Signs and Meanings of Adolescence*, Toronto, University of Toronto Press.

Darnell, S.C. (2007) 'Playing with Race: Right to Play and the Production of Whiteness in Development through Sport', *Sport in Society*, 10, pp. 560–79.

Darwin, C. (2009) *On the Origin of Species*, Harmondsworth, Penguin.

Daynes, S. and Lee, O. (2008) *Desire for Race*, Oxford, Oxford University Press.

Deci, R. and Ryan, E. (2000) 'Intrinsic and Extrinsic Motivations: Classic Definitions and New Directions', *Contemporary Educational Psychology*, 25, pp. 54–67.

Delgado, F. (1999) 'Sport and Politics Major League Soccer, Constitution, and (The) Latino Audience(s)', *Journal of Sport and Social Issues*, 23, pp. 41–54.

Denham, D. (2000) 'Modernism and Postmodernism in Professional Rugby League in England', *Sociology of Sport Journal*, 17, pp. 275–94.

Descartes, R. (2003) *Meditations and Other Metaphysical Writings*, Harmondsworth, Penguin.

Dimeo, P., Hunt, T.M. and Horbury, R. (2011) 'The Individual and the State: A Social Historical Analysis of the East German Doping System', *Sport in History*, 31, pp. 218–37.

Dittmer, J. and Dodds, K. (2008) 'Popular Geopolitics Past and Future: Fandom, Identities and Audiences', *Geopolitics*, 13, pp. 437–57.

Donaldson, M. (1993) 'What is Hegemonic Masculinity?', *Theory and Society*, 22, pp. 643–57.

Douglas, M. (1991) *Purity and Danger: An Analysis of the Concepts of Pollution and Taboo*, London, Routledge.

Duke, V. and Crolley, L. (1996) 'Football Spectator Behaviour in Argentina: A Case of Separate Evolution', *The Sociological Review*, 44, pp. 272–93.

Dun, S., Spracklen, K. and Wise, N. (2014) *Game Changer: The Transformative Potential of Sport*, Oxford, Inter-Disciplinary Press.

Duncan, M.C. and Klos, L.A. (2012) 'Paradoxes of the Flesh: Emotion and Contradiction in Fitness/Beauty Magazine Discourse', *Journal of Sport and Social Issues*, published on-line at DOI: 10.1177/0193723512467190.

Dunkle, R. (2008) *Gladiators: Violence and Spectacle in Ancient Rome*, London, Longman.

Dunn, M., Thomas, J.O., Swift, W., Burns, L. and Mattick, R.P. (2010) 'Drug Testing in Sport: The Attitudes and Experiences of Elite Athletes', *International Journal of Drug Policy*, 21, pp. 330–2.

Dunning, E. (1986) 'Sport as a Male Preserve: Notes on the Social Sources of Masculine Identity and its Transformation', *Theory, Culture and Society*, 3, pp. 79–90.

Dunning, E. (1994) 'Sport in Space and Time: "Civilizing Processes", Trajectories of State Formation and the Development of Modern Sport', *International Review for the Sociology of Sport*, 29, pp. 331–48.

Dunning, E. and Rojek, C. (1992) *Sport and Leisure in the Civilizing Process*, London, Macmillan.

Dunning, E. and Sheard, K. (2005) *Barbarians, Gentlemen and Players*, second edition, London, Routledge.

Durkheim, E. (1997) *The Division of Labor in Society*, New York, Simon and Schuster.

Dyreson, M. (2003) 'Globalizing the Nation-Making Process: Modern Sport in World History', *The International Journal of the History of Sport*, 20, pp. 91–106.

Dyreson, M., Mangan, J.A. and Park, R.J. (eds) (2013) *Mapping an Empire of American Sport: Expansion, Assimilation, Adaptation and Resistance*, Abingdon, Routledge.

Edgar, A. (2012) 'Who Needs Classical Music? Cultural Choice and Musical Value', *The British Journal of Aesthetics*, 52, pp. 209–11.

Eitzen, D.S. (2012) *Fair and Foul: Beyond the Myths and Paradoxes of Sport*, New York, Rowman and Littlefield Publishers.

Eliade, M. (1963) *Myth and Reality*, New York, Harper and Row.

Elias, N. (1978) *The Civilizing Process: Volume One*, Oxford, Blackwell.

Elias, N. (1982) *The Civilizing Process: Volume Two*, Oxford, Blackwell.

Elias, N. and Dunning, E. (1986) *The Quest for Excitement*, Oxford, Blackwell.

Elias, N. and Scotson, J. (1994) *The Established and the Outsiders*, London, Sage.

El-Zatmah, S. (2012) 'From Terso into Ultras: The 2011 Egyptian Revolution and the Radicalization of the Soccer's Ultra-Fans', *Soccer and Society*, 13, pp. 801–13.

Emmison, M. (2003) 'Social Class and Cultural Mobility: Reconfiguring the Cultural Omnivore Thesis', *Journal of Sociology*, 39, pp. 211–30.

Entine, J. (2000) *Taboo*, New York, Public Affairs.

Evans, J., Davies, B. and Wright, J. (eds) (2003) *Body Knowledge and Control: Studies in the Sociology of Physical Education and Health*, London, Routledge.

Fausto-Sterling, A. (2012) *Sex/Gender: Biology in a Social World*, Abingdon, Routledge.

Featherstone, M. (1987) 'Lifestyle and Consumer Culture', *Theory, Culture and Society*, 4, pp. 55–70.

Featherstone, M. (2007) *Consumer Culture and Postmodernism*, London, Sage.

Fitzgerald, H. (2005) 'Still Feeling like a Spare Piece of Luggage? Embodied Experiences of (Dis)ability in Physical Education and School Sport', *Physical Education and Sport Pedagogy*, 10, pp. 41–59.

Flintoff, A. and Scraton, S. (2001) 'Stepping into Active Leisure? Young Women's Perceptions of Active Lifestyles and their Experiences of School Physical Education', *Sport, Education and Society*, 6, pp. 5–21.

Foucault, M. (1970) *The Order of Things*, London, Tavistock.

Foucault, M. (1972) *The Archaeology of Knowledge*, London, Tavistock.

Foucault, M. (1973) *The Birth of the Clinic*, London, Tavistock.

Foucault, M. (1980) *Power/Knowledge, Selected Interviews and Other Writings*, New York, Pantheon.

Foucault, M. (1991) *Discipline and Punish: The Birth of the Prison*, Harmondsworth, Penguin.

Foucault, M. (2006) *The History of Madness*, London, Routledge.

Frank, T. (1997) *The Conquest of Cool: Business Culture, Counterculture, and the Rise of Hip Consumerism*, Chicago, University of Chicago Press.

French, S. and Saatsi, J. (2006) 'Realism about Structure: The Semantic View and Nonlinguistic Representations', *Philosophy of Science*, 73(5), pp. 548–59.

Freud, S. (1997) *The Interpretation of Dreams*, London, Wordsworth.

Freud, S. (2003) *Beyond the Pleasure Principle*, Harmondsworth, Penguin.

Freud, S. (2005) *The Unconscious*, Harmondsworth, Penguin.

Friell, G. and Williams, S. (1998) *Theodosius: The Empire at Bay*, London, Routledge.

Fullagar, S. (2002) 'Governing the Healthy Body: Discourses of Leisure and Lifestyle within Australian Health Policy', *Health*, 6, pp. 69–84.

Fuller, S. (1993) *Philosophy of Science and its Discontents*, New York, Guilford.

Fuller, S. (2000) *The Governance of Science*, Milton Keynes, Open University.

Fulton, G. and Bairner, A. (2007) 'Sport, Space and National Identity in Ireland: The GAA, Croke Park and Rule 42', *Space and Polity*, 11, pp. 55–74.

Galton, F. (1883) *Inquiries into Human Faculty and its Development*, London, Macmillan.

Gans, H. (2008) *Popular Culture and High Culture: An Analysis and Evaluation of Taste (Revised and Updated)*, New York, Basic Books.

Gard, M. and Wright, J. (2001) 'Managing Uncertainty: Obesity Discourses and Physical Education in a Risk Society', *Studies in Philosophy and Education*, 20, pp. 535–49.

Gard, M. and Wright, J. (2005) *The Obesity Epidemic: Science, Morality and Ideology*, London, Routledge.

Gibson, J. (1993) *Performance versus Results*, Albany, State University of New York Press.

Giddens, A. (1991) *Modernity and Self-Identity: Self and Society in the Late Modern Age*, Cambridge, Polity.

Gillette, A. (2007) *Eugenics and the Nature–Nurture Debate in the Twentieth Century*, Basingstoke, Palgrave.

Gilroy, P. (2000) *Between Camps: Nations, Culture and the Allure of Race*, London, Allen Lane.

Giulianotti, R. (2002) 'Supporters, Followers, Fans, and Flaneurs: A Taxonomy of Spectator Identities in Football', *Journal of Sport and Social Issues*, 26, pp. 25–46.

Giulianotti, R. and Robertson, R. (2007) 'Forms of Glocalization: Globalization and the Migration Strategies of Scottish Football Fans in North America', *Sociology*, 41, pp. 133–52.

Goldacre, B. (2008) *Bad Science*, London, Fourth Estate.

Goldacre, B. (2012) *Bad Pharma: How Drug Companies Mislead Doctors and Harm Patients*, London, Fourth Estate/Harper Press.

Gorn, E.J. and Goldstein, W. (1993) *A Brief History of American Sports*, Urbana-Champaign, University of Illinois Press.

Gould, S.J. (1997) *Mismeasure of Man*, Harmondsworth, Penguin.

Grainger, A., Falcous, M. and Jackson, J. (2012) 'Postcolonial Anxieties and the Browning of New Zealand Rugby', *The Contemporary Pacific*, 24, pp. 267–95.

Gramsci, A. (1971) *Selections from Prison Notebooks*, London, Lawrence and Wishart.

Green, M. and Houlihan, B. (2005) *Elite Sport Development: Policy Learning and Political Priorities*, London, Routledge.

Griffiths, C., Gately, P., Marchant, P.R. and Cooke, C.B. (2012) 'Cross-Sectional Comparisons of BMI and Waist Circumference in British Children: Mixed Public Health Messages', *Obesity*, 20, pp. 1258–60.

Guibernau, M. (2013) *Belonging: Solidarity and Division in Modern Societies*, Cambridge, Polity.

Guttmann, A. (1981) 'Sports Spectators from Antiquity to the Renaissance', *Journal of Sports History*, 8, pp. 5–27.

Guttmann, A. (1986) *Sports Spectators*, New York, Columbia University Press.

Habermas, J. (1984) *The Theory of Communicative Action, Volume One: Reason and the Rationalization of Society*, Cambridge, Polity.

Habermas, J. (1987) *The Theory of Communicative Action, Volume Two: The Critique of Functionalist Reason*, Cambridge, Polity.

Habermas, J. (1989) *The Structural Transformation of the Public Sphere*, Cambridge, Polity.

Habermas, J. (1990) *The Philosophical Discourse of Modernity*, Cambridge, Polity.

Hall, R. (2001) 'The Ball Curve: Calculated Racism and the Stereotype of African American Men', *Journal of Black Studies*, 32, pp. 104–19.

Hall, S. (1993) 'Culture, Community, Nation', *Cultural Studies*, 7, pp. 349–63.

Hamilton, M. (2012) 'Verbal Aggression: Understanding the Psychological Antecedents and Social Consequences', *Journal of Language and Social Psychology*, 31, pp. 5–12.

Hanley, S.B. (1999) *Everyday Things in Premodern Japan: The Hidden Legacy of Material Culture*, Sacramento, University of California Press.

Hanstad, D.V. and Waddington, I. (2009) 'Sport, Health and Drugs: A Critical Re-examination of some Key Issues and Problems', *Perspectives in Public Health*, 129, pp. 174–82.

Hardman, K. and Naul, R. (2002) *Sport and Physical Education in Germany*, London, Routledge.

Hargreaves, J. (1994) *Sporting Females: Critical Issues in the History and Sociology of Women's Sport*, London, Routledge.

Hargreaves, J. and Vertinsky, P. (2006) *Physical Culture, Power, and the Body*, London, Routledge.

Harman, G. (1975) 'Moral Relativism Defended', *The Philosophical Review*, 84, pp. 3–22.

Hartley, H. (2013) 'Modahl v British Athletic Federation (1994–2001)', in *Leading Cases in Sports Law*, pp. 155–74, The Hague, Asser Press.

Harvey, J., Rail, G. and Thibault, L. (1996) 'Globalization and Sport: Sketching a Theoretical Model for Empirical Analyses', *Journal of Sport and Social Issues*, 20, pp. 258–77.

Hearn, J. (1987) *The Gender of Oppression: Men, Masculinity and the Critique of Marxism*, Brighton, Wheatsheaf.

Hebdige, D. (1979) *Subcultures: The Meaning of Style*, London, Routledge.

Henry, I. (1993) *The Politics of Leisure Policy*, London, Macmillan.

Heywood, I. (2006) 'Climbing Monsters: Excess and Restraint in Contemporary Rock Climbing', *Leisure Studies*, 25, pp. 455–67.

Hiller, H. and Wanner, R. (2011) 'Public Opinion in Host Olympic Cities: The Case of the 2010 Vancouver Winter Games', *Sociology*, 45, pp. 883–99.

Ho, D. (1995) 'Selfhood and Identity in Confucianism, Taoism, Buddhism, and Hinduism: Contrasts with the West', *Journal for the Theory of Social Behaviour*, 25, pp. 115–39.

Hoberman, J. (1997) *Darwin's Athletes: How Sport has Damaged Black America and Preserved the Myth of Race*, Boston, Manner.

Hobsbawm, E. and Ranger, T. (1983) *The Invention of Tradition*, Cambridge, Cambridge University Press.

Holder, M., Coleman, B. and Sehn, Z. (2009) 'The Contribution of Active and Passive Leisure to Children's Well-being', *Journal of Health Psychology*, 14, pp. 378–86.

Holt, R. (1989) *Sport and the British: A Modern History*, Oxford, Clarendon.

Horne, J. (2006) *Sport in Consumer Culture*, Basingstoke, Palgrave.

Houlihan, B. (1991) *The Government and Politics of Sport*, London, Routledge.

Houlihan, B. (2005) 'Public Sector Sport Policy: Developing a Framework for Analysis', *International Review for the Sociology of Sport*, 40, pp. 163–85.

Houlihan, B. and Green, M. (2006) 'The Changing Status of School Sport and Physical Education: Explaining Policy Change', *Sport, Education and Society*, 11, pp. 73–92.

Hume, D. (1978) *A Treatise of Human Nature*, Oxford, Oxford University Press.

Huta, V. (2012) 'Linking People's Pursuit of Eudaimonia and Hedonia with Characteristics of their Parents: Parenting Styles, Verbally Endorsed Values, and Role Modeling', *Journal of Happiness Studies*, 13, pp. 47–61.

Innes, M. (1998) 'Memory, Orality and Literacy in an Early Medieval Society', *Past and Present*, 158, pp. 3–36.

Inwood, B. (1985) *Ethics and Human Action in Early Stoicism*, Oxford, Oxford University Press.

Ivy, J.L. (2007) 'Exercise Physiology: A Brief History and Recommendations Regarding Content Requirements for the Kinesiology Major', *Quest*, 59, pp. 34–41.

Jacoby, S.M. (1997) *Modern Manors: Welfare Capitalism since the New Deal*, Princeton, Princeton University Press.

James, W. (1890) *The Principles of Psychology*, Cambridge, Harvard University Press.

Jay, M. (2010) 'Liquidity Crisis: Zygmunt Bauman and the Incredible Lightness of Modernity', *Theory, Culture and Society*, 27, pp. 95–106.

Jeanes, R. (2005) 'Girls, Football Participation and Gender Identity', in J. Caudwell and P. Bramham (eds) *Sport, Active Leisure and Youth Cultures*, pp. 75–96, Eastbourne, Leisure Studies Association.

Jenkins, H. (2012) *Textual Poachers: Television Fans and Participatory Culture*, Abingdon, Routledge.

Jennings, A. (2011) 'Investigating Corruption in Corporate Sport: The IOC and FIFA', *International Review for the Sociology of Sport*, 46, pp. 387–98.

Jindra, M. (1994) 'Star Trek Fandom as a Religious Phenomenon', *Sociology of Religion*, 55, pp. 27–51.

Jones, A. and Greer, J. (2011) 'You Don't Look Like an Athlete: The Effects of Feminine Appearance on Audience Perceptions of Female Athletes and Women's Sports', *Journal of Sport Behavior*, 34, pp. 358–77.

Jones, I. (2000) 'A Model of Serious Leisure Identification: The Case of Football Fandom', *Leisure Studies*, 19, pp. 283–98.

Jones, O. (2012) *Chavs: The Demonization of the Working Class*, London, Verso.

Jonsson, K. (2010) 'Sport beyond Gender and the Emergence of Cyborg Athletes', *Sport in Society*, 13, pp. 249–59.

Judd, D. and Surridge, K. (2013) *The Boer War: A History*, London, I.B. Tauris.

Kane, R. (2011) *The Oxford Handbook of Free Will*, Oxford, Oxford University Press.

Kant, I. (1996) *The Metaphysics of Morals*, Cambridge, Cambridge University Press.

Kay, T. and Bradbury, S. (2009) 'Youth Sport Volunteering: Developing Social Capital?', *Sport, Education and Society*, 14, pp. 121–40.

Keil, F.C. (2010) 'The Feasibility of Folk Science', *Cognitive Science*, 34, pp. 826–62.

Kerr, A.K. and Gladden, J.M. (2008) 'Extending the Understanding of Professional Team Brand Equity to the Global Marketplace', *International Journal of Sport Management and Marketing*, 3, pp. 58–77.

Keys, B. (2004) 'Spreading Peace, Democracy, and Coca-Cola', *Diplomatic History*, 28, pp. 165–96.

Kidd, B. (2013) 'Sports and Masculinity', *Sport in Society*, 16, pp. 553–64.

Kieckhefer, R. (2000) *Magic in the Middle Ages*, Cambridge, Cambridge University Press.

King, A. (1997) 'The Lads: Masculinity and the New Consumption of Football', *Sociology*, 31, pp. 329–34.

King, C. (2007) 'Staging the Winter *White Olympics* Or, Why Sport Matters to *White* Power', *Journal of Sport and Social Issues*, 31, pp. 89–94.

Kirk, D. (1998) 'Educational Reform, Physical Culture and the Crisis of Legitimation in Physical Education', *Discourse: Studies in the Cultural Politics of Education*, 19, pp. 101–12.

Kirk, D. (1999) 'Physical Culture, Physical Education and Relational Analysis', *Sport, Education and Society*, 4, pp. 63–73.

Kirk, D. (2005) 'Physical Education, Youth Sport and Lifelong Participation: The Importance of Early Learning Experiences', *European Physical Education Review*, 11, pp. 239–55.

Kirk, D. (2010) *Physical Education Futures*, London, Routledge.

Klein, A. (2012) 'Chain Reaction: Neoliberal Exceptions to Global Commodity Chains in Dominican Baseball', *International Review for the Sociology of Sport*, 47, pp. 27–42.

Kohn, M. (1995) *The Race Gallery*, London, Verso.

Kosut, M. (2006) 'An Ironic Fad: The Commodification and Consumption of Tattoos', *The Journal of Popular Culture*, 39, pp. 1035–48.

Kraaykamp, G., Oldenkamp, M. and Breedveld, K. (2013) 'Starting a Sport in the Netherlands: A Life-Course Analysis of the Effects of Individual, Parental and Partner Characteristics', *International Review for the Sociology of Sport*, 48, pp. 153–70.

Krawietz, B. (2012) 'The Sportification and Heritagisation of Traditional Turkish Oil Wrestling', *The International Journal of the History of Sport*, 29, pp. 2145–61.

Krien, A. (2013) *Night Games: Sex, Power and Sport*, New York, Black Inc.

Kristiansen, K. and Larsson, T.B. (2005) *The Rise of Bronze Age Society: Travels, Transmissions and Transformations*, Cambridge, Cambridge University Press.

Kuhn, T. (1962) *The Structure of Scientific Revolutions*, Chicago, University of Chicago Press.

Kuwahara, M. (2005) *Tattoo: An Anthropology*, Oxford, Berg.

Latour, B. (1987) *Science in Action*, Cambridge, Harvard University Press.

Lawlor, D. and Hopker, S. (2001) 'The Effectiveness of Exercise as an Intervention in the Management of Depression: Systematic Review and Metaregression Analysis of Randomised Controlled Trials', *British Medical Journal*, 322, pp. 1–8.

Lechner, F.J. (2009) *Globalization: The Making of World Society*, New York, John Wiley.

Lefebvre, H. (1991) *Critique of Everyday Life*, London, Verso.

Lewis, T. and Gray, N. (2013) 'The Maturation of Hip-Hop's Menswear Brands: Outfitting the Urban Consumer', *Fashion Practice: The Journal of Design, Creative Process & the Fashion Industry*, 5, pp. 229–44.

Lieberson, S. (2000) *A Matter of Taste: How Names, Fashions, and Culture Change*, London, Yale University Press.

Lile, E. (2000) 'Professional Pedestrianism in South Wales During the Nineteenth Century', *The Sports Historian*, 20, pp. 94–105.

Llewellyn, M.P. (2011) 'The Curse of the Shamateur', *The International Journal of the History of Sport*, 28, pp. 796–816.

Loland, S. (2002) *Fair Play in Sport: A Moral Norm System*, London, Routledge.

Lomax, M. (1998) 'If He were White: Portrayals of Black and Cuban Players in Organized Baseball, 1880–1920', *Journal of African American Studies*, 3, pp. 31–44.

Long, J., Carrington, B. and Spracklen, K. (1997) ' "Asians Cannot Wear Turbans in the Scrum": Explorations of Racist Discourse within Professional Rugby League', *Leisure Studies*, 16, pp. 249–60.

Long, J. and Spracklen, K. (2010) *Sport and Challenges to Racism*, Basingstoke, Palgrave Macmillan.

Lorenz, C. (1994) 'Historical Knowledge and Historical Reality: A Plea for Internal Realism', *History and Theory*, 33, pp. 297–327.

Ludwig, M. and Schierl, T. (2013) 'Sport, Media and Migration: Use of Sports Media by Turkish Migrants and its Potential for Integration', *Sport in Society*, 16, pp. 94–105.

Lumpkin, A., Stoll, S.K. and Beller, J.M. (1999) *Sport Ethics: Applications for Fair Play*, New York, McGraw-Hill.

Maehr, M.L. and Meyer, H.A. (1997) 'Understanding Motivation and Schooling: Where We've Been, Where We Are, and Where We Need to Go', *Educational Psychology Review*, 9, pp. 371–409.

Magdalinski, T. (2008) *Sport, Technology and the Body: The Nature of Performance*, London, Routledge.

Malcolm, D. (2005) 'The Emergence, Codification and Diffusion of Sport – Theoretical and Conceptual Issues', *International Review for the Sociology of Sport*, 40, pp. 115–18.

Malthus, T. (2008) *An Essay on the Principle of Population*, Oxford, Oxford University Press.

Mandler, G. (2007) *A History of Modern Experimental Psychology*, Cambridge, MIT Press.

Mangan, J.A. (1981) *Athleticism in the Victorian and Edwardian Public Schools*, Cambridge, Cambridge University Press.

Mangan, J.A. (1986) *The Games Ethic and Imperialism: Aspects of the Diffusion of an Ideal*, London, Frank Cass.

Mangan, J.A. and Ritchie, A. (2005) *Ethnicity, Sport, Identity: Struggles for Status*, London, Routledge.

Mangan, J.A. and Vertinsky, P. (eds) (2013) *Gender, Sport, Science: Selected Writings of Roberta J. Park*, London, Routledge.

Marks, J. (2003) *What it Means to be 98% Chimpanzee*, London, University of Chicago Press.

Markula, P. and Pringle, R. (2006) *Foucault, Sport and Exercise*, London, Routledge.

Marx, K. (1992) *Capital*, Harmondsworth, Penguin.

Marx, K. and Engels, F. (2004) *The Communist Manifesto*, Harmondsworth, Penguin.

McArdle, W.D., Katch, F.I. and Katch, V.L. (2001) *Exercise Physiology*, fifth edition, Baltimore, Lippincott, Williams and Wilkins.

McCann-Mortimer, P., Augoustinos, M. and LeCouteur, A. (2004) 'Race and the Human Genome Project: Constructions of Scientific Legitimacy', *Discourse and Society*, 15, pp. 409–32.

McComb, D.G. (2012) *Sports in World History*, London, Routledge.

McDonald, R. (1984) ' "Holy Retreat" or "Practical Breathing Spot"? Class Perceptions of Vancouver's Stanley Park, 1910–1913', *Canadian Historical Review*, 65, pp. 127–53.

McDonald, M., Mihara, T. and Hong, J. (2001) 'Japanese Spectator Sport Industry: Cultural Changes Creating New Opportunities', *European Sport Management Quarterly*, 1, pp. 39–60.

McNamee, M. (2013) 'The Integrity of Sport: Unregulated Gambling, Match Fixing and Corruption', *Sport, Ethics and Philosophy*, 7, pp. 173–4.

McRobbie, A. (2004) 'Post feminism and Popular Culture', *Feminist Media Studies*, 4, pp. 255–64.

Mead, M. (1929) 'The History of Tattooing and Its Significance, with Some Account of Other Forms of Corporal Marking', *American Anthropologist*, 31, pp. 176–7.

Mello, M.M., Studdert, D.M. and Brennan, T.A. (2006) 'Obesity: The New Frontier of Public Health Law', *New England Journal of Medicine*, 354, pp. 2601–10.

Merton, R.K. (1973) *The Sociology of Science: Theoretical and Empirical Investigations*, Chicago, University of Chicago Press.

Messner, M. (1989) 'Masculinities and Athletic Careers', *Gender and Society*, 3, pp. 71–88.

Miah, A. (2007) 'Genetics, Bioethics and Sport', *Sport, Ethics and Philosophy*, 1, pp. 146–158.

Mill, J.S. (1998) *On Liberty and Other Essays*, Oxford, Oxford University Press.

Millward, P. (2013) 'New Football Directors in the Twenty-First Century: Profit and Revenue in the English Premier League's Transnational Age', *Leisure Studies*, 32, pp. 399–414.

Minton, H. (2002) *Departing from Deviance: A History of Homosexual Rights and Emancipatory Science in America*, Chicago, University of Chicago Press.

Monaghan, L. (2001) 'Looking Good, Feeling Good: The Embodied Pleasures of Vibrant Physicality', *Sociology of Health and Illness*, 23, pp. 330–56.

Moore, A. (2000) 'Opera of the Proletariat: Rugby League, the Labour Movement and Working-Class Culture in New South Wales and Queensland', *Labour History*, 79, pp. 57–70.

Morgan, W. (1976) 'On the *Path* – Towards an Ontology of Sport', *Journal of the Philosophy of Sport*, 3, pp. 25–34.

Morgan, W. (2005) *Why Sports Morally Matter*, London, Routledge.

Morgan, W. (2008) 'Some Further Words on Suits on Play', *Journal of the Philosophy of Sport*, 35, pp. 120–41.

Morris, B.S. and Nydahl, J. (1985) 'Sports Spectacle as Drama: Image, Language and Technology', *The Journal of Popular Culture*, 18, pp. 101–10.

Murray, S. (2004) 'Celebrating the Story the Way it is: Cultural Studies, Corporate Media and the Contested Utility of Fandom', *Continuum: Journal of Media and Cultural Studies*, 18, pp. 7–25.

Musto, D.F. (1991) 'Opium, Cocaine and Marijuana in American History', *Scientific American*, 265, pp. 40–7.

Nash, R. (2001) 'English Football Fan Groups in the 1990s: Class, Representation and Fan Power', *Soccer and Society*, 2, pp. 39–58.

Nauright, J. (1996) 'A Besieged Tribe? Nostalgia, White Cultural Identity and the Role of Rugby in a Changing South Africa', *International Review for the Sociology of Sport*, 31, pp. 69–86.

Nevill, A.M. and Whyte, G. (2005) 'Are There Limits to Running World Records?', *Medicine and Science in Sports and Exercise*, 37, pp. 1785–8.

Nicholls, J.G. (1979) 'Quality and Equality in Intellectual Development: The Role of Motivation in Education', *American Psychologist*, 34, pp. 1071–108.

Nichols, G. (2004) 'Crime and Punishment and Sports Development', *Leisure Studies*, 23, pp. 177–94.

Nichols, G., Tacon, R. and Muir, A. (2013) 'Sports Clubs' Volunteers: Bonding In or Bridging Out?', *Sociology*, 47, pp. 350–67.

Nocon, M., Hiemann, T., Muller-Riemenschneider, F., Thalau, F. *et al.* (2008) 'Association of Physical Activity with All-cause and Cardiovascular Mortality: A Systematic Review and Meta-analysis', *European Journal of Cardiovascular Prevention and Rehabilitation*, 15, pp. 239–46.

Norton, P. (2008) *Fighting Traffic: The Dawn of the Motor Age in the American City*, Cambridge, MIT Press.

Opotow, S. (1990) 'Moral Exclusion and Injustice: An Introduction', *Journal of Social Sciences*, 46, pp. 1–20.

Ortner, S.B. (1984) 'Theory in Anthropology since the Sixties', *Comparative Studies in Society and History*, 26, pp. 126–66.

Papineau, P. (1996) *The Philosophy of Science*, Oxford, Oxford University Press.

Parker, S. (1972) *The Future of Work and Leisure*, London, Paladin.

Parker, S. (1976) *The Sociology of Leisure*, London, Allen and Unwin.

Parlebas, P. (2003) 'The Destiny of Games Heritage and Lineage', *Studies in Physical Culture and Tourism*, 10, pp. 15–26.

Parry, J. (1987) 'The Devil's Advocate', *Sport and Leisure*, November, pp. 33–4.

Parsons, T. (1964) *The Social System*, New York, Macmillan.

Paxton, F.S. (1996) *Christianizing Death: The Creation of a Ritual Process in Early Medieval Europe*, Ithaca, Cornell University Press.

Peers, D. (2012) 'Patients, Athletes, Freaks: Paralympism and the Reproduction of Disability', *Journal of Sport and Social Issues*, 36, pp. 295–316.

Perkins, N., Smith, K., Hunter, D.J., Bambra, C. and Joyce, K. (2010) 'What Counts is What Works? New Labour and Partnerships in Public Health', *Policy and Politics*, 38, pp. 101–17.

Phillpots, L. and Grix, J. (2014) 'New Governance and Physical Education and School Sport Policy: A Case Study of School to Club Links', *Physical Education and Sport Pedagogy*, 19, pp. 76–96.

Plato (2007) *The Republic*, translated by H.D.P. Lee and D. Lee, Harmondsworth, Penguin.

Polanyi, M. (1958) *Personal Knowledge: Towards a Post-critical Epistemology*, Chicago, University of Chicago Press.

Pope, S. (2011) 'Like Pulling Down Durham Cathedral and Building a Brothel: Women as "New Consumer" Fans?', *International Review for the Sociology of Sport*, 46, pp. 471–87.

Poplak, R. (2013) *Braking Bad: Chasing Lance Armstrong and the Cancer of Corruption*, New York, Random House.

Popper, K. (2005) *The Logic of Scientific Discovery*, New York, Routledge.

Porter, D. and Smith, A. (eds) (2013) *Sport and National Identity in the Post-war World*, London, Routledge.

Poston, W.S.C. and Foreyt, J.P. (1999) 'Obesity is an Environmental Issue', *Atherosclerosis*, 146, pp. 201–9.

Pratkanis, A.R., Pratkanis, A. and Aronson, E. (2001) *Age of Propaganda: The Everyday Use and Abuse of Persuasion*, New York, Macmillan.

Provine, D.M. (2008) *Unequal under Law: Race in the War on Drugs*, Chicago, University of Chicago Press.

Psillos, S. (1999) *Scientific Realism: How Science Tracks Truth*, London, Routledge.

Pucher, J. and Dijkstra, L. (2003) 'Promoting Safe Walking and Cycling to Improve Public Health: Lessons from the Netherlands and Germany', *American Journal of Public Health*, 93, pp. 1509–16.

Rahman, M. and Lockwood, S. (2011) 'How to "Use Your Olympian": The Paradox of Athletic Authenticity and Commercialization in the Contemporary Olympic Games', *Sociology*, 45, pp. 815–29.

Rawls, J. (1971) *A Theory of Justice*, New York, Routledge.

Riordan, J. (1991) *Sport, Politics, and Communism*, Manchester, Manchester University Press.

Riordan, J. and Jones, R. (1999) *Sport and Physical Education in China*, London, Taylor and Francis.

Riordan, J. and Kruger, A. (2003) *European Cultures in Sport: Examining the Nations and Regions*, Bristol, Intellect.

Robbins, B. (2004) 'That's Cheap: The Rational Invocation of Norms, Practices, and an Ethos in Ultimate Frisbee', *Journal of Sport and Social Issues*, 28, pp. 314–37.

Roberts, K. (1978) *Contemporary Society and the Growth of Leisure*, London, Longman.

Roberts, K. (2004) *The Leisure Industries*, Basingstoke, Palgrave.

Rojek, C. (1995) *Decentring Leisure*, London, Sage.

Rojek, C. (2001) *Celebrity*, London, Reaktion Books.

Rojek, C. (2006) 'Sports Celebrity and the Civilizing Process', *Sport in Society*, 9, pp. 674–90.

Rojek, C. (2010) *The Labour of Leisure*, London, Sage.

Rojek, C. (2013) *Event Power: How Global Events Manage and Manipulate*, London, Sage.

Rokholm, B., Baker, J.L. and Sorensen, T.I.A. (2010) 'The Levelling Off of the Obesity Epidemic since the year 1999: A Review of Evidence and Perspectives', *Obesity Reviews*, 11, pp. 835–46.

Rousseau, J.J. (2008) *The Social Contract*, Oxford, Oxford University Press.

Rowe, D. (1997) 'Rugby League in Australia: The Super League Saga', *Journal of Sport and Social Issues*, 21, pp. 221–6.

Rowe, D. (2003) 'Sport and the Repudiation of the Global', *International Review for the Sociology of Sport*, 38, pp. 281–94.

Rowe, D. (ed.) (2004) *Critical Readings: Sport, Culture and the Media*, Milton Keynes, Open University Press.

Rowe, D. (2012) 'The Bid, the Lead up, the Event and the Legacy: Global Cultural Politics and Hosting the Olympics', *The British Journal of Sociology*, 63, pp. 285–305.

Russell, D. (1988) 'Sporadic and Curious: The Emergence of Rugby and Soccer Zones in Yorkshire and Lancashire, 1860–1914', *International Journal of the History of Sport*, 5, pp. 185–205.

Rylance, R. (2000) *Victorian Psychology and British Culture*, Oxford, Oxford University Press.

Sacchetti, S. and Tortia, E.C. (2013) 'Satisfaction with Creativity: A Study of Organizational Characteristics and Individual Motivation', *Journal of Happiness Studies*, 14, pp. 1789–811.

Sack, A. and Suster, Z. (2000) 'Soccer and Croatian Nationalism: A Prelude to War', *Journal of Sport and Social Issues*, 24, pp. 305–20.

Saeki, T. (1994) 'The Conflict between Tradition and Modernization in a Sport Organization: A Sociological Study of Issues Surrounding the Organizational Reformation of the All Japan Judo Federation', *International Review for the Sociology of Sport*, 29, pp. 301–15.

Sahlins, M. (2009) *Historical Metaphors and Mythical Realities: Structure in the Early History of the Sandwich Islands Kingdom*, Ann Arbor, University of Michigan Press.

Sallis, J.F., Carlson, J.A., Mignano, A.M., Lemes, A. and Wagner, N. (2013) 'Trends in Presentations of Environmental and Policy Studies Related to Physical Activity, Nutrition, and Obesity at Society of Behavioral Medicine, 1995–2010: A Commentary to Accompany the Active Living Research Supplement to *Annals of Behavioral Medicine*', *Annals of Behavioral Medicine*, 45, pp. 14–17.

Schlosser, E. (2001) *Fast Food Nation*, Boston, Houghton Mifflin.

Schultz, S.K. and McShane, C. (1978) 'To Engineer the Metropolis: Sewers, Sanitation, and City Planning in Late-Nineteenth-Century America', *The Journal of American History*, 65, pp. 389–411.

Schweinbenz, A.N. (2010) 'Against Hegemonic Currents: Women's Rowing into the First Half of the Twentieth Century', *Sport in History*, 30, pp. 309–26.

Scraton, P. (2004) *Childhood in Crisis*, London, Routledge.

Scraton, S., Caudwell, J. and Holland, S. (2005) 'Bend it like Patel: Centring "Race", Ethnicity and Gender in Feminist Analysis of Women's Football in England', *International Review for the Sociology of Sport*, 40, pp. 71–88.

Scully, D., Kremer, J., Meade, M.M., Graham, R. and Dudgeon, K. (1998) 'Physical Exercise and Psychological Well Being: A Critical Review', *British Journal of Sports Medicine*, 32, pp. 111–20.

Scully, G.W. (1995) *The Market Structure of Sports*, Chicago, University of Chicago Press.

Serazio, M. (2013) 'The Elementary Forms of Sports Fandom: A Durkheimian Exploration of Team Myths, Kinship, and Totemic Rituals', *Communication and Sport*, 1, pp. 303–25.

Shogan, D. (2002) 'Characterizing Constraints of Leisure: A Foucaultian Analysis of Leisure Constraints', *Leisure Studies*, 21, pp. 27–38.

Silvia, T. (2007) *Baseball over the Air: The National Pastime on the Radio and in the Imagination*, Jefferson, McFarland.

Simons, Y. and Taylor, J. (1992) 'A Psychosocial Model of Fan Violence in Sports', *International Journal of Sport Psychology*, 23(3), pp. 207–26.

Singh, A., Uijtdewilligen, L., Twisk, J.W.R., van Mechelen, W. and Chinapaw, M.J.M. (2012) 'Physical Activity and Performance at School: A Systematic Review of the Literature Including a Methodological Quality Assessment', *Archives of Pediatrics and Adolescent Medicine*, 166, pp. 49–55.

Skinner, Q. (1969) 'Meaning and Understanding in the History of Ideas', *History and Theory*, 8, pp. 3–53.

Smigel, E. (1963) *Work and Leisure: A Contemporary Social Problem*, New Haven, College and University Press.

Smith, A.D. (2009) *Ethno-symbolism and Nationalism: A Cultural Approach*, London, Routledge.

Smith, B. (2013) 'Disability, Sport and Men's Narratives of Health: A Qualitative Study', *Health Psychology*, 32, pp. 110–19.

Spaaij, R. (2012) 'Beyond the Playing Field: Experiences of Sport, Social Capital, and Integration among Somalis in Australia', *Ethnic and Racial Studies*, 35, pp. 1519–38.

Sparling, P.B. (2013) 'The Lance Armstrong Saga: A Wake-up Call for Drug Reform in Sports', *Current Sports Medicine Reports*, 12, pp. 53–4.

Spracklen, K. (1996) *Playing the Ball: Constructing Community and Masculine Identity in Rugby*, unpublished PhD Thesis, Leeds Metropolitan University, Leeds.

Spracklen, K. (2007) 'Negotiations of Belonging: Habermasian Stories of Minority Ethnic Rugby League Players in London and the South of England', *World Leisure Journal*, 49, pp. 216–26.

Spracklen, K. (2008) 'The Holy Blood and the Holy Grail: Myths of Scientific Racism and the Pursuit of Excellence in Sport', *Leisure Studies*, 27, pp. 221–7.

Spracklen, K. (2009) *The Meaning and Purpose of Leisure*, Basingstoke, Palgrave Macmillan.

Spracklen, K. (2011) *Constructing Leisure*, Basingstoke, Palgrave Macmillan.

Spracklen, K. (2013a) *Leisure, Sports and Society*, Basingstoke, Palgrave Macmillan.

Spracklen, K. (2013b) *Whiteness and Leisure*, Basingstoke, Palgrave Macmillan.

Spracklen, K. (2014) 'Why PE Should be Made Voluntary', in S. Dun, K. Spracklen and N. Wise (eds) *Game Changer: The Transformative Potential of Sport*, Oxford, Inter-Disciplinary Press.

Spracklen, K., Long, J. and Hylton, K. (2006) 'Managing and Monitoring Equality and Diversity in UK Sport', *Journal of Sport and Social Issues*, 30, pp. 289–305.

Spracklen, K. and Spracklen, C. (2008) 'Negotiations of Being and Becoming: Minority Ethnic Rugby League Players in the Cathar Country of France', *International Review for the Sociology of Sport*, 43, pp. 201–18.

Spracklen, K., Timmins, S. and Long, J. (2010) 'Ethnographies of the Imagined, the Imaginary, and the Critically Real: Blackness, Whiteness, the North of England and Rugby League', *Leisure Studies*, 29, pp. 397–414.

Spray, C., Biddle, S. and Fox, K. (1999) 'Achievement Goals, Beliefs about the Causes of Success and Reported Emotion in Post-16 Physical Education', *Journal of Sports Sciences*, 17, pp. 213–19.

Stebbins, R. (1982) 'Serious Leisure: A Conceptual Statement', *Pacific Sociological Review*, 25, pp. 251–72.

Stebbins, R. (2009) *Leisure and Consumption*, Basingstoke, Palgrave Macmillan.

St Louis, B. (2004) 'Sport and Common-sense Racial Science', *Leisure Studies*, 23, pp. 31–46.

Strutt, J. (1801) *The Sports and Pastimes of the People of England from the Earliest Period*, London, Methuen and Company.

Suits, B. (2005) *The Grasshopper: Games, Life and Utopia*, Orchard Park, Broadview Press.

Sumino, M. and Harada, M. (2004) 'Affective Experience of J. League Fans: The Relationship between Affective Experience, Team Loyalty and Intention to Attend', *Managing Leisure*, 9, pp. 181–92.

Svare, B. (2004) *Reforming Sports: Before the Clock Runs Out*, Delmar, Sports Reform Press.

Tajfel, H. (ed.) (1978) *Differentiation between Social Groups: Studies in the Social Psychology of Intergroup Relations*, Oxford, Academic Press.

Tatz, C. (2009) 'Coming to Terms: "Race", Ethnicity, Identity and Aboriginality in Sport', *Australian Aboriginal Studies*, 2, pp. 15–31.

Taylor, B. and Garratt, D. (2010) 'The Professionalisation of Sports Coaching: Relations of Power, Resistance and Compliance', *Sport, Education and Society*, 15, pp. 121–39.

Taylor, M. (2010) 'Football's Engineers? British Football Coaches, Migration and Intercultural Transfer, c.1910–c.1950s', *Sport in History*, 30, pp. 138–63.

Taylor, T.D. (2009) 'Advertising and the Conquest of Culture', *Social Semiotics*, 19, pp. 405–25.

Thin, N. (2012) *Social Happiness: Theory into Policy and Practice*, Bristol, The Policy Press.

Thomas, D. (1997) 'The Rugby Revolution: New Horizons or False Dawn?', *Economic Affairs*, 17, pp. 19–24.

Tinning, R. (2012) 'The Idea of Physical Education: A Memetic Perspective', *Physical Education and Sport Pedagogy*, 17, pp. 115–26.

Tomlinson, A. (2002) 'Theorising Spectacle: Beyond Debord', in J. Sugden and A. Tomlinson (eds) *Power Games: A Critical Sociology of Sport*, pp. 44–60, London, Routledge.

Trayhurn, P. and Beattie, J.H. (2001) 'Physiological Role of Adipose Tissue: White Adipose Tissue as an Endocrine and Secretory Organ', *Proceedings of the Nutrition Society*, 60, pp. 329–39.

Tribby, J. (1992) 'Body/Building: Living the Museum Life in Early Modern Europe', *Rhetorica: A Journal of the History of Rhetoric*, 10, pp. 139–63.

Tucker, R., Santos-Concejero, J. and Collins, M. (2013) 'The Genetic Basis for Elite Running Performance', *British Journal of Sports Medicine*, 47, pp. 545–9.

Turner, V. (1969) *The Ritual Process: Structure and Anti-structure*, Ithaca, Cornell University Press.

Twietmeyer, G. (2012) 'What is Kinesiology? Historical and Philosophical Insights', *Quest*, 64, pp. 4–23.

Vamplew, W. (2004) *Pay Up and Play the Game: Professional Sport in Britain, 1875–1914*, Cambridge, Cambridge University Press.

Van Damme, R. and Wilson, R. (2002) 'Athletic Performance and the Evolution of Vertebrate Locomotor Capacity', in P. Aerts (ed.) *Topics in Functional and Ecological Vertebrate Morphology*, pp. 257–92, Maastricht, Shaker Publishing.

Van Fraassen, B. (1980) *The Scientific Image*, Oxford, Clarendon.

Van Ree, E. (1997) 'Fear of Drugs', *The International Journal of Drug Policy*, 8, pp. 93–100.

Veblen, T. (1970) *The Theory of the Leisure Class*, London, Unwin.

Velija, P., Mierzwinski, M. and Fortune, L. (2013) 'It made me feel Powerful: Women's Gendered Embodiment and Physical Empowerment in the Martial Arts', *Leisure Studies*, 32, pp. 524–41.

Von Eschenbach, W. (1980) *Parzival*, translated by A. Hatto, Harmondsworth, Penguin.

Wachs, F.L. and Chase, L.F. (2013) 'Explaining the Failure of an Obesity Intervention: Combining Bourdieu's Symbolic Violence and Foucault's Microphysics of Power to Reconsider State Interventions', *Sociology of Sport Journal*, 30(2), pp. 111–31.

Wagg, S. (ed.) (2011) *Myths and Milestones in the History of Sport*, Basingstoke, Palgrave Macmillan.

Waldron, J.J., Lynn, Q. and Krane, V. (2011) 'Duct Tape, Icy Hot and Paddles: Narratives of Initiation onto US Male Sport Teams', *Sport, Education and Society*, 16, pp. 111–25.

Walseth, K. (2006) 'Sport and Belonging', *International Review for the Sociology of Sport*, 41, pp. 447–64.

Walsh, A.J. and Giulianotti, R. (2001) 'This Sporting Mammon: A Normative Critique of the Commodification of Sport', *Journal of the Philosophy of Sport*, 28, pp. 53–77.

Warren, J. (2009) *The Cambridge Companion to Epicureanism*, Cambridge, Cambridge University Press.

Watson, J.B. (1913) 'Psychology as the Behaviorist Views It', *Psychological Review*, 20, pp. 158–77.

Watson, J.B. (1930) *Behaviorism*, New York, W.W. Norton & Co.

Watts, E. (2004) 'Justinian, Malalas, and the end of Athenian Philosophical Teaching in AD 529', *The Journal of Roman Studies*, 94, pp. 168–192.

Weber, M. (1992) *Economy and Society*, Sacramento, University of California Press.

Weber, M. (2001) *The Protestant Ethic and the Spirit of Capitalism*, London, Routledge.

Weinberg, R.S. and Gould, D. (2011) *Foundations of Sport and Exercise Psychology*, Champaign, Human Kinetics.

Welch, M. (1997) 'Violence against Women by Professional Football Players: A Gender Analysis of Hypermasculinity, Positional Status, Narcissism, and Entitlement', *Journal of Sport and Social Issues*, 21: pp. 392–411.

Whannel, G. (2013) *Media Sport Stars: Masculinities and Moralities*, Abingdon, Routledge.

Wiesemann, C. (2011) 'Is There a Right Not to Know One's Sex? The Ethics of "Gender Verification" in Women's Sports Competition', *Journal of Medical Ethics*, 37, pp. 216–20.

Wilkinson, R. and Pickett, K. (2009) *The Spirit Level: Why Equality is Better for Everyone*, Harmondsworth, Penguin.

Williams, A. (2011) *The Architecture of Theology: Structure, System, and Ratio*, Oxford, Oxford University Press.

Williams, P.T. (2001) 'Physical Fitness and Activity as a Separate Heart Disease Risk Factor: A Meta-analysis', *Medicine and Science in Sports and Exercise*, 33, pp. 754–61.

Williams, R.J. (1972) 'Scribal Training in Ancient Egypt', *Journal of the American Oriental Society*, 92, pp. 214–21.

Wilson, A. and Ashplant, T. (1988) 'Whig History and Present-Centred History', *The Historical Journal*, 31, pp. 1–16.

Wittgenstein, L. (1968) *Philosophical Investigations*, Oxford, Blackwell.

Wong, D.B. (2006) *Natural Moralities: A Defense of Pluralistic Relativism*, New York, Oxford University Press.

Woo, H.J. and Kim, Y. (2003) 'Modern Gladiators: A Content Analysis of Televised Wrestling', *Mass Communication and Society*, 6, pp. 361–78.

Woolgar, S. (1981) 'Interests and Explanation in the Social Study of Science', *Social Studies of Science*, 11, pp. 365–94.

Wright, J. (1996) 'The Construction of Complementarity in Physical Education', *Gender and Education*, 8, pp. 61–80.

Wright, J., O'Flynn, G. and Macdonald, D. (2006) 'Being Fit and Looking Healthy: Young Women's and Men's Constructions of Health and Fitness', *Sex Roles*, 54, pp. 707–16.

Wrynn, A. (2003) 'Contesting the Canon: Understanding the History of the Evolving Discipline of Kinesiology', *Quest*, 55, pp. 244–56.

Yeates, A. (2013) 'Queer Visual Pleasures and the Policing of Male Sexuality in Responses to Images of David Beckham', *Visual Studies*, 28, pp. 110–21.

Young, D. (2005) 'Mens Sana in Corpore Sano? Body and Mind in Ancient Greece', *International Journal of the History of Sport*, 22, pp. 22–41.

Young, K. (2012) *Sport, Violence and Society*, New York, Routledge.

Zimbalist, A. (2003) 'Sport as Business', *Oxford Review of Economic Policy*, 19, pp. 503–11.

Zorzoli, M. and Rossi, F. (2010) 'Implementation of the Biological Passport: The Experience of the International Cycling Union', *Drug Testing and Analysis*, 2, pp. 542–7.

Index